Alchemy of the Quran

A GATEWAY TO THE SUPERNATURAL

Indeed we show (manifest) clear miracles for those who firmly believe.

(2:118)

And those who do not know say, why God does not speak to us or send us a miracle? And there were others who said the same before them. Their hearts are alike. Indeed we make clear miracles for those who firmly believe.

(2:118)

FARAMARZ FRANCO DAVATI

In the Name of Most Kind and Most Forgiving God

I dedicate this book to all the moderate Muslims around the world.

Caramelized will be the camels in this caravan

From this Persian sugar they carry to the Muslim world

— Faramarz Franco Davati

Table of Contents

Brief Background and History 1
The Quran, Early Islam, and Verses 5
Who Is Our God? 21
General Fundamentals of Islam 27
Alchemy of the Quran and Islam 33
Choosing Verses 41
There Is No God but the One God 51
Believe 55
Faith in God 65
"Trust-In" (God) (Tawakkul in Arabic) 73
Praising and Thanking God 79
Glorify and Elevate Your God 85
Prayers 91
Charity 109
Patience and Expectation in Receiving from God 121
Blessings of God 127
Submitting and Surrendering to God 133
God Testing You 137
Fear of God 143
Satan 147
Repent 163
Path of God 171
Forgiveness 177

Choosing Your Friends	179
Hope	183
Miracles	187
Karma in Islam	201
Revenge	205
Life, Death, and the Afterlife	209
Life	213
Death	221
Afterlife	225
Paradise	229
God's Pick for His Plans	235
Competition between Religions	245
Parallels with Science	249
Parallels with Other Religions	255
Noah	261
Abraham	269
Children of Israel	281
Moses	295
Jesus & Mary	319
Dealing with Our Enemies	331
Our Relationship with Other Abrahamic Faiths	341
Loving God and Why Are We Here?	353
Appendix – I	361
Appendix – II	403
References	453
Biography	455

In the Name of Most Kind and Most Forgiving God

Brief Background and History

What is the Quran?

The Quran is the holy book of Muslims. According to us Muslims, God chose Muhammad as His last prophet and messenger on earth. Muhammad was not an educated man, but the Quran was revealed to him word by word by the angel Gabriel some 1,400 years ago.

Muhammad was born and raised in Arabia. Arabs are Semite people, and they are the children of Ishmael, son of Ibrahim and Hagar. At that time, Arabia was going through a period known as an "ignorance period" (*jahiliyyah*[1]), and Arabs were pagans. Muhammad was chosen as a last prophet to guide these people out of that period and show them the right path. At the beginning Muhammad preached to his family and friends. His circle of friends got bigger, and eventually he was preaching to the whole town.

The Quran's message is universal; however, it is very much blended with the culture of the people it was intended to save in the first place. The Quran and its message are very much directed toward the people of Muhammad's time, as he was one of them and part of that community 1,400 years ago in Arabia.

The Quran is the time line of Muhammad and his journey to the top. It is also a reflection of the culture and customs of the people in Arabia some 1,400 years ago when Islam was born. No

---

[1] The word *jahiliyya* means "ignorance," which is taken to refer to the pre-Islamic period. It was the age of tribalism and is reckoned to cover the period of about a century before the advent of Islam. In pre-Islamic literature, and to a considerable degree in the Quran, the word from the root *j-h-l* means not ignorance but something like barbarism. The term *jahiliyya* occurs four times in the Quran (33:33, 48:26, 5:50. and 3:154). Ref: Ismaili.net

one has ever done as much for the people of Arabia as Muhammad did. He was able to unite the people under one monotheistic religion and have them give up their pagan beliefs and believe only in the One God who created the universe.

After Muhammad, his successors, with the help of this One Book, gained confidence and raised an army to spread Islam by force. Despite their inferiority in weaponry and numbers, they defeated the two superpowers of that time, the Persians and Romans, and spread Islam throughout the region, all the way to Southern Europe.

What is it about this book, the Quran, that can bring down empires, lead revolutions, and withstand back-breaking sanctions? What is it about this book that enables the weakest to pick a fight against superpowers and expel them out of the lands they have invaded? It cannot be the people, as they are too beaten and underequipped or trained to do so. So what is it that guides these beaten, underequipped people to overcome such adversities against all odds?

What is it about this book that when Muslims seek refuge in it during their hard times, it calms their heart and gives them hope, peace of mind, and strength to withstand and overcome all adversities and survive against all odds?

Is there something special about this book? Is there something supernatural about this book? Is the Quran really the exact words of God? Was the Quran written by Muhammad? Did Muhammad add to God's words to benefit himself or as he saw fit? Was Muhammad really God's last prophet, as he claimed?

These questions have been asked by many non-Muslims and Muslims alike for centuries.

In the following chapters we will get to know and discover the extraordinary book known as the Quran a little closer, though we may be able to touch only the tip of the iceberg. Although I

BRIEF BACKGROUND AND HISTORY

originally wrote this book for the young Muslims who live in the West, I think all those who are interested in the subject can use and enjoy it.

As much as I tried not to bring politics into this book, the recent Muslim ban by the Trump administration provoked me to make a few comments in several places in the book regarding the actions of the US toward the Muslim countries in general, as well as some of the events in the Muslim world, as it was due.

I finish the introduction with a poem from Rumi, one of the great Persian Muslim scholars, theologians, and poets. Rumi's work is mostly in the Persian language of Farsi, but he also occasionally used Arabic, Turkish, and Greek in his poems and writings. He analyzed the Quran extensively and figured out more of the secrets of this extraordinary book than many others did.

Here is how Rumi describes the Quran:

Words of the Quran, though they have a simple front
A deep inside layer exists, under that front

A third layer exists, beneath the deep layer
All wisdom will be lost, in the third layer

The fourth layer, was only seen by the Nabi (Prophet Muhammad)
And the unseen Lord, was the only one to see

Don't judge the Quran, by its simple front
Satan saw Adam, only as soil and mud

Rumi, Persian Poet 13th century
Translation and Rhyme
Faramarz Franco Davati

The Quran, Early Islam, and Verses

❖

The Quran is a book for mankind. It was sent to help the people of Arabia out of their difficult period. Naturally it embodies the cultural aspects of the very first people that it was intended to save, which were the Bedouins of Arabia. God sent His angel Gabriel to pass the words of the Quran to His prophet, Muhammad. Muhammad was chosen by God to save the Bedouin people from their wrong way of living. Some verses are naturally mixed with the culture and customs of the Bedouin people of Arabia at that time, as the Quran was intended for them in the first place. The Quran calls itself a "cure" (41:44) meant to rescue them from the bad period of time they were going through. God promised Abraham that each of his offspring would father a nation. Ishmael fathered the nation of Islam, and Isaac fathered the children of Israel. God kept His promise to them, and when either son got to a point where they needed rescuing, God sent a messenger to help them out. The same way the children of Israel were rescued from slavery by Moses and the Ten Commandments, Muhammad was sent with the Quran to rescue the descendants of Ishmael from their "period of ignorance."

It is mentioned in several places in the Quran that it was sent in their language (Arabic) by one of their own people (Muhammad) as a cure; therefore, the people have no excuse to turn away from it. And every community has its own teacher.

14:01
Alif, Lam, Ra. [This is] a book which We have revealed to you, [O Muhammad], that you might bring mankind out of darkness into

the light by permission of their lord to the path of Almighty, the praiseworthy.

41:44
And if We had made it a non-Arabic Qur'an, they would have said, "Why are its verses not explained in detail [in our language]? Is it a foreign [recitation] and an Arab [messenger]?" Say, "It is, for those who believe, a guidance and cure." And those who do not believe - in their ears is deafness, and it is upon them blindness. Those are being called from a distant place.

19:97
So, [O Muhammad], We have only made Qur'an easy in the Arabic language that you may give good news thereby to the righteous and warn thereby a hostile people.

26:199
And had him recite it (in Arabic), they could not possibly believe in it.

And he had recited it to them [in Arabic], they would [still] not have been believers in it.

43:3
Indeed, We have made it an Arabic Qur'an that you might understand.

44:58
And indeed, We have eased the Qur'an in your tongue that they might be reminded.

13:7
The unbelievers say, "Why has God not sent him, (Muhammad), some miracles." (Muhammad), you are only a warner. For <u>every nation</u> there is a guide.

THE QURAN, EARLY ISLAM, AND VERSES

One of the reasons God chose Muhammad and sent him to save the people of Arabia during their "bad period" was their wrong way of thinking when their wives would give birth to a girl. Bedouin men were ashamed of having daughters and only wanted to have sons to help them with work and in battle. So when their wife would give birth to a girl, they would bury the child alive out of shame. Islam changed all that and made that practice forbidden and a sin.

16:58
And when of them is informed of (the birth of a female), their face turns gloomy and black with anger.

16:59
He hides himself from the people because of the disgrace of such news. Shall he keep their new born with disgrace or bury it alive in the ground? How sinful is their judgement.

Today, wherever Muslims are allowed to freely practice their religion, moderate Muslims around the world pick and choose the parts of the Quran they will follow, using the verses that are agreeable to their culture and within the rules and laws of their societies. If someone wanted to practice the whole book of the Quran word for word, he or she would have to regress, scale down, and go backward to 1,400 years ago to the Bedouin culture, to match the lifestyle of that time. Today you will see that some very conservative Islamic countries have turned the clock back to almost 1,400 years ago, as they have been incapable of growing themselves and Islam with the rest of the world. Unfortunately their comfort zone is the "ignorance period." Not only have they destroyed God's religion, but they also have caused the suppression and suffocation of their own citizens. The extreme cases are ISIS, Al-Qaida, the Taliban, and similar organizations.

They defend their way of life as "pure Islam." Some fanatic Muslims put a catchy phrase on what was being practiced 1,400 years ago and call it *Sunnah*[2] (the way of Prophet Muhammad) so it cannot be questioned, regardless of if it was really his way or not! These groups don't want people to think or ask questions about what they do or what they preach; they just want people to accept it without questioning it.

God warns us about this and these people in the Quran:

21:10
We have sent down to you a Book which is a message for you, Then will you not reason?

8:22
Verily, the worst of living creatures in the sight of God are the deaf and dumb who will not think and use reason.

About 1,400 years ago, Muhammad tried very hard to bring the people in that region out of the "ignorance period." Unfortunately, after 1400 years, he has not been able to bring the "ignorance" out of some Muslims, in all the Muslims countries, in that part of the world.

Unfortunately, some Muslims today try to compete with this ignorance. They search through hadiths from 1,400 years ago and try to revitalize everything that was wrong or questionable at that time, and label it as a reliable Hadith or Sunnah! They either draw from it or make it a law or a custom; from female genital mutilation (female circumcision) to barring women from driving, singing, dancing, attending stadiums to watch sports or even riding a bicycle. The list can go on. At the time of Muhammad there were no stadiums, bicycles, or cars to draw from in any Hadith! Just be-

---

2   *Sunnah* is the verbally transmitted record of the teachings, deed, and any sayings, silent permissions, or disapproval of Muhammad, as well as various reports about Muhammad's companions. Wikipedia.

THE QURAN, EARLY ISLAM, AND VERSES

cause one of the descendants of Muhammad, six generation later after him, had made a statement that it is better for women to sing in a group than solo in public. The religious leaders have made that into a law barring women from singing solo on any stage, in the media or in public, and prohibiting the entire population of women in a nation from singing!

Ironically, some of the orders come from the highest religious leaders in that part of the world from different Islamic sects. Is this what they have learned from the religion of God and Islam after 1,400 years? They have shown they are incapable of adapting to the modern world even at a very basic level. Their vision for the future of Islam and its youth in the world does not go beyond their mosque!

Do you want your children to learn their Islam from these religious leaders and live their lives according to their teachings?

In today's world, we Muslims have to be our own mentor, especially in the West. None of the Muslim leaders have the capacity to do so or have a vision for the future of Islam. Many of these leaders still live in the "ignorance period" and are willing to see generations of young Muslim lives wasted on those wrong and backward ways of thinking and living, as long as nobody is rocking their boat and shaking their comfort zone.

All they have to do is say, "We uphold the *Sunnah*," and they are good for another fifty to one hundred years. While the whole world is moving forward and enjoying God's blessings in this dance of life, another generation of young Muslims come and go, with no joy, no music, no dance, no art, no happiness in another Muslim wasteland, with the hope of a better life in the afterlife! This is what our religious leaders have learned from the Quran and brought us after 1,400 years.

We moderate Muslims in the West are on our own and have to take the responsibility of the religion into our own hands. We have to separate ourselves from the fanatics. Nobody likes to be called a fanatic in any religion, and they refer to themselves "conservatives." The conservatives in any religion or organization come in a wide range of different opinions and ideas. We Muslims simply have to make a better Muslim community for ourselves, our families, and future generations of young Muslims in the West.

We have to pick and choose verses from the Quran, instead of following it blindly word for word. This is not something new. Jews and Christians, whose religion is older than ours, have come to the same conclusion. Especially Christians, when they went through their own Dark Ages in Christianity. When was the last time you heard Jews stoned someone for adultery, despite the fact that is in their scripture?

Picking and choosing verses from the Quran, instead of following it blindly word for word, is not something new. Many Muslim scholars and philosophers in the past came to the same conclusion.

When Rumi was questioned, criticized, and harassed by the fundamentalists and the hardliners of his time for his free thinking and dancing with music, his response to them was this:

From the Quran we only picked the kernel
We left the shell and the skin for the donkeys

As a Muslim living in the West or in a country where we can practice our religion freely, it is us and the Quran. We simply have to read all of it. We have to pick and choose the verses that are logical and agree with our own custom, culture, and the provisional rules and laws of the country we live in.

Some criticize the Quran for having contradicting verses. The verses in the Quran were revealed to Muhammad at different times throughout his struggles. I personally think the Quran is a book for all the seasons, good and bad. We can use its verses to heal our wounds, look for guidance, and have faith and hope in the Almighty. There are reasons some of the verses contradict each other.

Muhammad, who was a reformer of his time by bringing a new religion, had enemies from other religions and tribes. They would either be fighting or be at peace. When they were at peace, Muhammad would receive verses of tolerance.

109:6
For you is your religion and for me is my religion

On the other hand, when the enemy was planning to undermine Muhammad and Islam, the Quran reveals to Muhammad and Muslims to defend themselves.

9:29
Fight against those People of the Book who have no faith in God or the Day of Judgment, who do not consider unlawful what God and His Messenger have made unlawful, and who do not believe in the true religion, until they humbly pay tax with their own hands.

Now, in today's world, the believers of all religions reach for the words of their own scriptures to gain confidence and direction to help them in their struggle against their oppressor.

So if I am a Muslim living in the Middle East and my country is constantly undermined by "false springs" or "*whatever* color revolution," as the enemies of Islam like to create what they call "positive chaos," bullying, threatening, sanctioning, invading, and attacking under the false pretense of "weapons of mass destruction," I would have to draw on verses from the Quran to combat these evils who appear at my doorstep in Christian, Jewish, or even Islamic clothing, such as ISIS. Verses such as the following would be more soothing verses for me:

10:88-89
Moses said, "Lord, You have given the Pharaoh and his people great riches and splendor in this life and this makes them stray from Your path. Lord, destroy their wealth and harden their hearts in disbelief so that they will suffer the most painful torment".

God said, "Your prayer has been answered, so be steadfast on the right course, and do not follow the ways of those who do not know."

2:216
Fighting has been commanded upon you while it is hateful to you. But perhaps you hate a thing and it is good for you; and perhaps you love a thing and it is bad for you. And God Knows, while you know not.

9:111
God has purchased the souls and property of the believers in exchange for Paradise. They fight for the cause of God to destroy His enemies and to sacrifice themselves. This is a true promise which He has revealed in the Torah, the Gospel, and the Quran. No one is more true to His promise than God. Let this bargain be glad news for them. This is indeed the supreme triumph.

47:4
If you encounter the disbelievers in a battle, strike-off their heads. Take them as captives when they are defeated. Then you may set them free as a favor to them, with or without a ransom, when the battle is over. This is the Law. Had God wanted, He could have granted them (unbelievers) victory, but He wants to test you through each other. The deeds of those who are killed for the cause of God will never be without virtuous results.

THE QURAN, EARLY ISLAM, AND VERSES

8:12
Your Lord inspired the angels saying, "I am with you. Encourage the believers. I shall cast terror into the hearts of the unbelievers and you will strike their heads and limbs.

4:76
The believers fight for the cause of God. The unbelievers fight for the cause of the Satan. So fight against the friends of Satan for the evil plans of Satan are certainly weak

3:195
Their Lord answered their prayers saying, "I do not neglect anyone's labor whether the laborer be male or female. You are all related to one another. Those who migrated from Mecca, those who were expelled from their homes, those who were tortured for My cause, and those who fought and were killed for My cause will find their sins expiated by Me and I will admit them into the gardens wherein streams flow. It will be their reward from God Who grants the best rewards."

This is true during war time, when the enemy is at your border and bullying you. Regardless if you like it or not or want to fight or not, you need to rise and stand up to your enemy and fight, because he has come all the way to your borders, by land or by sea, to kill you!

What was that old saying by John Wayne? "Courage is being scared to death but saddling up anyway!"

And that's the way it is for Muslims. In Islam it is not important if you win or lose a war, it is important that you stand up to evil and follow the path of God. If you die, you have died and become a martyr on His path, which is the highest honor for a Muslim, and your afterlife in Paradise is guaranteed.

If you are meant to die in a war, it is far better and comforting for you, your next of kin, relatives, and the people around you if you die on the path of God, defending your country and people and standing up to evil, instead of dying for the greed and benefits of a bunch of politicians, lobbyists, neocons, and special interests of various kinds. The worst thing that can happen for you and your family is for you to die or get injured in vain for these characters, who try to paint their greed and tyranny with patriotism or security.

Sometimes people ask the non-Arab Muslims, who come from different nationalities and cultures, why do we stick to this religion and not change our religion to one that already has been reformed and polished, and makes common sense in its treatment of others, respects other beliefs and cultures, does not impose a burden not only on people who practice it but also on people outside that religion, and live by social rules that are internationally accepted and respected around the world? Why are we stuck to what was practiced 1,400 years ago by those Bedouin people?

The number one reason we stick to this religion is, we believe it is the word of God that was revealed to Muhammad 1,400 years ago, regardless of who it was sent for. Number two, we are born into it just like Jews and Christians who are born into their religion. Number three, we don't have any control over the behavior or way of thinking of Muslim leaders. We practice our religion regardless of who the leader is, regardless if we agree with them or not, similar to Christians who practice their Christianity regardless of who the pope is.

The Quran may have some controversial verses like the Bible and Torah, but when you go through hard times, there is nothing like the Quran to calm your heart, give you hope, teach you all about Powerful God and how He controls everything, how temporary this life is, and how you should restrain from temptations, do good, and save yourself for the afterlife.

In my opinion, the confidence and trust in God you receive from the Quran is unmatched by any other religious book on the planet, as I have read them all!

When you read it, you come across verses you know did not come from Muhammad or anybody else at that time, which seals your confidence in its divine connection.

When I come across verses such as the following:

24:45
God has created every living being from water: Some of them creep on their bellies; some walk on two feet and some of them walk on four legs. God creates whatever He wants. He has power over all things

51:47
The universe, We have built it with power, Verily We are expanding it.

It was just recently discovered that the universe is expanding.

21:32
And we made the sky a protected ceiling, but they turn away (neglected) from its sign (evidence).

21:30
Have those who disbelieved not considered that the heavens and the earth were a joined entity, and We separated them and made from water every living thing? Then will they not believe?

4: 118-119 (cloning)
God cursed Satan when he said, "I will surely take from among your servants a specific portion

And I will mislead them, and I will arouse in them [sinful] desires, and I will command them so they will slit the ears of cattle, and I will command them so they will change the creation of God." And whoever takes Satan as an ally instead of God has certainly sustained a clear loss.

Verses 4:118-119 are directly talking about cloning. I read several articles that stated cloning cows is easier compared to cloning other animals, as they take an ear cell from a healthy adult cow and use it to create a new clone. Or the following verse, when God created heaven and earth in six days, earth was covered with water. So for all those who say Muhammad wrote the Quran, what would Muhammad know about earth being covered with water, especially being a Bedouin man, standing in the sands of the desert, with no water in sight!

11:7
And it is He who created the heavens and the earth in six days - and His Throne had been on water - that He might test you as to which of you is best in deed. But if you say, "Indeed, you are resurrected after death," those who disbelieve will surely say, "This is not but obvious magic."

13:2
It is God who erected the heavens (universe) without pillars that you [can] see; then He established Himself above the Throne and made subject the sun and the moon, each running [its course] for a specified term. He arranges [each] matter; He details the signs that you may, of the meeting with your Lord, be certain.

31:29
Have you not seen that God causes the night to enter into the day and the day into the night. He has made the sun and moon subser-

vient (to Himself). Each running (its course) for an appointed time. God is certainly All-aware of what you do

39:5
He created the heavens and earth in truth. He wraps the night over the day and wraps the day over the night and has subjected the sun and the moon, each running [its course] for a specified term. Unquestionably, He is the Exalted in Might, the Perpetual Forgiver.

36:38
How the sun moves in its orbit and this is the decree of the Majestic and All-knowing God;

It is verses like these and many others like them that give validity to the Quran as God's word, as the things talked about in it had not yet been discovered when the Quran was revealed to Muhammad. The Quran clearly says that before you, there were other humans and animals on earth, and that "we" (God) wiped them off and started with new, to see how they would do (10:13, 14). An idea or a statement other religions have a hard time accepting is that there were other people and animals on this earth before us, and they have a really hard time explaining the dinosaurs!

10:13,14
We destroyed certain generations who lived before you because of their injustice. Our Messengers came to them and showed them miracles, but they would not believe. Thus do We punish the criminals. We have made you their successors in the land so that We could see how you behaved.

The Quran does say Adam was created from clay and that God blew from his spirit into him, but it also says humans and animals came from water. This was way before modern science. And what would Muhammad, this forty-plus-year-old Bedouin man walking in the deserts of Arabia, know about the atmosphere protecting the earth like a shield (21:32)! Or every living thing coming from water (24:45, 21:30), or about cloning (4:118-119)?

It's verses like these that make me and the likes of me more of "Quran explorers" rather than just people who read the Quran and try to follow it word for word. As the Quran says, we need to think and reason.

When I see verses like the ones mentioned above, I know there is something in this book for me to mine and extract. Some dismiss the Quran with arrogance and say, "Why should I practice a religion that was sent to these Bedouin people during their 'rough period,' 1,400 years ago?"

I say, "Nonsense, never mind the kind of people it was sent for." That is specifically why you should take a closer look at this religion. If this book can cultivate the "lost" descendants of Ishmael 1,400 years ago and give them a better life today, it can do wonders for you!

Dust off and clean up this old religion from its 1,400-year-ago Bedouin culture and customs, and you will find gold underneath. Read the Quran as God recommends it. Think and reason (21:10, 8:22). See what fits today's world and what does not. Use the fundamentals of religion that can help you and others in this life. It will put you on a better path and give you a better life.

Think of it as a tool box that was sent for those people, mixed with their culture and customs. You do not have to pick all the tools in the box or adopt their culture and customs. Simply pick and choose the tools that can help you in this life. That is precisely why you should mine and excavate the Quran and separate the diamonds from the rough Bedouin culture and customs the same way pearls are sought from the bottom of the sea and extracted from their hard shell. There are pearls of wisdom in the Quran that you can comb through and find and benefit from for a lifetime.

THE QURAN, EARLY ISLAM, AND VERSES

When the book of the Lord, the Quran, came to us
Unbelievers laughed, made foolish remarks

They said it's stories and myths of the past
It doesn't have depth, it's short of grand

The little children can understand it so
It's nothing but what to do and not to do.

Say, if it looks so easy to you
Then tell us one easy chapter, that came to you!

> Rumi, Persian poet 13th century (deducted from 2:23)
> Translation and Rhyme
> Faramarz F. Davati

Who Is Our God?

2: 255 (Ayat 'ol korsi)
God - there is no deity except Him, the Ever-Living, the Sustainer of [all] existence. Neither drowsiness overtakes Him nor sleep. To Him belongs whatever is in the heavens and whatever is on the earth. Who is it that can intercede with Him except by His permission? He knows what is [presently] before them and what will be after them, and they encompass not a thing of His knowledge except for what He wills. His Dominion extends over the heavens and the earth, and their preservation tires Him not. And He is the Most High, the Most Great.

Who is our God? Our God is the God of the universe, the One and only One who created this earth, universe, and everything in it. He is the owner of this world and afterlife. He was not born from anyone and does not give birth to anyone. He is the Master of the Day of Judgment. He is at the throne and is the ruler of the universe.

If there is one Abrahamic faith that could encompass all three Abrahamic faiths in one, it would be Islam. By completely setting aside and differentiating the real teachings of Islam from its Bedouin culture and customs, it can be practiced by anybody from any culture and with any customs around the world.

2:136
Say we have believed in God and what is revealed to Abraham and Ismail and Isaac and Jacob (Yaqub) and the descendants (Jacob), and what was given to Moses and Jesus, and was

given to the prophets for their Lord. We make no distinction between any of them. And to Him we are submissive (Muslims)

In comparison with other religions, our concept of God and fear of God is closer to the concept of God in Judaism than Christianity. God is absolute and feared in Judaism also.

Christianity sees God differently. In Christianity, God, the creator of the universe, is in the background and referred to as "Father." Jesus is believed to be His son, the God of the universe, and the savior on the Day of Judgment, and everything happens through Jesus.

In Islam, our belief in God is different. He is the One and only God. He is the King of the Universe and does not share power with anybody. He is the One and only that you pray to and ask for help. No intermediary. He is Absolute and the Almighty. Everything can come through Him. He is in control and capable over all affairs. He is eternal and His power is simply above All powers. If He orders something "to be" or "behold," it will be done. That is our God that we Muslims worship, pray to, and ask for forgiveness and help. We have no intermediary. One of the main differences between Islam and Christianity is we do not believe we have a savior. We Muslims believe that on Judgment Day we are paid back for all the good and all the bad we have done in this life.

The enemies of Islam and Muslims, or those who are prejudiced against Islam, constantly try to portray Islam and our God as something different than the God of the universe. When they talk to you or in the TV or media coverage, they say, "So you believe in Allah," as if He is different from the God of Abraham, Moses, and Jesus. Well, in fact, He is the God of all of them. *Allah* is simply the Arabic word for God. The Western media makes remarks such as, "This Allah you believe in..." or "This Allah that you pray to..." as if He is some different entity than the Almighty God. Some of them may really not know, and some persist in their ignorance.

When you explain it to them, their response is either, "I did not know that," or "Is that what you believe?" as they believe Prophet Jesus is God. They refer to God, the creator of the universe, as Father. He is somewhat in the background and is hardly mentioned, asked helped from, prayed to, or asked forgiveness from. Everything goes through Jesus, as they call him the son of God and worship him.

I have read the Bible and have never seen Jesus tell anyone, "Worship ME!"

That is why in this book, I have emphasized the word **God** instead of the Arabic translation (Allah), so there is no misunderstanding for the non-Muslims in regard to who we worship and believe in, as some of them may simply not know and are victims of the bias and controlled media here in the US.

That is why we have to educate the public about who our God is, since some of our enemies in the West own the media and constantly try to influence the people against us, our beliefs, and Islam, similar to what the Nazis did to the Jews.

They do this by referring to us Muslims as terrorists and saying it over and over in the media, loud enough and long enough, for people to believe it.

But let's get back to the subject of our God and only God of the universe that we believe in.

There are hundreds of verses about God and God's interaction with us in the Quran. I am going to mention just a few, as it would take over 130 pages of this book to mention all the verses. I leave the rest for you to find for yourself.

The following are some verses describing the God of Islam and who we worship:

3:18
GOD bears witness that there is no God except He, and so do the angels and those who possess knowledge. Truthfully and equitably, He is the absolute God; there is no God but He, the Almighty, Most Wise.

59:23
He is the One GOD; there is no other God besides Him. The King, the Most Sacred, the Peace, the Most Faithful, the Supreme, the Almighty, the Most Powerful, the Most Dignified. GOD be glorified; far above having partners.

2:62
Indeed, those who believed and those who were Jews or Christians or Sabeans [before Prophet Muhammad] - those [among them] who believed in God and the Last Day and did righteousness - will have their reward with their Lord, and no fear will there be concerning them, nor will they grieve

1:1
In the name of God, Most kind, Most Merciful.

1:2
Praise be to God, Lord of the universe.

1:4
Master of the Day of Judgement

1:5
We only worship You and we only ask help from You.

112:1
Say, He is the One and only GOD.

WHO IS OUR GOD?

112:2
The Eternal Refuge (the one you go to when in need).

112:3
He was not born from anyone and He does not give birth to anyone.

114:3
The God of the people.

114:4
There is no one equal to Him

2:22
The One who made the earth habitable for you, and the sky a structure. He sends down from the sky water, to produce all kinds of fruits for your sustenance. You shall not set up idols to rival God, now that you know.

2:163
Your God is one God; there is no God but He, Most Gracious, Most Merciful.

2:107
Do you not recognize the fact that God possesses the kingship of the heavens and the earth; that you have none besides God as your Lord and Master?

2:255
God; there is no other God besides Him, the Living, the Eternal. Never a moment of unawareness or slumber overtakes Him. To Him belongs everything in the heavens and everything on earth. Who could intercede with Him, except in accordance with His will? He knows their past, and their future. No one attains any knowledge, except as He wills. His dominion encompasses the heavens

and the earth, and ruling them never burdens Him. He is the Most High, the Great.

4:26
God wants to make clear to you [the lawful from the unlawful] and guide you to the [good] practices of those before you and to accept your repentance. And God is Knowing and Wise.

4:27
God wishes to redeem you, while those who pursue their lusts wish that you deviate a great deviation.

4:28
God wishes to lighten your burden, for the human being is created weak.

General Fundamentals of Islam

Islam is the strongest religion in the world. The more the West and dark forces try to push it down or portray it as bad, the stronger it gets. The beauty and strength of Islam come from its foundation: believing in One God. We do not take any other deity except God. Our complete belief and devotion in One God and the only God who created the universe is unmatched by any other religion. Judaism may come close, but their lack of belief in the afterlife makes it seem incomplete and without a destination or a direction.

The beauty of Islam is how easy it is to be a Muslim and be close to God by just following the fundamentals of Islam. Here in the US, you do not have to dress in Arabian fashion, grow a beard, or even wear a burqa or scarf. It's up to you. Those things are done mostly overseas in some of the Muslim countries, where the religious authorities rule or influence the system in their country.

Islam is like learning how to swim correctly. Once you learn it, you can always swim and be saved from drowning in any water, anywhere in the world. God has not tried to put any hardship on you in Islam.

22:78
Strive steadfastly for the Cause of God. He has chosen you but has not imposed on you hardship in your religion, the noble religion of your father, Abraham. God named you Muslims before (former scriptures) and in this Book (revelation), so that the Messenger will witness (your actions) and will be the witness over mankind. Be

steadfast in your prayer, pay the religious tax, and seek protection from God; He is your Guardian, a gracious Guardian and Helper.

In order to be a Muslim, you have to believe and act on the following five items which are the main pillars of Islam:

1- **(*Shahada*) Declaring there is only one God and one God alone we worship and Muhammad is God's messenger.**

   (All you have to say to become Muslims is, "I testify there is no other God but God, and Muhammad is God's messenger," and you are Muslim.)

2- **Ritual prayers five times a day.**

3- **Charity, giving 2.5 percent of your income to the poor and needy.**

4- **Fasting and self-control between sunrise and sunset during the month of Ramadan. (If you can. If you are sick, have a health problem, or are pregnant or too old, you do not have to.)**

5- **Pilgrimage to Mecca for the ceremony of Hajj at least once in a lifetime (only if you can afford it).**

The above are fundamentals of Islam and all you need to do to be a Muslim. The Quran does not tell you that you have to be a member of a certain sect (Shia or Sunni). All it tells you is to be a Muslim and submit to God.

Islam has been divided into two major groups of Sunni and Shia. There are other smaller sects too, but these two are the major ones. The majority of the Muslims in the world are Sunnis.

Both groups have added their own rules and interpretations of the Quran and claim their rules have come directly from Muhammad or *hadiths*, which are stories they claim happened at the time of Muhammad; whatever they claim Muhammad or his companions said verbatim; and anything else they consider relevant after his death.

In any religion, once people have messed with the foundation of the religion or have set the first stone wrong, either the walls have gone up crooked or the whole house is on shaky ground and they have to spend the rest of the time constantly explaining, repairing, and defending their version of the religion or sect, regardless of if they are Jews, Christians, or Muslims.

Many different sects of Islam have not gone through any reformations, and the ones who did have been attacked by the major two. The major two (Shia and Sunni) mostly follow the Quran word for word without putting any logic or common sense first. As a result, not only have they led their people backward to 1,400 years ago, but they have also done a disservice to Islam and Muslims by directing them the wrong way, alienating not just Muslims but also other people around the world.

After all, if the Quran is the exact word of God, how come Muslim countries are competing for the last place on earth culturally? Obviously they have been going the wrong way, and it will not fix itself, unless the people decide to reform.

Here in the US, thank God we are not under any religious authority and we can practice our Islam freely and without any fear from religious or Hijab police.

In the US all you need is the Quran. Find a good and easy-to-read translation of it in order to understand, and pick and choose the verses that are logical and can be used for a better life.

I personally found "Sahih International" to be the closest word-by-word translation of the Quran, and "Muhammad

Sarwar's" translation to be the most common-sense translation of the scripture.

For a free PDF download of Muhammad Sarwar's translation of the Holy Quran with Arabic and English text (made possible by the Sajjad Foundation) visit our website:

www.IslamIsGrand.com.

For an in-depth meaning of any verse, I like to recommend http://corpus.quran.com/translation.jsp, where you can compare seven translations of the same verse, including "Sahih International" and also exact word-by-word translations of each verse. Click on the "English Translation" on the left vertical column. This is where you can see the seven translations of each verse. This is a wonderful website, and I am sure a lot of hard work and dedication has gone toward it. More power to the people who made it.

Another good website I like to recommend if you like to hear the recitation of the Quran is http://www.allahsquranQuran.com/.

If you are non-Muslim and are thinking about attending a mosque, each mosque has its own personality. Men and woman do not sit together, similar to at synagogue. Not all mosques are the same, as there are different sects of Islam. Just like churches, they all have their own personality. Most mosques import their *imam* from overseas. The *imam* is equivalent to a pastor or preacher in the Christian world. The imam of a mosque represents the branch of Islam he comes from. All you have to do is listen to the Friday sermon once and decide if that is the right mosque for you. Unfortunately, most imams are imported from overseas and carry the same old baggage from wherever they come. We still have a long way to go here in the US. I personally believe in the US, Islam should be reformed for the better by US-educated moderate Muslims who are familiar with the American culture and way of life, instead of some imam who has gone to a Muslim school in the Middle East and recently just landed and has no real clue about life in America.

Fundamentals of Islam can be practiced by anybody in the world. There is nothing unusual about believing in One God, testifying that Muhammad is a prophet of God, praying five times a day to God, and giving charity to poor. Fasting once a year for one month is a great tool for self-discipline, self-control and giving up bad habits. Fasting is not mandatory for those who are sick, have a health problem, have to take prescription drugs or are pregnant. Pilgrimage to Hajj is required only if you can afford it.

In short, "you" become a "better you" by practicing the fundamentals of Islam, regardless of your current belief. This is why Islam is the strongest religion in the world.

Alchemy of the Quran and Islam

❖

I believe if anyone tries to read the Quran as a Quran Explorer, he or she can get a lot more out of it than by just following it word for word without even thinking. They can discover the alchemy of the Quran in simple words that can lead them to a better life.

The Quran is written in simple language, and when followed, a person will supernaturally have a better life, no matter what he or she does. The unshakable confidence and belief in One God that is received from this book creates a certain self-assured feeling and vibes around the person that makes things happen for the person and to his or her benefit, over and over, which is not by accident.

Getting on your knees and privately praying and talking to God five times a day not only changes you as a person, but it also brings blessings to your house. The relationship you develop with God is much stronger and surpasses all the other religions in which their believers go to their temple, church, synagogue, or any house of worship once a week.

Singing and dancing in church once or twice a week is having a "fun" relationship with God, and there is nothing wrong with it. But getting on your knees, praying, and having your quiet moment with the Almighty five times a day is a "serious" relationship with God.

For successful Muslims, it is not what they do for a living that makes them successful. It is the right path that God lays in front of them, tailored just for each of them, their personal treasure that makes them successful. God has put a certain treasure for everyone in their heart. By reading the Quran, people will have their "trust-in-God" (*tawakkul*) to follow it and get it. Reading the Quran and having a one-on-one meeting, conference, dialog, whatever you may call it, in the form of prayer five times a day with the Almighty Himself, creator of the universe, will create an invisible spiritual connection between you and God. No intermediaries, no one but One God, the Only God of the universe. It is this kind of praying that makes your prayers more potent and powerful compared to praying to his intermediaries!

With the Quran, by repeating certain sayings, phrases, beliefs, or prayers, or reciting them out loud in life over and over again, repeated every day at least five times a day and followed religiously and believed with confidence, people can make the universe turn upside down and give them what they asked for, and receive it supernaturally. That is the alchemy of the Quran. It is the simplest way to success in life. The stronger you believe in God, the faster you see results.

The more you pray... the more blessings you receive (2:186, 7:170, 20:132, 22:41)!

The more you thank... the more blessings you receive (14:7)!

The more you praise God... the more you get his attention!

To get the best of the Quran, you have to go through it yourself and pick and choose the verses that can give an answer to your cause, or healing to your wounds, knowing that God is the ultimate redeemer, vindicator, and absolute power and that His hand is above all hands. Anything is possible through God.

As you read the Quran, completely set aside its Bedouin culture and customs, as they belong to 1,400 years ago. Only read and concentrate on the main teachings of Islam and the Quran. This will become your one-on-one journey with God, all the way till you reach the end of the Quran. When you finish the Quran, you feel you are not alone anymore. There is someone with you at all times, and He is God. He hears you, He is all-aware of you. He sees everything you do and backs you up in everything. He lays the right path in front of you, for your own good, even if it is against what you were looking for. You are no longer worried when going through ups and downs in life, as you know He will catch you if you fall. By thanking Him throughout the day, over and over, you remind yourself of his blessings in your life and get to enjoy the "treasure of the moment" more and more throughout the day. You know everything will be fine as you glide through life. The hardships of life seem temporary and like background noise, as your focus is on Him and you know this life is impermanent and short. Everything will turn out okay. Put your trust in Him and enjoy the treasure of the moment and the ride of your life as long as you are in this world. He is your backup in everything you do, and you understand how this world works! When you go through ups and downs in life, you go through them with assurance.

As the Persian poet Saadi puts it,

With the hands of the Lord on your back what to worry of any
With Noah in command, not worrisome of the waves when in the sea

Saadi, Persian poet 13th century
Translation and Rhyme
Faramarz F, Davati

It is this kind of assurance, comfort, trust, faith, and submission to God that you receive when reading the Quran.

In the following chapters I will try to explain some of the main concepts you will find in the Quran, but this will not replace you reading and deriving what you can from it. We all have different talents and capabilities, and I am sure many of you will have a better grasp than me when it comes to absorbing from the Quran, and will be able to do extraordinary things with it. Anything is possible through God!

You should keep in mind as you read through that the Quran sometimes does not explain all the stories like a story book. It appears it assumes we know some of the Old Testament stories. For example, it seems the Quran assumes we know the story of Saleh[3] (who was the seventh descendant of Noah) and the camel God sent, as well as Moses splitting the sea or hitting the rock with his staff to create nine fountains for the nine tribes of Israel. So from time to time you may see bits and pieces of stories that have been mentioned to remind us of the event.

Below is what I call a partial list of what I found to be repeated and emphasized over and over in different parts of the Quran. These messages have been repeated between verses or stories in the Quran and are easy to detect.

I am sure there are more if you look for them. Many of them

---

[3] Saleh invited the tribe of Thamud to worship only God, as they were idol worshipers. The idol worshipers told Saleh, "If your God is true ask Him to make a beautiful she camel that is ten months pregnant, out of a rock." Saleh asked them if God were to send what they were asking, would they then believe in his teachings. They said yes.

So Saleh took a vow from them and prayed to God. God ordered a distant rock to split, and a beautiful ten-month-pregnant camel came out of it. The people were amazed by the miracle. Some believed his teachings and some became skeptical and later on conspired against that camel. Saleh warned people not to do anything bad with the camel God had sent. But the idol worshipers conspired against the camel and killed her. Saleh gave them three days to repent and ask forgiveness from God. They all laughed at him and said, "Why wait three days, why don't you ask your God to send something now?" God saved Saleh and his followers, as they moved to another place. After the third day, thunderbolts filled the sky and a violent earthquake destroyed all their homes and killed all the idol worshipers who were left behind. The story of Saleh has been mentioned in various chapters and sections: 11:61-62, 15:80-81, 17:59, 17:80-81, 27:45-53, 7:73-79, and 11:64. You may see stories or verses in different parts of the Quran that refer to this incident and what happened to the tribe of Thamud for disobeying God.

Courtesy of http://www.islamawareness.net/Prophets/salih.html.

have become short sayings people recite throughout the day. I know in the Farsi language, some of them have been made into one-line poems so you can memorize them smoothly and easily and say them throughout the day.

Here are some of the messages that have been repeated many times, or draw from the Quran that I believe supernaturally open gates and create possibilities for everyone. The verse that was the first key for me and opened up the Quran in a completely different way was verse 2:118. I will explain that further in the "Believe" section:

- **You believe in Me, and I will show you a miracle in your life (2:118)!**

God tells his followers through the Quran to have faith in the unseen; to be patient in their prayers and have faith and believe and it will happen; to be certain and expect that it will happen, and it will happen.

The following is the message that has been repeated many times in the Quran:
- Anything is possible through God.
- He has power over all things.
- Have faith in the unseen, be patient in your prayers, expect and believe it will happen.
- God is in total control of everything, with power.
- God is the greatest.
- There is no God but the One God.
- Put your trust in God.
- God's hand is above all hands.
- God has power over everything.

- Thank you, God the King of the universe.
- Thank you, God, for all the blessings you have given me.
- Powerful God has control over everything.
- God is in control of everything.
- Thank you, God, for protecting me against evil.
- God, I will be patient and leave everything to you.
- Believe in God.
- Have faith in God.
- Trust in God.
- Trust in God and move forward.
- Praise God.
- Do your daily prayers.
- Give charity.
- Put everything in God's hands.
- Be patient and expect to receive it from God with confidence.
- The more you thank God for your blessings, the more blessings you receive.
- The more you pray, the more blessing you receive.
- The more you praise God, the more you get His attention.
- God listens to those who praise Him.
- God is the One you go to when in need.
- God is an eternal refuge.

- God has power over all things.
- And many more that hopefully you will find and share with the rest of us.

Some of the above do get preached and practiced in other religions too, but perhaps are not repeated or reminded as often as in the Quran.

In Islam, the more you pray, the more blessings you receive from God. That is why we are commanded to pray five times a day. And the more you praise the Lord, the more you get his attention. God listens to those who praise Him.

The more charity you give, the more God will repay you as He says in the Quran (57:11, 57:18). When you give charity consider it a loan to God, as He will pay you back in multiples of what you have given.

57:11
Whoever gives a "good deed" loan to God will receive multiple from Him in addition to a noble reward.

57:18
Indeed, the men who practice charity and the women who practice charity and [they who] have loaned God a goodly loan - it will be multiplied for them, and they will have a noble reward

The following chapter also describes in general how I picked and chose verses, even though I veered off many times. But it is simply a general template. There are many, many topics you can draw from, and I hope you will continue your study far beyond the guide I provide here. This book is only a very small tip of a huge iceberg underneath. It has taken me over ten years to extract and find the information contained here by using various translations. It took me so long, because I simply enjoyed every minute of it. I hope you enjoy it too!

ALCHEMY OF THE QURAN

If the Lord meant for this work to get accepted
It wasn't out of the temptation that I did this work

Whatever came to me the credit goes to Him
Whatever I did, I did it all with the grace of the Quran

Hafez, Persian poet 14th century
Translation and Rhyme
Faramarz F, Davati

Choosing Verses

In order to tap into the supernatural verses of the Quran, one has to separate the main teachings of the Quran from its Bedouin culture and customs. The verses are a combination of the stories, customs, and culture of these people, intertwined with universal laws to be read and followed.

Muhammad was not an educated man, or as the Quran states a "learned man," and he was far from being an eloquent writer to write the Quran. The Quran, at first glance, may read similarly to the Bible or the Old Testament, except it is easier to understand and it is written in a more layman language compared to the King James English version of the Bible today.

Like other religious books, it does have its share of controversial and questionable verses that I do not have an answer for. Most of the Quran is about stories of the past. Moses has been mentioned over 140 times in the Quran. The fundamentals of Islam are a small portion of the Quran and are mixed with these stories and between the chapters, or *Surahs* as they are called. Among these verses the supernatural laws of the universe are placed so beautifully that you can memorize them with the least amount of effort.

One of the beauties of Islam is that there is no intermediary between you and God. All you need is to read the book and create your own connection with God. You do not need or have to follow any clergyman, as they may put their own spin on the message, based on their background, belief, or branch of Islam or for their own benefit, which these days is true in almost all religions.

The big question is, how do you find and recognize the important, meaningful verses? For that you have to read the Quran in its entirety in order to feel the essence of the Quran. The good news is, you do not have to know Arabic. With the advent of the Internet and plenty of websites offering various translations in almost every language in the world, you can conveniently read the Quran in your own language. Perhaps English is the most common and best one, as there are a variety of translations you can compare, and also word-by-word translations.

When you read the Quran, find verses that encourage you to press on and give you hope and confidence. Think of it as a toolbox you reach into to find the right tool to help you fix your problem. But understand that you do not become the toolbox, as the toolbox by itself does not have any intelligence.

Anyone who follows any religious book word for word is simply a fanatic. Only follow verses that are logical and make sense.

21:10
We have sent down to you a Book which is a message for you, Then will you not reason?

I have gathered some of these verses and listed them in different chapters. I have also included topics that are mostly asked about Islam by non-Muslims, like our beliefs about Mary, Jesus, Moses, the children of Israel, the afterlife, Paradise, and who our God is.

I have written this book for second-generation Muslims in general and young Muslims in particular. I think for non-Muslims who are interested in Islam and would like to know more about Islam this would be a good sampler of the verses in the Quran. In my opinion, it is perhaps one of the best miniatures or collected verses of the Quran available in English today.

CHOOSING VERSES

When I was writing this book, I mostly had in mind the second-generation Muslims here in the US, as most of them are Muslim by name but have never read the Quran and may not know enough about Islam. Their parents may be Muslim, but their devotions to the religion may vary, like with many other religions.

Some of the young Muslims have a good start, but as they grow older they lose interest, as they want something "cool" in their teenage years and may stray away. Perhaps in the near future we can create a "cooler" environment for the teenagers. I have tried very hard not to discuss politics and stain this book and leave that subject for another book. However, given the current situation in the US, I know I have slipped a few times!

To come up with my list of verses, I generally tried to follow the steps below, which I am sure I might have deviated from a few times. Using this method, I am sure you can find your own pearls of wisdom from this book as well.

Here are my suggestions:

1- For practicing your Islam, pick and choose verses that can help you in this life and do not impose a burden for people around you regardless if they are Muslim or non-Muslim.

2- Arabian and Middle Eastern customs are respected and are good for Arabian and Middle Eastern people, regardless of their country of origin. If you do not live there, though, separate those customs from the main teachings of the Quran.

3- Try to pick and choose verses that can be followed by all the Muslims in this world, not just the fundamentalists in the mosque!

ALCHEMY OF THE QURAN

4- Go around any verse you think was sent for the people of the "ignorance period" 1,400 years ago.

5- The best verses are those that would make sense to and benefit a non-Muslim you are trying to help.

6- In your Quran search, completely put aside any *hadith* [4](story) and *Sunnah* regardless of whether or not the *hadith* or *Sunnah* has been confirmed by the highest religious figure of any sect. Only concentrate on the Quran itself.

31:6
But there are among men those who buy ridiculous Hadiths without knowledge, to mislead (men) from the Path of God and throw ridicule; for such there will be a humiliating penalty.

Although there are many good hadiths, sometimes fabricated hadiths accompany the good ones. Hadiths and the Sunnah are second or third in ranking anyway compared to the Quran. We are focusing first on examining what verses to choose from the Quran, which would make the hadiths and Sunnah somewhat irrelevant and non-essential compared to the Quran. There are hadiths and Sunnah that have been fabricated by different groups or people, either for their own benefit or for competing with different branches in Islam, competing with Christians and Jews, or elevating Muhammad far above what he was. Muhammad was just a messenger as he and the Quran have said over and over again. When reading the Quran, you want to look at a bigger picture, and your bigger picture is the Quran and God.

---

4   *Hadith: a collection of traditions containing sayings of the prophet Muhammad that, with accounts of his daily practice (the Sunna), constitute the major source of guidance for Muslims apart from the Koran.*

CHOOSING VERSES

Here is an example of a false hadith: Dogs are known around the world as man's best friend. As a matter of fact, if you live in the countryside or remote areas, having a dog is a necessity, as a dog is the best security alarm and protector of the house you can have. However, a dog is considered by many Muslims and Muslim countries as unclean and untouchable, and Muslims try not to touch a dog, or if they do, they are advised to wash their hands immediately before touching anything else or they will make whatever they have touched unclean also! However, Muslims do not have this phobia against cats, even though they may be as unclean as dogs. There is not one verse in the Quran that would justify this, and this belief is simply one of the results of untrue and made up hadiths that have deprived Muslims from man's best friend for 1,400 years! Here are all the verses in the Quran that talk about dogs: 5:4, 7:176, 18:18, 18:22.

7- Last but not least, if Arabic is not your first language, do not waste your time trying to learn Arabic first or at the same time as reading the Quran. With the convenience of the Internet, plenty of translations are available for comparison, you can read and understand the Quran in English or your own language instead of trying to read in a foreign language and then translating it and getting tired and giving up after a few verses. Just read the whole book either in English or your own language; do not bother with the Arabic words. There is always time in the future if you are interested in learning Arabic. The Quran is a voluminous book, and it will take you quite a while to read the whole thing; I would say approximately a year and half by reading a few pages every day. Highlight the verses you like and write notes. If you reach some verses you don't understand or don't make sense, don't get stuck. Simply go around them and continue reading to the end. I personally have read the Quran in its entirety six or seven times, with five separate English translations, and every time, I have noticed something new that I did not notice before.

Don't worry about the people who tell you have to read it in pure Arabic and it should be read correctly with an Arabic accent otherwise it is a sin and you will go to hell!

Push them aside and do not even associate with them! As a matter of fact, do not even associate with any Muslim who comes across as a fanatic backward Muslim. He is bad for you, your beliefs, and Islam.

As I mentioned earlier, some of the verses in the Quran are reflections of the events around Muhammad as he was going through his struggles. The numbers on the chapters (*surahs*) of the Quran do not reflect the time or the order in which the Quran was revealed to Muhammad. These numbers were arranged later when the Quran was being put together by the third caliph, Uthman. It starts with bigger chapters at the beginning and gets smaller as it nears the end.

In the following chapters, I have touched on the surface of the Quran and Islam and what makes this extraordinary book so powerful. Hopefully this sampler will encourage you to get involved and dig deeper.

Start your own journey with God! It will be a journey that you will never forget, for years and years to come.

I know some Muslims may not agree with this book or me, as they believe only their way is the right way and the Quran should be followed word for word, and they probably would like to show me a verse or two from the Quran to prove their point. I have read all of them!

I am sure the hardliners of all sects of Islam would hate this book and accuse me of "cherry picking." Well, cherry picking it is.

CHOOSING VERSES

This book is not intended for them anyway.

This book is for moderate Muslims who are tolerant of the rest of the world and understand not only us Muslims but most religions of the world all worship the same God, the creator of universe, but we all do it in different manners, customs, languages, and traditions.

I think the story of *"Moses and Shepherd"* by Rumi would be an appropriate way to finish this chapter.

My translation and rhyme, no matter how hard I tried, would neither come close nor do justice to the beauty of the original poem by Rumi in Farsi, but here is a shorter version of the original:

Moses and Shepherd

Saw Moses a Shepherd on his way
Calling on God, the Lord O Yahweh

Where can I find you to be your waitron?
Mend and sew your shoes, your hair I brush

Will be at service kissing your hands and feet
Will sweep your bed when it's sleepy time

If an illness comes to you all of sudden
Will be sharing it as if my own pain

Sacrifice myself for you, Mighty Lord
Included children my livelihood

Sacrifice for You, all my sheep and goats
Thinking of You every call I holler out

ALCHEMY OF THE QURAN

This manner was false worship by the shepherd
Heard Moses asked, "Who you talk to O shepherd?"

Said shepherd, "Talking to our only creator the One
Who created this earth, this spread, sky above."

Said to him Moses, "You are insulting God.
You've become pagan, before bowing to God.

If you don't stop talking in this manner
Fire and hell from above will come to us."

Said shepherd, "Moses you sewed my mouth shut
You broke my soul, your words burnt my heart."

Then shepherd tore his clothes his headdress walking away
He cried and burned inside as he headed for the desert

God saw that, sent Moses a message,
"A believer's ties to us, you did sever.

We sent you to create a connection
Didn't send you to cause disconnection

We don't look on the outside or what they say
We look inside their soul, not the lips say."

When Moses heard the Lord's objection to him
He chased after the shepherd in that desert

CHOOSING VERSES

Finally caught up with him and said to him,
"Good news I have, the Lord sent a command!"

No worry what order or manner to choose
Talk to Almighty, any way that you choose."

Rumi, Persian poet 13th century
Translation and Rhyme
Faramarz F, Davati

There Is No God but the One God

❖

M*onotheism* is the cornerstone of Islam; that is, to believe in One God and One God alone. There is no God but the One God. This belief and saying, "no God but One God," is the foundation of the house of Islam. **Muslims are not to bring anyone else to share the throne with Him.** This is emphasized in Islam over and over more than in any other religion in the world.

In Islam, it is this force of the All-Powerful One God that is above all other forces in nature, that can control everything at any time in the universe. God is the creator and sits at the throne of this vast universe. He is the undisputed Supreme Power. His power is above all powers and overrides any natural or supernatural power in the world. **Through Him, everything is possible no matter what.** When He "wills it," "it is done."

It is this One All-Powerful God that is the main driving force of Islam that can make everything possible, no matter what the circumstances and situation. The stronger your belief in Him, the more happens for you.

Chapter (*Surah*) 112 of the Quran describes this very well and clearly.

In the name of Most kind and Most forgiving God
Say He is the Only God
God, the Eternal Refuge (on Whom all depend [the one you go to when in need])
He neither gives birth nor was He born.
And there is nothing like Him.

In Islam, He is the One and Only, He is the All-Seeing, All-Powerful, All-Eternal, All-Just, Absolute, and Complete, with no equal to Him. Everything depends on Him. He is All-Capable over everything, and everything is possible through Him. He is at the throne of this universe. He created all of it, and it all belongs to Him.

As Mahmoud Shabestari, fourteenth-century Persian poet, describes His Oneness:

See One, say One, and know One
This is how the main and branches of Islam have come

Mahmood Shabestari, Persian poet 14th century
Translation and Rhyme
Faramarz F, Davati

In the Quran in many verses God emphasizes not to take another God besides him. He is the One and Only God. Verse 2:165 is one example of it.

[2:165]
And [yet], among the people are those who take other than God as equals [to Him]. They love them as they [should] love God. *But those who believe are stronger in love for God. And if only they who have wronged would consider [that] when they see the punishment, [they will be certain] that all power belongs to God and that God is severe in punishment*

Rumi takes from above verse as follow:

Don't take another Love beside Him
Your soul shouldn't think of other Ones beside Him

THERE IS NO GOD BUT THE ONE GOD

Another Love another way, is a curse, not our ways
Don't stain religion, with these other ways

Your soul mirrors what you say in words
It can't be hidden, don't you try it

Rumi, Persian poet 13th century
Translation and Rhyme
Faramarz F, Davati

In Islam, God is beyond all comprehension, imagination, shape, measurement, or manifestation. He is above all, He is the One and only God, the One you go to when in need, the eternal refuge. He is not born from anyone and does not give birth to anyone, and there is nothing like Him.

The thirteenth-century Persian poet *Saadi* puts it nicely:
You, who are beyond imagination, comprehension, thoughts, and doubts
From whatever we've heard, read, and has been said about You

This party is coming to an end as our life is nearing end
And we are still in the first chapter of describing You!

Saadi, Persian poet 13th century
Translation and Rhyme
Faramarz F, Davati

The following are a few of the verses as samplers, emphasizing the Oneness of God in Islam. There are a lot more as you read through the Quran.

2:163
*And your God is one God; there is no God except **Him**, the most kind and forgiving.*

3:18
God bears witness that there is no God except He, and so do the angels and those who possess knowledge. Truthfully and equitably, He is the absolute God; there is no God but He, the Almighty, Most Wise.

4:171
O People of the Scripture, do not exaggerate in your religion or say about God except the truth. The Messiah, Jesus, the son of Mary, was but a messenger of God and His word which He directed to Mary and a soul [created at a command] from Him. So believe in God and His messengers. And do not say, "Three"; God - it is better for you. Indeed, God is but one God. He is too Grand to give birth to a son. To Him belongs whatever is in the heavens and whatever is on the earth. And He (God) is enough to take care of the affairs.

14:52
This [Qur'an] is notification for the people that they may be warned thereby and that they may know that He is but one God and that those of understanding will be reminded

16:51
And God has said, "Do not take for yourselves two deities. He is but one God, so fear only Me."

[64:13]
God is the only Lord and in Him the believers should trust

Believe

Indeed we make clear miracles for those who firmly believe (2:118).

You believe in Me (God), and I will show you a miracle in your life.
After "the Oneness of God," perhaps the most important word or subject in the Quran would be "believe." Other holy books or testaments ask you, advise you, or invite you to believe in God in a somewhat mild manner, compared to Islam. Somehow by reading the Quran, you don't just believe in God. **You believe and trust in God with confidence.** Perhaps it is the way it is written or put together in the Quran. I do not know how to describe it, but maybe it is because the message has come from above, as Muhammad didn't even know how to read and write, and certainly was not an eloquent writer! But your belief in God is much stronger when you learn about Him through the Quran. How much stronger, you may ask? Strong enough for many people to be willing to put their lives on the line when push comes to shove. The events in the Middle East are a prime example of this.

A few years ago, when I decided to write this book, I had a moment of clarity when I was comparing Muhammad with his predecessors.

The main prophets before Muhammad would show people miracles, and people would see the miracle and would believe in his word and his God. Then I came across the following verse, and it suddenly opened up the entire Quran for me and gave me an entirely different perspective.

2:118
And those who do not know say, why does God not speak to us or send us a miracle? And there were others who said the same before them. Their hearts are alike. Indeed we make clear miracles for those who firmly believe.

The main difference between Muhammad and his predecessors is this:

Previous prophets would preach to people about God, and then either God would send a miracle or they would show you a miracle. Then you would believe in God and the teachings of that prophet.

But in 2:118 and other parts of the Quran, God, through his last prophet on earth, tells people,

"You believe in Me, and I will show you a miracle in your life!"

God tells his followers through the Quran to have faith in the unseen; to be patient in their prayers and have faith and believe, and it will happen; to be certain and expect that it will happen, and it will happen. Faith says for and encourages you to believe it. Once you believe it, then you can see it and bring it into your life.

That is the supernatural way of the Quran, the power of belief in the Almighty! Once I saw that, the rest of the book opened up completely differently to me. It was as if I had discovered a "key" to see the laws of the universe embedded among the stories and verses in the Quran. I found signs, advice, and mandatory disciplined routine actions, such as prayer, gratitude, expectancy from God, hope, faith, unbreakable trust and belief in God, and knowing there is no power above God's power, His power overtakes and is above all powers, and He is capable of doing everything. The Quran teaches you; by simply following it, it will lead you to the direct path and a better life.

If followed correctly with an open mind, it is simply an "ignorant-period"-proof guide for a better life. You can simply achieve and get whatever you like in this life and have the opportunity to plant a seed and save for the afterlife.

The teachings, religious rituals, prayers, and habits are emphasized over and over in the Quran a lot more than in other religious or holy books. And this is a book that was revealed 1,400 years ago, to an uneducated Bedouin man, in the deserts of Arabia, with no sign of any advanced civilized world around him. If the teachings and essence of this book can turn those people into a group of people with monotheistic beliefs and a much better status today, compared to before, it can do wonders in the modern times for anybody, regardless if he or she is Muslim or not.

This book can be used as a torch, or as the Quran calls it, "as a light to illuminate your path" (42:52), as it can guide you to a better life.

42:52
Thus, We have revealed to you an inspiration of Our command, (Muhammad). Before, you did not even know what a Book or Faith was, but We have made the Quran as a light by which We guide whichever of Our subjects We want. You certainly guide (people) to the right path.

The main focus in Islam is your absolute trust and belief in God. The power of belief alone has been repeated over and over in different content in the Quran. When followed religiously in your prayers and sayings throughout the day, it can do wonders!

I always like to finish each chapter by sharing a poem. Here is a much shorter version of a forty-seven-line poem about "belief" by the twelfth-century poet Nizami Ganjavi:

Anyone whose belief turns into his will
The good fortune awaits him in the final

A path that you believe-in, find searching
The best state to be-in, when believing

Errand boy turns to Master, when behaving in belief
See the rock turn into gold with your belief

If you stand confident with your belief
Lift the sea fog, wetness of fire you can with your belief

Anyone who blended his believe with his trust-in-Lord
Wrote a chapter, in the Greatness of the Lord

Nizami Ganjavi, Persian poet 12 the century
Makhzan ul Asrar (treasury of secrets)
Translation and Rhyme
Faramarz F, Davati

I have listed some of the verses emphasizing believing in God below. There were so many verses, I even put some in Appendix 1 and still could not include all of them in this book. Besides, I prefer that you do your own research in the Quran and become astonished by this powerful book!

23:01
Indeed the believers are successful.

2:03
Those who believe in the unseen, and establish prayer and they spend out (give charity) of what we have provided them

BELIEVE

2:153

Oh you who believe! Seek help through patient and prayer. Indeed God is with the patient ones.

[2:186]

(Muhammad), if any of My servants ask you about Me, tell them that the Lord says, "I am near; I accept the prayers of those who pray." Let My servants answer My call and believe in Me so that perhaps they may know the right direction.

[10:104]

(Muhammad), say, "People, if you have doubt about my religion, know that I, certainly, do not worship the idols which you worship instead of God, but I worship God who causes you to die. I am commanded to believe (in His existence)

2:177

Righteousness is not determined by facing East or West during prayer. Righteousness consists of the belief in God, the Day of Judgment, the angels, the Books of God, His Prophets; to give money for the love of God to relatives, orphans, the destitute, and those who are on a journey and in urgent need of money, beggars; to set free slaves and to be steadfast in prayer, to pay the religious tax (zakat) to fulfill one's promises, and to exercise patience in poverty, in distress, and in times of war. Such people who do these are truly righteous and pious.

[3:160]

If God is your helper, no one can defeat you. However, if He abandons you, who would help you? The true believers trust in God.

[3:171]

That they will be rewarded with bounties and favors from their Lord and that God will not neglect the reward of the true believers

9:112
(The believers) who repent for their sins, worship God, praise Him, travel through the land (for pious purposes), kneel down and prostrate themselves in obedience to God, make others do good and prevent them from sins and abide by the laws of God, will receive a great reward. Let this be glad news for the believer

9:119
Believers, have fear of God and always be friends with the truthful ones.

10:9
The righteously striving believers receive, through their faith, guidance from their Lord to the bountiful gardens wherein streams flow.

[10:57]
People, good advice has come to you from your Lord a (spiritual) cure, a guide and a mercy for the believers

[13:29]
The righteously striving believers will receive abundant blessings and the best eternal dwelling.

[18:30]
The righteously striving believers should know that We do not neglect the reward of those who do good deeds.

[18:88]
As for those who believe and do good, they will receive virtuous rewards and We will tell them to do only what they can.

[18:107]
The righteously striving believers will have the gardens of Paradise as their dwelling place and therein they will live forever

BELIEVE

[19:96]
Surely, those who believe and lead a righteous life, the God will shower them with love.

[20:75]
But whoever comes to Him as a believer having done righteous deeds - for those will be the highest degrees [in position]:

[20:82]
But indeed, I am the Perpetual Forgiver of whoever repents and believes and does righteousness and then continues in guidance.

[23:1]
Successful indeed are the believers

And following related verses

23:02
Who are submissive to God during their prayers

23:03
Those who turn away from unproductive (useless) talk.

23:04
And they pay their charity (Zakah)

23:05
And those who guard their private part (from illegal sexual act)

23:07
Then whoever seeks beyond that they are sinners (wrongdoers).

23:08
Those who keep their trust and their covenant.

23:09
And those who maintain their prayer.

23:10
Those are the inheritors

23:11
Who will inherit the Paradise and they will stay there forever.

[29:2]
Do the people think that they will be left to say, "We believe " without being put to the test?

[39:10]
Say, "O My servants who believed, you shall Fear your Lord." For those who worked righteousness in this world, a good reward. GOD's earth is spacious, and those who steadfastly persevere will receive their recompense generously, without limits.

[42:26]
And He answers [the supplication of] those who have believed and done righteous deeds and increases [for] them from His bounty. But the disbelievers will have a severe punishment.

[42:36]
Whatever you have received is just a means of enjoyment for this life but the reward of God for the believers and those who trust in their Lord will be better and everlasting.

[47:11]
That is because God is the protector of those who have believed and because the disbelievers have no protector

BELIEVE

[57:21]
Compete with one another to achieve forgiveness from your Lord and to reach Paradise, which is as vast as the heavens and the earth, and is prepared for those who believe in God and His Messenger. This is the blessing of God and He grants it to whomever He wants. The blessings of God are great.

[64:13]
God is the only Lord and in Him the believers should trust

2: 277
Indeed, those who believe and do good deeds and establish the prayer and give the zakat (charity) they will have their reward from their Lord, and they will have no fear nor will they grieve.

[2:82]
As for the righteously striving believers, they will be among the people of Paradise wherein they will live forever.

[2:103]
And if they had believed and feared God, then the reward from God would have been [far] better, if they only knew

[2:153]
Believers, help yourselves (in your affairs) through patience and prayer; God is with those who have patience.

[2:208]
Believers, submit yourselves to the will of God as a whole. Do not follow the footsteps of Satan; he is your sworn enemy.

[2:212]
This worldly life is adorned in the eyes of the disbelievers, and they ridicule those who believe. However, the righteous will be far above

them on the Day of Resurrection. GOD blesses whomever He wills, without limits.

2:118
And those who do not know say, why does God does not speak to us or a sign (miracle) comes to us? And there were others who said the same before them. Their hearts are alike. **We have indeed made the signs (miracles) clear (manifest) for those people who firmly believe.**

2:136
Say we have believed in God and what is revealed to Abraham and Ismail and Isaac and Jacob (Yaqub) and the descendants, and what was given to Moses and Jesus, and was given to the prophets for their Lord. We make no distinction between any of them. And to him we are submissive (Muslim means submissive).

[2:165]
And [yet], among the people are those who take other than God as equals [to Him]. They love them as they [should] love God. But those who believe are stronger in love for God. And if only they who have wronged would consider [that] when they see the punishment, [they will be certain] that all power belongs to God and that God is severe in punishment

Faith in God

Faith in Islam is the unshakable trust and expectancy you have in God. Faith is a constant relation you have to God, as your faith in God is 100 percent. He is the Hand above all hands that has always reached from above and helped you through thick and thin. When you look back on your life, you see it has always been Him that has miraculously pulled you out of any bad situation, trouble, or sickness. Sometimes He has placed a person on your path to help you or has created a situation that has ultimately turned to your favor.

Looking back, He has pulled you out of trouble over and over again and has never disappointed you. That is why you have faith in Him as you always reach back and ask Him for help. As we say in our daily prayers, "Allah hu Samad," which has been translated and explained in several ways: "God the eternal refuge" or "God, the one on Whom all depend" or "God is the One to go to when in need." It is simply your faith, belief, trust, and expectancy in Him that sets you apart from others.

Having faith is like a farmer who looks far into the horizon and prays for some rain, despite the fact that he does not see a single cloud in the sky. You have faith in the unseen God, as you remember He has always pulled you out of trouble and delivered you. You remember when you have been in distress, He has always put people or circumstances in front of you that miraculously have pulled you out of the difficulty. You look into your past and remember how many times He has helped you and rescued you when you were struggling and needed Him most.

Here is a good definition of *faith* by Wikipedia:

> *Faith in God is to believe and trust in God with confidence despite the absence of proof and evidence. Faith is the steadfast, persistent, tireless, and industrious constant belief in God. Faith is redoubling your effort with enthusiasm, with your aim and belief in God, when there is no proof in sight.*

In Islam one of the conditions of faith is to believe in One God alone, who is the creator of the universe and who you worship. Your entire faith is in this One God alone.

A closely related subject to faith in Islam is "trust-in" God (*tawakkul* in Arabic) that goes hand in hand with faith, and we will discuss it in the next chapter.

Faith is Hagar running in the deserts of Arabia to find water for her son, Ishmael.

Faith is Joseph in the prison of the pharaoh, not forgetting his God, and praying to Him, knowing one day God somehow would bring him out.

Faith is when you are hit with the strongest storm in your life and you seek refuge in Him for help, when there is no help in site. The storm could be anything, including your family life, job, finances, sickness, or anything else you could think of, and you find yourself in a situation and expect a Hand from above to come rescue you. And miraculously He does!

I always thank God that I was raised in a religious family. It doesn't matter what religion you were born into; I believe religious people have a much better and easier life compared to non-religious people. Religious people have faith in God, but non-religious people do not have anyone. We all go through some hard times in life no matter who we are or what we do. And that's what sets religious people apart from non-religious people. Religious people have God to go to when in need, while non-religious people do not have anyone and try to find an escape through alcohol and drugs.

Religious people do have faith in God, so they find refuge in Him during the hard times, and ultimately He pulls them out of difficult situations and they get rescued. It's that expectancy, hope, and our faith in our God that sets us apart from the atheists or non-believers. The stronger our belief in God, the better the outcome and the faster we see results. If your belief is so strong you literally see it and can visualize it, God's help will be there!

Non-religious people like to refer to themselves as self-reliant and refer to God as some energy source up there who has created all of this, but they have no personal relationship with God as religious people do. When non-religious people are hit with a storm of life and feel they no longer have control and have lost the reins and are sinking to rock bottom, that's when they lose their self-reliance they lectured you about over your beliefs! And unfortunately you see them falling apart without any comeback or return to their old self. Their life keeps getting worse and worse. They become someone far away and apart from whoever they were before.

Their previous illusion of self-reliance is gone, and they have no hope since they have no faith in, trust in, or relationship with God. It is that "steadfast, persistent, tireless, and industrious constant belief in God" that pulls religious people out of trouble. Non-religious people simply do not have that, and therefore do not get the benefit of it!

That's one of the main differences between the believers of any religion compared to non-believers. When they go through a crisis or disaster, the believers are on their knees praying and seeking refuge in God, while non-believers have no one to go when in need, and that's when they go astray.

The good news for the non-believer is, God does not disappoint those who are asking for help and trying to get in. In Islam they can repent of their sins, ask God for forgiveness, and submit themselves to Him. To become a Muslim means submitting to God and starting to live a righteous life.

Islam also warns people that after they ask for help and receive it from God, they should keep their covenant with God.

5:7
Remember God's favors to you and the firm covenant that He has made with you. You said because of this covenant, "We have heard (the words of the Lord) and have obeyed Him." Have fear of God; He knows well all that the hearts contain.

7:170
And those who cling (refuge) to the Book and establish the prayer, We indeed will not let the reward of the reformers go to waste. (We will not disappoint them)

16:91
And fulfill the covenant of God when you have taken it, [O believers], and do not break oaths after their confirmation while you have made God, over you, a witness. Indeed, God knows what you do.

Simply by having faith—no matter how big the task or how small your resources, no matter how much public and media pressure or opinion you may experience in the country in which you live, regardless of if it is a Muslim or non-Muslim country—you can achieve your goals and are capable of monumental tasks. Simply by having "your faith and trust in God," keeping God in first place in your life, you can move forward with trust in the Lord.

FAITH IN GOD

In the desert, with joy of Kaaba, when you are walking through
Not worrisome of the thorns in the desert when they brush

If the destructive flood can destroy one's livelihood
With Noah as the Ships' captain, not worrisome of flood.

Hafez, Persian poet 14th century
Translation and Rhyme
Faramarz F, Davati

The following are some of the Quran's verses on *faith*:

3:173
When the people say to them, "People have mobilized against you; you should fear them," this only strengthens their faith and they say, "GOD suffices us; He is the best Protector."

3:186
You (believers) will certainly be tested by the loss of your property and lives and you will hear a great many insults from the People of the Book and the pagans. If you steadfastly persevere and lead a righteous life, this will prove the strength of your faith.

3:193
Lord, we have heard the person calling to the faith and have accepted his call. Forgive our sins, expiate our bad deeds, and let us die with the righteous ones.

8:2
Believers are those who when God is mentioned they feel fear (out of respect) in their heart and when his verses are recited to them, they increase his faith. And they put their trust (with courage) in their God.

10:09
Indeed those who believed and did good deeds their Lord will guide them by their faith, underneath them will flow rivers in Gardens of Delight (Paradise).

14:24
Have you not considered how God presents an example, [making] a good word (with faith) like a good tree, whose root is firmly fixed (in the ground) and it branches (high) in the sky.

Interpretation/commentary:
With your strong faith firmly in the ground as your foundation, you can reach high in the sky. With your strong and firm faith in God, you can reach the sky.

21:30
Have the unbelievers not ever considered that the heavens and the earth were one piece and that We tore them apart from one another. From water We have created all living things. Will they then have no faith?

30:60
Be patient. The promise of God is certainly true. Let not the faithless shake the firmness of the promise of God.

33:22
When the true believers saw the parties (ready to attack), they said, "This is what GOD and His messenger have promised us, and GOD and His messenger are truthful." This (dangerous situation) only strengthened their faith and augmented their submission (to the Will of God).

42:52
Thus, We have revealed to you an inspiration of Our command, (Muhammad). Before, you did not even know what a Book or Faith

was, but We have made the Quran as a light by which We guide whichever of Our servants We want. You certainly guide (people) to the right path.

44:07
He is the Lord of the heavens and the earth and all that is between them, if only you would have strong faith.

45:20
This (Quran) is an enlightenment for the people and a guide and mercy for the people who have strong faith

47:36
The worldly life is only a play and amusement. And if you believe and fear God, He will grant your rewards and will not ask you to pay for them.

48:4
He is the One who places contentment into the hearts of believers to expand more faith, in addition to their faith. To God belongs all forces of the heavens and the earth. God is All Knowing, All Wise.

49:7
And know that God's messenger has come in your midst. Had he listened to you in many things, you would have made things difficult for yourselves. But God made you love faith and adorned it in your hearts, and He made you abhor disbelief, wickedness, and disobedience. These are the guided ones.

49:11
O you who believe, no people shall ridicule other people, for they may be better than they. Nor shall any women ridicule other women, for they may be better than they. Nor shall you mock one another, or make fun of your names. Evil indeed is the reversion to

wickedness after attaining faith. Anyone who does not repent after this, these are the transgressors.

57:25
We sent our messengers supported by clear proofs, and we sent down to them the scripture and the law, that the people may uphold justice. And we sent down the iron, wherein there is strength, and many benefits for the people. All this in order for God to distinguish those who would support Him and His messengers, on faith. God is Powerful, Almighty.

"Trust-In" (God) (Tawakkul in Arabic)

❖

The phrase "trust-in," translated from the word *tawakkul* in Arabic, means your complete trust in God. The phrase *tawakkal ta al Allah* means "trust-in God," knowing He is there to back you up. "Trust-in God" is having trust in God at the onset of doing something, and is followed by a forward movement or action in starting a task. "Trust-in God" is when you start a task without knowing the outcome and how it ends, and you put your whole trust in God and move forward. The essence of "trust-in God" has a forward movement in it, an action to follow, whatever it is. It is not passive, but very active.

Where I grew up in Iran, when people wanted to start a new task, new business, or new adventure of any type, at the beginning they would say the Quranic Arabic phrase, *"tawakkul ta al Allah,"* or "trust-in God," and would move forward. Anytime here in the US when I want to start a new task or a new business adventure, after all my thinking and preliminary research, I say, "Trust in God and move forward. God is the greatest!" "Trust in God" and "faith" go hand in hand.

"Trust in God" is Abraham breaking the idols by simply having trust and faith in God.

"Trust in God" is Muhammad relocating (Higrat) his people across the desert of Arabia from Mecca to Yasrib (former name of Madinah) to protect them against the Ghoraish, without any promise from God, but simply having faith and trust in Him.

Trust in God is when Muhammad's followers (Muhagereen) gave up their house, packed their bags, and followed him in the desert to their next homeland, as they had trust and faith in God.

Trust in God is when Ali stood up as the champion of Muslims against the Quraysh's strong man, Amr ibn Abdu Wuud, when he challenged Muslims to fight in the Battle of the Trench.

Trust in God is when Dawood (David) stood up against Goliath (2:251).

Trust in God is when you know it all ends well at the end no matter what the outcome, even if you are in the middle of a crisis.

Trust in God is when you know everything will be fine, and continue with your daily activity, even if you are in the middle of turmoil.

As Rumi says,

If you put trust in the Lord, use it for work
Then plant your seeds and lean on the Lord

Rumi, Persian poet 13th century
Translation and Rhyme
Faramarz F, Davati

One thing to notice, as I mentioned earlier, "Trust in God" is always followed by *you* doing the work and activity. It is not that we just sit around and do nothing and expect God to do everything for us!

It says in the Quran in 3:159, when you will it and have made the preparation for it, try it and get it done, as your real confidence is with God, as His Will is supernatural: **"But, when you reach a decision, trust God. God loves those who trust Him.** God loves those who put their trust in Him." Here are a few verses regarding "trust in God" :

3: 159
Only through the Divine Mercy have you (Muhammad) been able to deal with your followers so gently. If you had been stern and hard-

"TRUST-IN" (GOD) (TAWAKKUL IN ARABIC)

hearted, they would all have deserted you a long time ago. Forgive them and ask God to forgive (their sins) and consult with them in certain matters. ***But, when you reach a decision, trust God. God loves those who trust Him.***

3:160
If God helps you, then no one can overcome you; and if He forsakes you, who is there who can help you after Him? And let the believers put their trust in God.

5:23 Two men who were reverent and blessed by God said, "Just enter the gate. If you just enter it, you will surely prevail. You must trust in God, if you are believers."

8:2

Believers are those who when God is mentioned they feel fear (out of respect) in their heart and when his verses are recited to them, they increase his faith. And they put their trust (with courage) in their God.

8:49
The hypocrites and those whose hearts are sick, say, "The (believers') religion has deceived them." Those who trust in God will find Him Majestic and All-wise.

9:129
So if they turn away, then say for me God is enough. There is no God except him. I put my trust in the God who is on the Throne of this Great (universe).

10:71
And recite to them the news of Noah when he said to his people, O' my people! If my stay with you and reminding you the signs of God

is hard, because I put my trust in God. So all of you resolve your plan with your partners and let there be no doubt in your plan and carry it out upon me without giving me any break.

10:84
And Moses said" O my people if you have believed in God then put your trust in him if you are surrounded (to God).

10:85
Then they said, we put our trust in God. Our Lord does not make us a trial for the people who are wrongdoers.

11:56
Indeed, I put my trust upon God, my Lord and your Lord. There is no creature but he has a hold on its forelock (life). Indeed my Lord is on a straight path.

11:88
He said O' my people Do you see if I am on a clear evidence from my Lord, and He has provided me a good provision from Himself. And not I intend that I differ from you in what I forbid you from it. Not I intend except that I reform as much as I am able. And not is my success except with God. I trust upon him and to Him I return.

11:123
And the hidden of the earth and skies is for him, and to him will be returned all of it. So worship Him and put your trust upon Him. And your Lord is not unaware of what you do.

12:67
And he (Jacob) said, O my sons! Do not enter from one gate but enter from different gates. I can not avail you against anything that is the decision of God, as I have trusted upon him. And those who trust Him (believe in Him), should put their trust in Him.

"TRUST-IN" (GOD) (TAWAKKUL IN ARABIC)

13:30
Thus we have sent you to a nation verily that other nation have passed before them, so that you may recite to them what We revealed to you, while they disbelieve in the Most Gracious, Say He is my Lord there is no God except Him, upon Him I put my trust and to Him is my return.

14:11
Their messengers (Prophets) said to them, we are only human like you, but God bestows His Grace on whom He wills of his subjects and it is not for us to bring you an authority except by the permission of God. And believers should put their trust in God.

14:12
Why should we not trust in God when He has shown us the right way? We shall exercise patience against the troubles with which you afflict us. Whoever needs a trustee should trust in God."

16:42
Those who are patients and put their trust in God.

16:99
Indeed he (Satan) has no authority over the believers who have trust in their God.

25:58
And trust in the Living One who never dies and glorify Him with His praise. He has sufficient knowledge of the sins of His servants.

26:217
And put your trust in the All-Mighty, the Most Merciful

27:79
So put your trust in God, indeed you are on manifesting the truth.

29:59
Those who are patient and put their trust on their Lord.

31:22
And whoever face toward God and commit to Him and be a gooddoer, then indeed he has grasped the most trustworthy handle. And the outcome of all matters is with God.

33:03
And Put your trust in God, And God is a sufficient guardian (protector, trustee, disposer of affairs)

33:48
Do not yield to the disbelievers or the hypocrites. Disregard their insult and put your trust in God. God is your all Sufficient Protector.

42:36
So whatever thing you have been given - it is but [for] enjoyment of the worldly life. But what is with God is better and more lasting for those who have believed and trust upon their Lord.

64:13
God- There is no God but Him and the believers should put their trust upon Him.

65:03
And He will provide for him from where he does not expect. And whoever puts his trust upon God, then God is sufficient for him. Indeed God will accomplish His purpose. God has set a measure for everything.

67:29
Say, "He is the Most Merciful; we believe in Him, and we put our trust upon Him. And you will [come to] know who it is that is in clear error."

Praising and Thanking God

Thanking God for the blessings he has given us is a part of all religions and cultural habits. In many Muslim countries, you see people carrying rosaries. I have seen Christians outside the US also having or carrying rosaries. Where I grew up, men carrying a rosary next to their car keys was a common thing. Many people didn't know, but by constantly advancing their rosary, praising the Lord, and thanking the Lord for their blessings as a daily habit, they were adding to their own blessings.

Some of the phrases people commonly say when advancing their rosary or playing with it or wrapping it around their finger are as follows:

- "Thank you, Lord."
- "Thank you, Lord, for all your blessings."
- "Glory to the Almighty."
- "Praise the Lord."
- "No God but One God"
- "There is no God but One God."
- "God listens to those who praise Him."
- "Praise the Lord, King of the universe."
- "God's hand is above all hands."
- "Through God anything is possible."
- "Help from God and victory over the enemy."
- "God has power over all things."

ALCHEMY OF THE QURAN

By saying the above phrases over and over again you are simply activating the universe, as the "new age" calls it, and getting God's attention. Many people do this as a habit, style, or tradition. But I am sure a good number of them know that by praising God or thanking Him over and over, they are getting His attention to add to their blessings.

This seems to be universal. I recently heard a good quote from a very respectable and famous American TV Christian pastor, who said, "When you praise God, you get His attention. When you pray to God, you get His favor. Talk like it is going to happen. Pray like it is going to happen. Think and behave like it is going to happen. It is better that you take your praise to God than your complaints."

Although he is a good Christian, I find his sermons a lot like some of the passages of our own teachings. Of course he teaches from the Bible, not the Quran. But what is amazing is the interconnection of different religions with each other. The last portion of his saying above, which he learned from the Bible, is similar to what we Muslims call (*tawakkul*) "trust-in" God, in Islam, which we covered in the previous chapters.

Regarding "thanking the Lord," here are two lines from one of Rumi's poems from what he has taken from the Quran (Abraham 14:7):

Thanking the Lord for your blessings, shows your power
Hurting others with your blessings, shows you denial
Thanking for your blessings, will add to your blessings
Hurting others with your blessings, will lose your blessings

Rumi, Persian poet 13th century
Translation and Rhyme
Faramarz F, Davati

PRAISING AND THANKING GOD

Deducted from Quran (Abraham 14:7)

1- *14:7: Remember when your Lord said to you, **'If you give thanks, I shall give you greater (favors), but if you deny, indeed, My punishment is severe.***

And see how Saadi so beautifully takes from the Quran (49:13 & 14:7) in the following passage:

*Praise the Lord full of glory and majesty that his obedience will cause closeness to Him and thankfulness to Him will cause blessings. Every breath we take in is necessary for our life, and when it's let out, continues our life. So in **every breath**, there are **two blessings,** and for every blessing, gratitude is a must.*

Who can ever in words or in deeds?
Be capable of praise and thanking Him?

Saadi, Persian poet 13th century
Translation and Rhyme
Faramarz F. Davati

Deducted from Quran:

49-13: People, We have created you all male and female and have made you nations and tribes so that you would recognize each other. ***The most honorable among you in the sight of God is the most righteous of you****. God is All-knowing and All-aware*

*14:7: Remember when your Lord said to you, **'If you give thanks, I shall give you greater (favors),** but if you deny, indeed, My punishment is severe.*

Here are some verses about praising the Lord:

10:10
Their prayer therein (will be) Glory to you O' God, and their greeting therein (will be) "Peace". And the last of their prayer will be, All the praise be to God, the Lord of the worlds.

11:73
They said are you amazed at the order of God? The mercy of God and his blessings be upon you, the people of the house. Indeed he is All-praiseworthy, All-glorious.

14:01
Alif, Lam, Ra. [This is] a book which We have revealed to you, [O Muhammad], that you might bring mankind out of darkness into the light by permission of their lord to the path of Almighty, the praise-worthy.

14:08
And Moses said, if you and everybody else on earth, disbelieves, the praiseworthy God is Free of needs.

14: 39
Praise to God, who has granted to me in old age Ishmael and Isaac. Indeed, my Lord is All- hearer of the prayer.

15:98
So (be thankful) and glorify your Lord with the praise and be among those who prostrate to him (prays to him with his head facing the ground)

20:33
So that we may praise you a lot.

PRAISING AND THANKING GOD

20:130
(Muhammad), have patience with what they say, glorify your Lord, and always praise Him before sunrise, sunset, in some hours of the night and at both the beginning and end of the day, so that you may become content (get what you want).

24:36
[Such guiding lights are] in mosques which God has ordered to be raised and that His name be mentioned therein; praising Him within them in the morning and the evenings.

Author's personal comment: Such guiding light can also be in your home. When you allocate a specific space or room for God and pray to Him throughout the day in that same space, you bring the guiding light of God to your house. When you pray, imagine you are talking directly to God. If you cannot do that, imagine God is watching you. I believe this originally came from Muhammad, when someone asked him how to pray.

I personally imagine talking to the burning bush that Moses was talking to from the original movie *The Ten Commandments*!

25:58
Also trust in the Living One who never dies and glorify Him with His praise. He has sufficient knowledge of the sins of His servants.

27:93
And say, "All praise be to God. He will show you His signs, and you will recognize them. And your Lord is not unaware of what you do."

35:01
All praise belongs to God, the creator of the heavens and the earth who has made the angels Messengers of two or three or four

wings. He increases the creation as He wills. God has power over all things.

35:15
O' people, you are always in need of God, while God is free of needs and praiseworthy.

45:36
It is only God, Lord of the heavens and the earth and Lord of the Universe who deserves all praise.

64:01
All that is in the heavens and the earth glorify God. To Him belongs the Kingdom and all praise. He has power over all things

110:03
Then Glorify and praise your Lord and ask for forgiveness. Indeed He is ever accepting of repentance.

Glorify and Elevate Your God

❖

How do we glorify God? By thanking Him and giving Him the credit for all the good he has done for us or made happen for us. Instead of giving all the credit to yourself for your accomplishments, glorify the Lord for making things happen for you.

It's only in the future failures that one realizes their earlier success for the same kind of task or business venture was not all theirs, and someone from above was watching over them.

We constantly glorify our God in our daily prayers. Every time we go to the bowing position (*ruku*) and say, "Glory to God," three times or, "Glory to my God, the Almighty," we have glorified Him. Also, every time we place our forehead on the ground in prostration to God (*sujud*) and say, "Glory to my God, the Most High," we have glorified Him. And when we are sitting on the ground at the end, finishing the prayer, and we say, "Indeed you are full of Glory, full of majesty," we are glorifying God. And of course at the beginning of prayer in Surah al-Hamd, when we say, "Praise the Lord, the King of the universe," we have glorified Him.

Here are some of the verses about glorifying the Lord:

3:41
He said oh my Lord give me a sign. "He said, "Your sign is that you will not speak with people for three days except with gestures. And remember your Lord much, and glorify (Him) in the evening and in the morning."

5:116
And when God said, O Jesus son of Maryam, did you tell people "Take me and my mother as two Gods beside God? He (Jesus) said Glory to you, it was not for that I say, what not I had the right if I had said it, then surely you would have known it. You know what is in me, and I do not know what is in you. Indeed you are all knower of the unseen.

7:143
And when Moses came to our appointment and spoke to Him, his Lord. He said "O my Lord" show me that I may look at You. God said never you can see me, but look at that mountain, if it remain in its place, then you will see me. Then God revealed himself to the mountain and the mountain crumbled to dust and Moses fell unconscious. And when he recovered he said glory be to you, I turn (in repentance). I am one of the first believers.

7:206
Indeed those who are close to God, do not turn away from worshipping him in arrogance. They Glorify him and they prostrate to him (face down, level to the ground).

10:10
Their prayer therein (will be) Glory to you O' God, and their greeting therein (will be) "Peace". And the last of their prayer will be, All the praise be to God, the Lord of the worlds.

11:73
They said are you amazed at the command of God? May be the mercy of God and his blessings be upon you, the people of the house. Indeed he is All-praiseworthy, All-glorious.

GLORIFY AND ELEVATE YOUR GOD

12:108
Say this is my way, I invite to God with insight, me and whoever follows me. And glory be to God and I am not of those) who puts a partner with God.

15:98
So (be thankful) and glorify your Lord with the praise and be among those who prostrate to him (prays to him with his head facing the ground)

20:130
(Muhammad), have patience with what they say, glorify your Lord, and always praise Him before sunrise, sunset, in some hours of the night and at both the beginning and end of the day, so that you may become content (get what you want).

21:22
Had there been within the heavens and earth Gods besides the Lord, there would have been disorder. Glorified is the Lord of the Throne. (He is above) of what they attribute (to Him).

21:26
And they said the Most merciful has taken a son. Glory be to Him, nay, but they are honored servants.

22:37
It is not the flesh and blood of your sacrifice that pleases God. What pleases God is your piety. God has made subservient to you the sacrificial animals so that perhaps you will glorify Him; He is guiding you. (Muhammad), give the glad news (of God's mercy) to the righteous people

23:91
God has not taken any son, nor has there ever been a God beside him. If there were, each God would have taken away his creatures and claimed superiority over the others. Glory be to God, He is above of what they describe Him.

23:92
He knows what is hidden and what is open, he is glories and above what they associate with Him.

25:58
And trust in the Living One who never dies and glorify Him with His praise. He has sufficient knowledge of the sins of His servants.

30:17
So Give glory to God, when you reach the evening and when you reach the morning.

32:15
Only those who believe in our verses, when they are reminded by them, fall down in prostration and glorify their Lord and they are not arrogant.

36:83
All glory belongs to the One in whose hands is the control of all things. To Him you will all return.

48:09
so that you (people) may believe in God and His Messenger, help, and respect God and glorify Him in the morning and the evening

56:74
So, glorify the name of your Lord, the All-Mighty

GLORIFY AND ELEVATE YOUR GOD

64:01
All that is in the heavens and the earth glorify God. To Him belongs the Kingdom and all praise. He has power over all things

76:26
Prostrate before Him and glorify Him extensively during the night

87:01
Glorify the Name of your lord, the Most High

110:03
Then Glorify and praise your Lord and ask for forgiveness. Indeed He is ever accepting of repentance.

Prayers

2:186
And when my servants ask you concerning Me, (tell them) then indeed I am near. I respond to the call (prayer) of the one who calls (prays to) Me. So let them respond to Me and believe in Me, so that they may be led the right way.

Prayer and "Dua" are the secret! Prayer in Islam is the acts of ritual praying (Salat) and believing in the Oneness of God and the All-Powerful Supreme Being who runs this world. We Muslims pray to Him five times a day at specified times. Dua on the other hand is the essence of worship. Dua is the list of praise, thanks, wishes and personal requests from God. Our Dua resembles what Christians refer to as prayer. We make Dua, at will during the day or night, and there are no specific times for it. The most potent time to make Dua is after we finish our ritual prayer, either when we are in prostration position or holding our hands in the air toward Him. They say Prophet Muhammad said "when you are making Dua, do not be shy or bashful. God is generous and owns it all. Ask from Him firm and ask big. What seems big to us for Him is nothing". When making Dua you can ask for anything you want from God.

We can also make Dua for family, friends or anybody in need of help. There is a deeper meaning and connection with Dua, compared to what is referred as prayer in the western societies. In Dua, we call out to God or ask Him to come in or summon as some may describe it. That is when we whisper too Him or ask

Him persistently what we want. It is reported that prophet Muhammad said, "when making Dua, raise your hand toward Him with humility, He is too generous and kind to let His humble servant to pull back his hand empty handed."

Another important factor is, when we make Dua we must never give up! We should never think, I pray and pray and God does not answer. We should have firm determination, hold steady, be bold and humble, (not arrogant) and be patient. We should also understand that God may not give us what we want and instead give us what is good for us. As He sees a lot further down the road that we can see. If you believe and pray, He will respond. ....***Tell them indeed I am near. I respond to the call of the one who needs Me.....2:186***

Nothing activates God's response like prayers. Simply put, the more you pray, the better line of connection you have with God. No other religion has prescribed more daily prayer than Islam. We pray five times a day: dawn, noon, afternoon, sundown, and night. We pray for our own good, to have a connection with Him, to be reminded of Him, and to put Him first and worldly life second after Him. I know it can be difficult to make time for prayer at noon or in the afternoon, and sometimes it is impossible, as you may be busy with work and simply cannot leave your work and attend to your prayer, as it would be unjust to your employer, customer, or client. But there are times when you can get away from your daily work or business and have your prayer time, and that is when you will realize the joy and comfort in the fact that you have put this earthly life second and God first.

Although I have my own business and you would think it would be easier for me to do all my prayers in the office during the day, it usually is not. There are many times that I simply cannot make the time. However, the afternoon prayer at the office, when I can do it, is the best. Usually by three or four o'clock you have had enough of the business world. A nice *wudhu* (wash up) and a nice noon and afternoon prayer gives you a break from the challenges of life, lifts the weight of the business world off your shoulders for a short time, and reminds you this is just the earthly life that we are playing in!

By putting the worldly life second, all the problems and challenges of life seem like background noise! You have your connection with your God, and all those problems and issues, they too will pass.

God knows we are busy during the day working and making our daily living. In the Quran, He has emphasized doing the night prayer (73:03-73:08). The night prayer leaves the strongest impression on one's soul, and at that time we have more time to spend with God, as we are free from our daily chores.

When we Muslims pray, we pray to the creator of the universe. As part of prayer, we bow, kneel, and prostrate in front of Him; there is no ego. He is the Almighty, and we are nothing but His subjects. We are humble in front of Him, no matter who we are. He is the Lord of the universe, and His hand is above all hands and He is in control. We have our trust in Him. Our prayer time is a time for communication between us and God alone. We are in the presence of God the Almighty, and we are praying directly to Him, the King of the universe. There is no intermediary. He is the One God that has built it all and owns it all, and we all return to Him one day. He is the One who can make you or break you. You love Him with respect, but you also fear Him.

When we pray, we are at full attention and concentration, like a soldier in front of a general, except we are humble and our head is down. There is no looking around, talking, eating, drinking, chewing gum, or lack of respect. We wash up clean (*Wudhu*[5]) before our appointment with God. We pray on a clean ground or in

---

[5] *Wudu is the Islamic procedure for washing parts of the body, a type of ritual purification. Wudu involves washing the hands, mouth, nostrils, arms, head, and feet with water, and is an important part of ritual purity in Islam. Wikipedia*

clean surroundings. We treat our appointment (prayer) with God as the most important appointment, and it overrules others. The more we learn and discipline ourselves to put our appointment with God in first place over other matters, the more it automatically puts the earthly life and other matters in second place. The prayer calms our heart and relaxes us. For a moment it lifts the weight and burdens of this earthly life off of our shoulders and helps us to relax a bit as we submit to God, acknowledging He is in control of this universe and our lives. We are experiencing a one-on-one connection and communication with Him. In those several minutes of prayer, it's us and Him alone with no distraction.

As in a previous chapter, Prophet Muhammad reportedly said, "When you pray to God, try to imagine that you are talking to Him directly. If you cannot do that, imagine He is looking at you."

When we compare our prayers to other religions' prayers, we see differences. Our prayers are disciplined, structured, and are in order, as we are in total submission to God. We are in total privacy and are having our quiet moment with God. We do not talk, eat, look around, or speak to anyone around us, or it will cancel our prayer with God and we will have to start over. We feel we are in total one-on-one communication with the Creator. There is no laughing, joking, looking around, lack of respect or attention, or playing around. It is serious, solid, and firm, like our belief.

Our prayers are a combination of the beginning chapter of the Quran (opening) plus other chapters of the Quran by tradition or choice. We praise the Lord during our bowing and kneeling and prostration. Our structured prayers are a combination of testifying and declaring He is the One and only One, we praise and give glory to Him, we only obey Him, and we ask Him to help us and show us the right path. We seek refuge in Him from the evils of this world, from the sorcery, jealousy, and temptations, declaring He is the One and only One and does not share the throne with anyone. We ask Him to forgive our sins. At the end when we finish our prayer we ask Him for forgiveness and thank Him for all the blessings He has sent us. After we finish the prayer, then we ask for our personal requests, wishes, and wants.

The main difference between Islamic prayer and prayers in other religions is, the bulk of our prayers is a mandatory acknowledgment of God's greatness and glory, giving praise, asking to be forgiven for our sins, and thanking Him for His blessings first. Then, after we finish the prayer and praising Him, we ask for our list of wishes and wants. Most other religions start their prayers with the list of their wishes and wants!

The Quran teaches us that in our prayers we first have to praise the Lord, and then we can ask him for favors. This way we practice and prove our belief in Him first.

I say my daily prayers in Arabic, as I was taught growing up, despite the fact we Iranians do not speak Arabic. But it is the tradition, and we try to learn the meaning of the words. But sometimes during prayer I find myself saying these Arabic words and asking myself what was meant by what I just said.

It is amazing that sometimes I forget some of the meanings of the Arabic words. Especially the sayings between the movements when we are rising from a bowing position or prostration or standing up. Some of these Arabic phrases I have been saying for years without really knowing the meaning of them! However, now, with the advent of the Internet, it is much easier to find the meanings.

Also, sometimes when I am tired and am praying, I drift away in autopilot mode. Although my words are said in Arabic, I find myself talking to God in my mind, telling Him my daily problems and so on, regardless of what I was just saying in Arabic. I believe we all may drift away momentarily every now and then during our prayers, but I think if I was saying my prayers in my native language of Farsi or in English, the meaning of them would get hammered in much more strongly and there would be less chance of drifting away or forgetting the meaning of what Arabic word I just said.

In 4:43 God says you have to understand what you are saying in your prayers:

4:43
Believers, do not pray when you are drunk, but, instead, wait until you can understand what you say. Also, do not pray when you have experienced a seminal discharge until after you have taken a bath, unless you are on a journey. If, while sick or on a journey, you can find no water after having defecated or after having had carnal relations, perform tayammum by touching your palms on the pure earth and wipe the (upper part of) your face and the backs of your hands. God is Gracious and All-forgiving.

So every once in a while, I say my prayers in English, just to remind myself of the meaning of every word I say. And I find it quite useful. I also found another helpful tip for praying on www.understandQuran.com. They say that when you are praying to God, imagine there is a curtain between you and God. When you drift away, that curtain comes down between you and God; when you are alert and talking to the Almighty the curtain goes up and you can see God.

I say my prayers in Arabic and sometimes in English just to remind myself of the meaning of every word. God said in 4:43 you have to understand what you say in your prayer. I personally think for the young Muslims growing up here in the US and the West, it would be much easier to learn the whole prayer in English first. Then when they have more confidence, they can learn the original Arabic version also.

For Arabic-speaking parents at home with their children, saying the prayer in their language comes easy. However, for non-Arabic-speaking parents in the US, trying to encourage their children to learn the prayers in Arabic is not that easy. Even if they do, a good portion of the children walk away in the teenage years. The proof is thousands of young Muslims in the US that are only Muslim by name, because their parents are Muslims. I think it is far better for children to say their prayers in English every day rather than to try to say them in Arabic and become frustrated after a few tries and give up for good. The important thing is to develop the habit of praying every day so they develop that sense of if they don't say their prayer one day, the entire day seems awkward, as if they have left their cell phone at home or something similar. They know and feel like they missed something that day and do not feel comfortable until they either find a moment and place to say that prayer on that day or make up for it the next day.

If Islam wants to be a universal religion with people from all races around the world, it needs to have a strong English language platform, especially in America or possibly Europe. New converts should be able to understand every word in the mosques in English. The number of commentaries or phrases said in Arabic should be minimized so the guests or the new converts do not feel left out or like outsiders!

Christians in Europe went through this when the priests spoke in Latin and the parishioners had no idea what they were saying. The churches decided to change for the better. Now when you attend a non-Catholic church, you can understand every word said in church or during the sermon. You don't have to worry about missing anything.

I believe one of the good traditions that we Muslims could pick up from other religions and encourage the young Muslims to do is something similar to the Bar-Mitzvah in Judaism.

We could encourage our young Muslims to read the entire Quran in English from start to finish, and when they finish we would throw a big party for them with gifts from parents, friends, and guests. Hopefully that day will come.

For those who are interested in learning the prayers, I have seen a number of YouTube illustrative cartoons with simple English subtitles. I have also put a very basic prayer in simple English in Appendix 2. If Arabic is not your native language, simply concentrate on the English words and their meaning. Saying the prayers in Arabic does not make them magical, as some people would like you to believe and possibly even try to prove by showing you a supporting verse in the Quran. The importance is the meaning of the prayer and your connection with God. It is good to know it in Arabic for the uniformity of the religion, Friday prayers, group prayers, and so on. But when it's you and God, you can say your prayer in any language and He will listen.

Remember, the more you pray, the more blessings you get!

Here are a few verses on prayer:

2:153
Oh you who believe! Seek help through patient and prayer. Indeed God is with the patient ones.

2:186
And when my servants ask you concerning Me, (tell them) then indeed I am near. I respond to the call (prayer) of the one who calls (prays to) Me. So let them respond to ME and believe in Me, so that they may be led the right way.

2: 277
Indeed, those who believe and do good deeds and establish the prayer and give the zakat (charity) they will have their reward from their Lord, and they will have no fear nor will they grieve.

2:03
Those who believe in the unseen, and establish prayer and they spend out of what we have provided them

PRAYERS

2:43

And establish the prayer and give Zakah and bow down with those who bow down.

2:45

And seek help through patience and prayer. And indeed it is difficult except for the humble ones.

2:83

And (recall) when we took the covenant from the Children of Israel (saying), Do not worship except God and be good to parents, relatives, orphans and the needy, and speak good to people and establish the prayers.

2:110

And establish prayer and give Charity (zakat). And whatever good you send forth for yourselves (investment for your afterlife), you will find it with God. Indeed God is All- seer of what you do.

2:125

And remember when we made the house of (Kabah) a place of return for mankind a place of security and said, "Take the standing place of Abraham as a place of prayer." And we made a covenant with Abraham and Ismail, (saying), Purify my house for those who circumambulate (walking in circle around) it and those who bow down and prostrate. (face down on the flat in worship and submission to God)

2:145

And even if you bring to those who were given the Book all the signs (miracles), they would not follow your direction of prayer, nor will you follow their direction of prayer. And nor would they be followers of each other's direction of prayer. And if you follow their desires after knowledge has come to you, then surely you will be among the wrong doers.

2:149
And from wherever you start forth (for prayer) turn your face in the direction of Al Masjid Al- haram (Kabah). And indeed, it is truth from your Lord. And God is not unaware of what you do.

2:150
And from wherever you start forth (for prayer) turn your face in the direction of Al- Masjid Al Haram (kabah). And wherever you are turn your face towards it, so that people will not have any argument against you except the wrongdoers among them, so do not fear them but fear Me, so that I may complete My favor upon you, perhaps you may guided.

2:177
It is not righteousness that you turn your faces towards the east or the west but righteous is he who believes in God, the Last Day, the Angels, the Book, and the Prophets and gives wealth in spite of love for it to the near relative the orphans, the needy, the drifter, and those who ask, and in freeing the slaves; and who establishes prayer and gives charity (zakat) and he who fulfills the covenant when makes it; and he who is patient in suffering, hardship, and periods of stress. Those are the ones who are true and it is those who are the righteous.

3:38
Zachariah prayed to his Lord, saying "My Lord grant me by Your Grace a pure offspring. indeed, You are all-Hearer of the prayer.

3:39
When he was standing during prayer in his place of worship, the angels called him saying, "God gives you the glad news of the birth

of your son, John who will be a confirmation of (Jesus) the Word of God. He will become a chaste, noble leader and one of the righteous Prophets.

3:113
They are not (all) the same among the people of the book (amongst) them is a group that stands (stands for) and recite the verses of God in the hours of night and they face down to the ground and pray to God.

4:103
Then when you have finished the prayer (always) remember God, standing, sitting, and lying on your sides. And when you are in a secure position do your regular prayer. Indeed the prayer is on the believers (to be performed) at the specified times.

5: 55
Your only ally is God and his messenger and those who believe; those who establish the prayer and give zakat (charity) while bowing down.

5:58
And when you make a call for prayer, they ridicule and make fun of it. Because they do not understand.

5:91
Satan tries to cause animosity between you and hatred through intoxicants and gambling and hinders you from remembering God and prayer. So will you stop doing it?

6:162
Say, "Indeed my prayers, my rites of sacrifice, my living and my dying are for God, Lord of the worlds.

7:170
And those who cling (refuge) to the Book and establish the prayer, We indeed will not let the reward of the reformers go to waste. (We will not disappoint them)

8:3
Those who do their daily prayers and from what we have given them they spend.

9:18
The masjids of God will maintain only by those who believe in God and the final day and establish the prayer and gives zakah (charity) and they do not fear anyone except God. Those are the guided ones.

9:71
And the believing men and believing women are allies and should be friends. They direct and tell to do the right thing and forbid doing the wrong thing. They (establish) do the prayer, give zakah, and the obey God and his messenger. Those, God will have mercy on them. Indeed God is all mighty and all wise.

10:10
Their prayer therein (will be) Glory to you O' God, and their greeting therein (will be) "Peace". And the last of their prayer will be, All the praise be to God, the Lord of the worlds.

10:87
And we inspired to Moses and his brother that, settle your people in Egypt in houses and make your houses a place of worship and establish the prayer and give good news to the believers.

10:89
The Lord replied, "Moses, the prayer of your brother and yourself has been heard. Both of you must be steadfast (in your faith) and must not follow the ignorant ones."

PRAYERS

10:106
And do not pray beside God something that neither benefit you nor harm you. But if you did so, indeed then you will be of the wrongdoers.

11:114
And establish the prayer at the two ends of the day and approach of the night and indeed the good deeds remove the evil deeds that is reminder for those who remember.

13:22
And those who exercise patience to gain God's pleasure, who are steadfast in prayer, who spend for the cause of God privately and in public, and who keep away evil with good will have a blissful end.

14:31
Say to My servants those who believe: "Establish the prayers and spend (Charity) from what we have provided them secretly and publicly," before that a day will come that there will not be any trade or friendship.

14:37
Our Lord, I have settled some of my descendants in an uncultivated valley near your sacred house., our Lord, that they may establish prayer. So make hearts among the people incline toward them and provide for them from the fruits that they might be grateful.

14: 39
Praise to God, who has granted to me in old age Ishmael and I sac. Indeed, my Lord is All- hearer of the prayer.

14:40
My Lord, make me an establisher of prayer, and (many) from my descendants. Our Lord, and accept my prayer.

15:98
So (be thankful) and glorify your Lord with the praise and be among those who prostrate to Him (prays to him with their head facing the ground)

17:78
Say your prayer when the sun declines until the darkness of night and also at dawn. Surely the recitation at dawn is witnessed.

20:14
Indeed I am God. There is no God, but I, so worship me and establish the prayer to remember Me.

20:132
Instruct your family to pray and to be steadfast in their worship. We do not ask any provision from you; it is We who give you provision. Know that (good) outcome is for the righteous.

21:73
And we made them leaders guiding by our command and We inspired them doing good deeds, establishment of prayer, and giving of Zakah (Charity) and they were worshiper of us.

22:41
He will certainly help those who, if given power in the land, will worship God through prayer, pay the religious tax, enjoin others do good, and prevent them from committing evil. The consequence of all things is in the hands of God

23:01
Indeed the believers are successful.

23:02
Who are submissive during their prayers

PRAYERS

23:03
Those who turn away from unproductive (useless) talk.

23:04
And they pay their charity (Zakah)

23:05
And those who guard their private part (from illegal sexual act)

23:07
Then whoever seeks beyond that they are sinners (wrongdoers).

23:08
Those who preserve their trust and their covenant.

23:09
And those who maintain their prayer.

23:10
Those are the inheritors

23:11
Who will inherit the Paradise and they will stay there forever.

24:37
Men whom neither commerce nor sale distracts from the remembrance of God and performance of prayer and giving of zakah. They fear a Day in which the hearts and eyes will [fearfully] turn about (Resurrection).

25:74
They pray, "Lord, let our spouses and children be the delight of our eyes and make us a leader for the righteous."

27:3

Those who establish the prayer and give zakah and they certainly believe in the Hereafter.

29:45
(Muhammad), recite to them what has been revealed to you in the Book and be steadfast in prayer; prayer keeps one away from indecency and evil. It is the greatest act of worshipping God. God knows what you do.

30:31
Turn in repentance to Him. Have fear of Him. Be steadfast in your prayer. Do not be of those who associate others with God.

30:33
When people face hardship, they begin praying to their Lord and turn in repentance to Him. When they receive mercy from Him, a group of them begin to take partner others with their God.

31:04
Those who establish the prayer and give Charity and they believe firmly in the hereafter.

31:17
(Luqman said) My son, be steadfast in prayer. Make others do good. Prevent them from doing evil. Be patient in hardship. Patience comes from faith and determination

35:29
Those who recite the Book of God, who are steadfast in prayer and, who spend out of what We have given them for the cause of God, both in public and in private, (can) Expect a profit that never perish.

PRAYERS

41:51
When We grant the human being a favor, he ignores it and turns away but when he is afflicted by hardship, he starts lengthy prayers

42:26
He answers the prayers of the righteously striving believers and grants them increasing favors. The unbelievers will suffer a severe punishment

48:29
Muhammad is the Messenger of God and those with him are stern to the disbelievers yet kind among themselves. You can see them bowing and prostrating before God, seeking His favors and pleasure. Their faces (foreheads) are marked due to the effect of their frequent prostrations. That is their description in the Torah and in the Gospel they are mentioned as the seed which shoots out its stalk then becomes stronger, harder and stands firm on its stumps, attracting the farmers. Thus, God has described the believers to enrage the disbelievers. God has promised forgiveness and a great reward to the righteously striving believers.

62:09
O you who have believed, when [the adhan] is called for the prayer on the day of Jumu'ah [Friday], then proceed to the remembrance of God and leave trade. That is better for you, if you only knew.

62:10
And when the prayer has been concluded, disperse within the land and seek from the bounty of God, and remember God often that you may succeed.

73 :06
Prayer at night leaves the strongest impression on one's soul and the words spoken are more consistent

73 :07
During the day, you are preoccupied with many activities.

73:08
And remember the name of your Lord and devote yourself to Him with [complete] devotion.

(Worship Him) for more or less than half of the night

73:20
Your Lord knows that you and a group of those who are with you get up for prayer sometimes for less than two-thirds of the night, sometimes half and sometimes one-third of it. God determines the duration of the night and day. He knew that it would be hard for you to keep an exact account of the timing of the night prayers, so He turned to you with forgiveness. Thus, recite from the Quran what is easy for you. He knew that some of you would be sick, others would travel in the land to seek God's favors, and still others would fight for the cause of God. Thus, recite what is easy from Quran, be steadfast in prayer, pay the zakat, and give righteous (honorable) loans to God. Whatever good deeds you save for the next life, you will certainly find them with God. This is the best investment, and for this you will find the greatest reward. Ask forgiveness from God. God is All-forgiving and All-merciful.

76:25
And mention the name of your Lord [in prayer] morning and evening

76:26
Prostrate before Him and glorify Him extensively during the night

Charity

The act of charity has been prescribed by all religions and organizations, as all religions come as a way of encouraging human beings to be benevolent toward one another. However, no other religion has emphasized more than Islam the importance of helping mankind, the poor, orphans, widowed and unprotected woman, and those who are traveling and have fallen short of their destination. Acts of charity have been advised and prescribed many, many times in the Quran. The Quran says to think of charity as a loan you give God for the poor, and He will return it to you tenfold.

Giving the obligatory charity or *zakat* (2.5 percent of your net income per year), helping the poor and the needy, helping the orphans, not arguing with the beggars (93:10) are all instructions that have been given in various sections of the Quran. There is a universal belief and fact that the more charity you give, the more blessings you will receive.

Do the kindnesses, give away, as you throw* in the river
As the Lord makes up for it, when stranded in the desert

Saadi, Persian poet 13th century
Translation and Rhyme
Faramarz F, Davati

*Throw here means when people throw leftover food for their domestic animals, or the fishes, if they are next to a body of water.

Here are some of the verses advising in *charity*:

2: 277
Indeed, those who believe and do good deeds and establish the prayer and give the zakat (charity) they will have their reward from their Lord, and they will have no fear nor will they grieve.

2:3
Who believe in the unseen, observe the Contact Prayers (Salat),* and from our** provisions to them, they give to charity.

2:43
You shall keep up the Contact Prayers (Salat) and give the obligatory charity (Zakat), and bow down with those who bow down.

2:83
And [recall] when We took the covenant from the Children of Israel, [enjoining upon them], "Do not worship except God; and to parents do good and to relatives, orphans, and the needy. And speak to people good [words] and establish prayer and give zakah." Then you turned away, except a few of you, and you were refusing.

2:110
And establish prayer and give Charity (zakat). And whatever good you send forth for yourselves (investment for your afterlife), you will find it with God. Indeed God is All- seer of what you do.

2:215
They ask you about giving: say, "The charity you give shall go to the parents, the relatives, the orphans, the poor, and the needy travelers." Any good you do, GOD is fully aware thereof.

2:177
It is not righteousness that you turn your faces towards the east or the west (praying) but righteous is he who believes in God, the

CHARITY

Last Day, the Angels, the Book, and the Prophets and gives wealth in spite of love for it to the near relatives, the orphans, the needy, the drifter, and those who ask, and in freeing the slaves; and who establishes prayer and gives charity (zakat) and he who fulfills the covenant when makes it; and he who is patient in suffering, hardship, and periods of stress. Those are the ones who are true and it is those who are the righteous.

2:219
(Muhammad), they ask you about wine and gambling. Tell them that there is great sin in them. Although they have (some) benefits for people, the sin therein is far greater than the benefit. They ask you about what they should give for the cause of God. Tell them, "Let it be what you can spare." This is how God explains for you His guidance so that perhaps you will think.

2:254
Believers, out of what We have given you, spend for the cause of God before the coming of the day when there will be no trading, no friendship, and no intercession. Those who deny the Truth are unjust.

2:262
Those who spend their money in the cause of GOD, then do not follow their charity with reminders (of it) or harm, will receive their recompense from their Lord; they have nothing to fear, nor will they grieve.

2:263
A kind word and (seeking) forgiveness are better than a charity followed by hurting (the feeling of the needy). And God is All- richly sufficient and All patiently tolerant.

2:264
O you who believe do not make your charities worthless by reminders of your generosity and by hurting (the feelings of the needy), like the one who spends his wealth to be seen by people and does not believe in God and the Last Day. Then his example is like that of a smooth rock on which is dust, then heavy rain fell on it and left it bare. (they will be transparent in their action). They have no control on anything of what they have earned. And God does not guide disbelieving people.

2:267
O you who believe, you shall give to charity from the good things you earn, and from what we have produced for you from the earth. Do not pick out the bad therein to give away, when you yourselves do not accept it unless your eyes are closed. You should know that GOD is Rich, Praiseworthy.

2:270
God knows all about whatever you spend for His cause or any vows that you make. The unjust people have no helper.

2:271
It is not bad to give charities in public. However if you give them privately to the poor, it would be better for you and an expiation for some of your sins. God is Well-Aware of what you do

2:272
(Muhammad), you do not have to guide them. God guides whomever He wants. Whatever you spend for the cause of God is for your own good, provided you do not spend anything but to please God. For anything good that you may give for the cause of God, you will receive sufficient reward and no injustice will be done to you.

CHARITY

2:273
[Charity is] for the poor who have been restricted for the cause of God, unable to move about in the land. An ignorant [person] would think them self-sufficient because of their restraint, but you will know them by their [characteristic] sign. They do not ask people persistently [or at all]. And whatever you spend of good - indeed, God is Knowing of it.

2:274
Those who spend their wealth [in God's way] by night and by day, secretly and publicly - they will have their reward with their Lord. And no fear will there be concerning them, nor will they grieve.

2:276
God condemns usury, and blesses charities. God does not love sinful unbelievers.

2:280
If the debtor is unable to pay, wait for a better time. If you give up the loan as a charity, it would be better for you, if you only knew.

3:92
You cannot attain righteousness until you give to charity from the possessions you love. Whatever you give to charity, GOD is fully aware thereof.

3:134
Who give to charity during the good times, as well as the bad times. They are suppressors of anger, and pardoners of the people. GOD loves the charitable.

4:38
They give money to charity only to show off, while disbelieving in GOD and the Last Day. If one's companion is the devil, that is the worst companion.

4:77
Have you noted those who were told, "You do not have to fight; all you need to do is observe the Contact Prayers (Salat) and give the obligatory charity (Zakat)," then, when fighting was decreed for them, they feared other men as much as they feared GOD, or even more? They said, "Our Lord, why did You force this fighting on us? If only You would give us a little time!" Say, "The materials of this world are nil, while the Hereafter is far better for the righteous, and you never suffer the slightest injustice."

4:114
There is nothing good about their private conferences, except for those who advocate charity, or righteous works, or making peace among the people. Anyone who does this, in response to GOD's teachings, we will grant him a great recompense.

4:162
However, the learned among them (the Jews) and the faithful believe in what God has revealed to you (Muhammad) and to the others before you and those who are steadfast in prayer, pay their religious tax, and believe in God and the Day of Judgment. They all will receive a great reward from Us

5:12
GOD had taken a covenant from the Children of Israel, and we raised among them twelve patriarchs. And GOD said, "I am with you, so long as you observe the Contact Prayers (Salat), give the obligatory charity (Zakat), and believe in My messengers and respect them, and continue to lend GOD a loan of righteousness. I will then remit your sins, and admit you into gardens with flowing streams. Anyone who disbelieves after this, has indeed strayed off the right path."

CHARITY

5:45
And we decreed for them in it that: the life for the life, the eye for the eye, the nose for the nose, the ear for the ear, the tooth for the tooth, and an equivalent injury for any injury. If one forfeits what is due to him as a charity, it will atone for his sins. Those who do not rule in accordance with GOD's revelations are the unjust.

5: 55
Your ally is none but God and His Messenger and those who have believed – those who establish prayer and give zakah, and they bow [in worship].

7:156
Grant us well-being in this life and in the life hereafter for we have turned ourselves to You." The Lord replied, "My torment only afflicts those whom I want to punish, but My mercy encompasses all things. I shall grant mercy to those who maintain piety, pay their zakat (charity) and those who have faith in Our revelations.

8:3
They are steadfast in prayer and spend part of what We have given them for the cause of God

9:18
The masjids (house of prayer) of God will maintain only by those who believe in God and the final day and establish the prayer and gives zakah (charity) and they do not fear anyone except God. Those are the guided ones.

9:67
The men and woman who are hypocrites are the same. They do what is wrong and they forbid what is right. Their hands are closed (from giving charity). They forget God, and God forgets them. Indeed the hypocrites are disobedient.

9:71
The believing men and women are allies of one another. They advocate righteousness and forbid evil, they observe the Contact Prayers (Salat) and give the obligatory charity (Zakat), and they obey GOD and His messenger. These will be showered by GOD's mercy. GOD is Almighty, Most Wise.

9:75-76
And among them are those who make a covenant with God that if he gives us his abundance, surely we will give charity and surely we will be among the righteous.

But when he gave them from His bounty, they were stingy with it and turned away while they refused.

9:104
Don't they know that God accepts repentance from his servants and takes charity. And God is the acceptor of repentance and he is most kind and forgiving.

14:31
Tell My believing servants to be steadfast in prayer and to spend for the cause of their Lord, both in private and in public, out of what We have given them. Let them do this before the coming of the day when there will be no merchandising or friendship.

16:90
Indeed, God orders justice and good conduct and giving (charity) to relatives and forbids immorality and bad conduct and oppression. He admonishes you that perhaps you will be reminded.

19:31
"He made me blessed wherever I go, and commanded me to observe the Contact Prayers (Salat) and the obligatory charity (Zakat) for as long as I live.

CHARITY

19:55-56
Mention in the Book (the Quran) the story of Ishmael; he was true to his promise, a Messengers and a Prophet.

He would order his people to worship God and pay the religious tax. His Lord was pleased with him

21:72-73
We granted him Isaac and Jacob as a gift and helped both of them to become righteous people.

We appointed them as leaders to guide the people through Our command and sent them revelation to strive for good deeds, worship their Lord, and pay religious tax. Both of them were Our worshipping servants.

22:35
They are the ones whose hearts are filled with awe upon mentioning GOD, they steadfastly persevere during adversity, they observe the Contact Prayers (Salat), and from our provisions to them, they give to charity.

22:41
He will certainly help those who, if given power in the land, will worship God through prayer, pay the religious tax, enjoin others do good, and prevent them from committing evil. The consequence of all things is in the hands of God

22:78
You shall strive for the cause of GOD as you should strive for His cause. He has chosen you and has placed no hardship on you in practicing your religion—the religion of your father Abraham. He is the one who named you "Submitters" originally. Thus, the messenger shall serve as a witness among you, and you shall serve

as witnesses among the people. Therefore, you shall observe the Contact Prayers (Salat) and give the obligatory charity (Zakat), and hold fast to GOD; He is your Lord, the best Lord and the best Supporter.

23:01-04
Indeed the believers are successful.
Who are submissive during their prayers
Those who turn away from unproductive (useless) talk.
And they pay their charity (Zakat)

24:56
And establish prayer and give zakah and obey the Messenger - that you may receive mercy.

27:3
Who establish prayer and give zakah, and of the Hereafter they are certain [in faith]

30:38
Give the relatives, the destitute, and the needy travelers their share (of charity). It is better for those who want to please God and they will have everlasting happiness

30:39
The usury that is practiced to increase some people's wealth, does not gain any increase with God. But if you give to charity, seeking God's pleasure, these are the ones who receive their reward multiplied.

57:7
Believe in GOD and His messenger, and give from what He has bestowed upon you. Those among you who believe and give (to charity) have deserved a great recompense.

CHARITY

57:18
Indeed, the men who practice charity and the women who practice charity and [they who] have loaned God a goodly loan - it will be multiplied for them, and they will have a noble reward.

63:10
And spend [in the way of God] from what We have provided you before death approaches one of you and he says, "My Lord, if only You would delay me for a brief term so I would give charity and be among the righteous.

73:20
Your Lord knows that you meditate during two-thirds of the night, or half of it, or one-third of it, and so do some of those who believed with you. God has designed the night and the day, and He knows that you cannot always do this. He has pardoned you. Instead, you shall read what you can of the Quran. He knows that some of you may be ill, others may be traveling in pursuit of God's provisions, and others may be striving in the cause of God. You shall read what you can of it, and observe the contact prayers (Salat), give the obligatory charity (Zakah), and lend God a loan of righteousness. Whatever good you send ahead on behalf of your souls, you will find it at God far better and generously rewarded. And implore God for forgiveness. God is Forgiver, Most Merciful.

98:5
All that was asked of them was to worship God, devoting the religion absolutely to Him alone, observe the contact prayers (Salat), and give the obligatory charity (Zakat). Such is the perfect religion.

Patience and Expectation in Receiving from God

❖

The Quran always advises having patience in receiving from God. It is not just patience alone, but patience with the constant expectation of receiving what you are asking for from God. One could say its patience combined with the relentless expectation to receive from your God, almost as if you are seeing it.

Remember that old saying, "Patience and virtue are two old friends, after patience comes, then it is time for the virtue to show up"? It was taken from the Quran in 2:153.

2:153
*Oh you who believe! Seek help through **patient and prayer**. Indeed God is with the **patient ones.***

Saadi takes from 2:153 and puts it like this:

Patience and Virtue's friendship goes afar
After Patience comes, the Virtue won't be far

Saadi, Persian poet 13th century
Translation and Rhyme
Faramarz F, Davati

Sometimes we may not receive what we are asking for from Him, and we may get disappointed, only to find out later that what we were asking from God was not good, and thank God we never received it. Or as they say here in the US, "Thank God for unanswered prayers."

God can see a lot further down our future path than we can. We predict and we think we know what's good for us, but He knows and can see a lot further.

We predict or think we can predict the next few years, but He has our schedule for the rest of our lives. As the Quran says:

31:34
Only God has the knowledge of the coming of the Hour of Doom. He sends down the rain and knows what is in the wombs. No soul is aware of what it will achieve tomorrow and no soul knows in which land it will die. God is All-knowing and All-aware.

Here are a few verses regarding patience:

2:155
Many of the People of the Scripture wish they could turn you back to disbelief after you have believed, out of envy from themselves [even] after the truth has become clear to them. So pardon and overlook until God delivers His command. Indeed, God is over all things competent.

2:177
*It is not righteousness that you turn your faces towards the east or the west but righteous is he who believes in God, the Last Day, the Angels, the Book, and the Prophets and gives wealth in spite of love for it to the near relative the orphans, the needy, the drifter, and those who ask, and in freeing the slaves; and who establishes prayer and gives charity (zakat) and he who fulfills the covenant when makes it; and he who is **patient** in suffering, hardship, and periods of stress. Those are the ones who are true and it is those who are the righteous.*

PATIENCE AND EXPECTATION IN RECEIVING FROM GOD

3:120
If any good touches you, it grieves them; and if any misfortune strikes you, they rejoice at it. And if you are patient and fear God, their plot will not harm you at all. Indeed God (knows) all-about of what they do.

7:128
Moses said to his people, seek help from God and be patient. Indeed the earth belongs to God. He causes, to whom He wills of his servants to inherit it. And the (best) end is for the righteous.

7:137
We gave the suppressed people the blessed eastern and western regions as their inheritance. Thus, the promises of your Lord to the children of Israel all came true because of the patience which they exercised. He destroyed all the establishments of the Pharaoh and his people

10:109
And follow what is revealed to you (O Muhammad) and be patient until God gives judgment. And he is the Best of the Judges.

11:11
Except those who are patient and do the good deeds, for those will be forgiveness and great reward.

11:49
That is from the news of the unseen which We reveal to you, [O Muhammad]. You knew it not, neither you nor your people, before this. So be patient; indeed, the [best] outcome is for the righteous

11:75
Indeed, Abraham was patient, grieving and [frequently] returning [to God].

11:115
And be patient for indeed God does not allow the rewards of those who do good go to waste.

12:90
They said," Are you indeed Joseph? He said" I am joseph, and this is my brother. God has certainly favored us. Indeed, he who fears God and is patient, then indeed, God does not allow to be lost the reward of those who do good".

13:22
Who exercise patience to gain God's pleasure, who are steadfast in prayer, who spend for the cause of God privately and in public, and who keep away evil with good will have a blissful end

13:24
saying, "Peace be with you for all that you have patiently endured. Blessed is the reward of Paradise."

14:05
We sent Moses and gave him miracles in order to lead his people from darkness into light and to remind them of the days of God. In this there is evidence (of the truth) for those who exercise patience and give thanks.

14:12
Why should we not trust in God when He has shown us the right way? We shall exercise patience against the troubles with which you afflict us. Whoever needs a trustee should trust in God."

16:42
Those who are patients and put their trust in God.

PATIENCE AND EXPECTATION IN RECEIVING FROM GOD

16:96
Whatever you have will end, but what God has is lasting. And We will surely give those who were patient their reward according to the best of what they used to do.

16:126 -127
If you want retaliation, let it be equal to that which you faced. But if you exercise patience it will be better for you.

Exercise patience (O Muhammad) and let it be only for the cause of God. Do not be grieved about them nor disappointed at their evil plans.

17:11
And man prays for evil (putting a curse on someone) as he prays for the good, and the man is ever hasty.

23:111
Indeed I have rewarded them this day for their patient. Indeed they are the successful ones.

29:58-59
We shall give mansions in Paradise wherein streams flow to the righteously striving believers and therein they will live forever. How blessed is the reward of the hard working people

Those who are patient and put their trust on their Lord.

30:60
Be patient. The promise of God is certainly true. Let not the faithless shake the firmness of the promise of God.

31:17
(And Luqman said) O' my son, establish the prayer and command the right, and forbid from wrong and be patient over what befalls you. Indeed that is something that requires determination.

38:17
Be patient over what they say, and remember our slave David, who had strength and indeed repeatedly repented and turned back (to God).

Blessings of God

--- ❖ ---

We all want the blessings of God, and we all wonder how we can get them. What are we supposed to do in order to receive His blessings, or what might we do wrong that would mess up our blessings?

In 2:268, it says:

Satan threatens you with poverty and commands you to commit sin. God promises you forgiveness and abundance. God is Bountiful and All-knowing.

There is more to this verse than comes across. When Satan threatens us with poverty, what do we do? We become negative and complain about "not having" any money, "not having" a good job, "not having this and that," and complain constantly about "not having," and that "not having" becomes the focus of our life and we bring it into our life by constantly thinking about it.

But God promises you forgiveness and abundance, and He is bountiful and all-knowing. So if I am choosing to follow God's way, I think to myself, no matter where I am in life, I am going to be "positive" and ask for His forgiveness and all the abundance and bountiful blessings He can send my way, as He is all-knowing and all-seeing of my bank account and my expenses! I will ask Him to send His bountiful blessings to me since He owns it all and can send in as much as He pleases, as I have been the righteous servant and have been knocking at His door and asking. So I will expect and have faith in Him to send me, his righteous servant, His bountiful blessings, as I have been righteous.

In order to receive His blessings, I always stay positive, do the prayers, give charity, do good deeds, stay patient, have faith and expectancy from Him, and I believe and I am certain that I will receive from Him.

Thank God for the Quran, as God has put it right in front of me.

In order to receive God's blessings, all you have to do is read the Quran on a daily basis and do the following as a habit:

1- Believe in One and only God. God is above All.

2- Believe God has power over all things.

3- Know anything is possible through God.

4- Have faith in God.

5- Trust in God.

6- Pray your daily prayers and give charity when you can.

7- Do the fasting if you are capable.

8- Be patient and expect things to happen.

9- Submit and surrender to God.

10- Do good deeds, as they return to you.

11- Thank God for all the blessings He has given you.

12- Glorify and elevate your God.

13- When good things happen, credit God for it and thank Him.

14- Give the mandatory charity.

15- Forgive and ask to be forgiven by God.

16- Ask God to settle the score with your enemies. Don't worry about them or project hate toward them, and continue peacefully with your life. Ask God to vindicate you against them, as His retribution is a lot harsher than what you can do.

17- Have hope and confidence in God that He will take care of you.

18- Have hope and confidence in God that it all ends well for you. Everything will be fine. Everything will end in your favor. God's hand is above all hands, and everything will be okay.

19- His power is above all powers, and His hand is above all hands.

20- Always say and believe, "Anything is possible through God!"

21- Always say positive words, and declare them loudly.

22- Always have positive thoughts, and never have doubts.

You will see the above ideas in various chapters and verses of the Quran. I am sure there are a lot more, but I'd like you to find them yourself and then share them with everyone.

Here are a few:

1:06-07
Guide us to the right path.

The path of those who you gave your blessings, not those who earned your anger and not those who went astray.

4:173
The righteously striving believers will receive the reward for their deeds and extra favors from God. But those who disdain the worship of God out of pride will suffer the most painful torment. They will find no guardian or helper besides God.

5:20
And when Moses said to his people, oh my people remember the blessings of God he put among you when he placed a prophet among you and made you kings and he gave you what He had not given any one else in the world.

7:69
Do you wonder that a man from among you has come to you a reminder from your lord? And remember when he made you the descendants after the tribe of Noah. And increased you in the Stature extensively. So remember the Rewards (blessings) of God, so that you may succeed.

7:96
And if the people of the cities had believed and feared God, we would have surely opened the blessings from the heaven and the earth, but they denied, so we held them from their earnings.

8:53
That is because God does not change the blessing that he had bestowed upon people until they change from within (toward wrong). And indeed God is All-Hearing and All-knowing.

9:21
Their Lord gives them the good news of mercy from Him and approval and of the gardens for them where in is enduring pleasure.

BLESSINGS OF GOD

9:99
Some of the Bedouins believe in God and the Day of Judgment. Whatever they spend for the cause of God they consider it as a means of getting nearer to God and have the prayers of the Messenger in their favor. This, certainly is a means to get nearer to God. God will admit them into His mercy. God is All-forgiving and All-merciful

13:29
Those who have believed and done righteous deeds, for them there is blessings and a beautiful place to return.

14:07
Remember when your Lord said to you, 'If you give thanks, I shall give you greater (favors), but if you deny the Truth, know that My retribution is severe.

16:18
Even if you wanted to count all of God's blessings, you would not be able to. God is All-forgiving and All merciful.

16:121
He (Abraham) was grateful for his blessings. And God chose him and guided him to a straight path.

17:21
Consider how We have given preference to some people above others, yet the life to come (Hereafter) has more honor and respect.

24:38
(They worship Him) And God may reward them with the Best of their deed and increase their blessings and God provides for whom he wills without any measure.

57:21
Compete with one another to achieve forgiveness from your Lord and to reach Paradise, which is as vast as the heavens and the earth, and is prepared for those who believe in God and His Messenger. This is the blessing of God and He grants it to whomever He wants. God is the possessor of Great Blessings

Submitting and Surrendering to God.

❖

What is submitting and surrendering to God? Submitting to God is a lot like *tawakkul*, "trust-in" the Lord, that was discussed earlier, but it is in a steady state. It is at all times, like oxygen. You do not worry about running out of oxygen as you go through your day, it is always there. You are not worried about the future as you go through your daily chores, as you know He will take care of you and is looking after you.

Submitting to God is like giving the steering wheel of your life to God and asking Him for guidance and putting the right path in front of you. I personally believe you have to be a believer first and have already established your own way of spiritually connecting to God, before relinquishing everything to God. I do not think a non-believer can all of a sudden, cold turkey, tell God, "Well here is the steering wheel of my life. Let's see if you can do any better." I don't think that will work. There has to be that connection first, no matter what religion you practice. Many times you may hear someone saying, "God is literally talking to me," with a series of events, answered prayers, or different events that are happening around them and their life. That is the connection I am talking about.

Personally speaking, I used to have a different business fourteen years ago. There was a change in the industry I was in, and that business started failing. It was as if I had lost the reins and had no control. I was sinking just like a rock that you drop in the ocean, and was heading nowhere but the bottom. I used to pray and pray and ask God to show me a way. I remember I was telling

Him that I would not let go until He showed me a way. After my prayers, I used to have my face on the ground in prostration and constantly pray to Him and ask Him to show me a way. And that is how the idea of my next business venture came to me, which fit my background perfectly. But my computer skills were not good enough to start that business venture alone. I had a good Irish friend who helped me tremendously to get the new business off the ground, and I believe God placed him on my path to help me. He was literally God sent! We spent the whole summer getting that business off the ground. I still have that business today and make a living from it.

Submitting to God should not be mistaken with not doing anything. We still have to do our daily work and handle our responsibilities. You cannot tell God, "I am going to live in this house or apartment, and I submit to you to pay my rent or mortgage," or car payment or anything else!

Saadi puts it very eloquently:

Though the bird is in trust of the Lord for daily bread
Yet she builds her own nest with her own hand

Saadi, Persian poet 13th century
Translation and Rhyme
Faramarz F. Davati

Submitting to God is asking God to guide you to the right path or put the right path in front of you for you to reach your destination. You still have to do your daily work and routine, but you no longer have to worry about the results, as you have submitted to God and you know He will take care of you and show you the right path. You put God in first place, keep your eyes on the stars, and keep those feet moving to achieve your goals.

Here are some verses regarding submitting to God:

SUBMITTING AND SURRENDERING TO GOD.

4:125
And who is better in religion than he who submits himself to God and he is a good-doer and follows the religion of the upstanding Abraham. And God took Abraham as a friend.

2:112
Yes, whoever submits himself to God and is a good -doer then his reward is with his Lord. And there will be no fear on them and nor will they have any sadness. No fear and sadness will be on them.

6: 14
Say, is there other than God that I should take as a protector, who has created Heaven and earth. While He is the one that feeds, Is (someone) feeding him? Say (O Muhammad), Indeed I am commanded that I am the first (among you) who submit to God and (was commanded) Do not ever bring a partner to him.

10:72
And if you turn away from my advice, I am not asking you for any reward. My reward is only from God, and I have been commanded that I be of surrenders to God (become a Muslim).

16:87
(On the Day of Judgment) the disbelievers will submit themselves to God and whatever they had falsely invented will disappear

21:108
Say, "It is revealed to me that there is only one Lord. So, will you submit to Him?"(become Muslim)

22:34
And for every nation we have appointed a (sacrifice) ritual, that they may mention the name of God over what He has provided

them of the beast of cattle your God is One, submit to him and (Muhammad) give good news (God's mercy) to the humble ones.

39:54
Turn in repentance to your Lord and submit to His will before you are afflicted with the torment after which you can receive no help.

6:163
He has no partner, and this I have been commanded, And I am the first of those who surrender to Him.

10:84
And Moses said" O my people if you have believed in God then put your trust in him if you are surrounded (to God).

10:90
And we took across the sea, the children of Israel and Ferro and his companions followed them in revolt and animosity until we over took them by drowning, he (Ferro) said I believe that there is no God except the One who the children of Israel believe and I am a surrender (to Him).

11:14
Then if they don't respond to you, then you know that Quran was sent down with the knowledge of God, and there is no God except Him. Then would you surrender to God (become Muslim)?.

God Testing You

29:2
Do the people think that they will be left to say, "We believe," without being put to the test?

God tests all of us through adversities and sickness to see if we stay faithful, believe in Him, and pray to Him. Sometimes people who are struck with adversity completely lose faith, as it seems such an injustice to anyone who experiences it. And you will see this in people from all faiths and religions.

Many of us have experienced when tragedy strikes one of our loved ones, especially the innocents, and we ask ourselves, "Why?" and "Where is the justice in that?" That's why in the Quran it has been emphasized so many times that this life is very temporary and is nothing but child's play, or not to be taken too seriously. It is simply an illusion compared to the final destination, which is the afterlife when we all return to Him.

47:36
The worldly life is only a play and amusement. And if you believe and fear God, He will grant your rewards and will not ask you to pay for them.

57:20
Know that the worldly life is only a game, a temporary attraction, a means of boastfulness among yourselves and a place for multiplying your wealth and children. It is like the rain which produces plants that are attractive to the unbelievers. These plants flourish,

turn yellow, and then become crushed bits of straw. In the life hereafter there will be severe torment or forgiveness and mercy from God. The worldly life is the enjoyment of an illusion.

But before we make it to the other side, He certainly tests all of us, to separate the real believers and the hypocrites. This has been shown in many stories in the Quran and the Old Testament.

21:111
"For all that I know, this world is a test for you, and a temporary enjoyment."

21:35
Every soul will taste death, after we put you to the test through adversity and prosperity, then to us you ultimately return.

A great example of God testing his prophets and subjects are the stories of Abraham and Job. Job is an exemplary figure in *patience* in Islam, and Abraham is an example of *submission and obedience* to God.

In the story of Abraham, there is a man that could not have any offspring, until he was old. Then God sent his three messengers to give the man good news of future children. At the end the man had to sacrifice one of these children. Now we Muslims believe God asked Abraham to sacrifice Ishmael. Jews and Christians believe God asked Abraham to sacrifice Isaac. This has become one of the differences between Islam and Judaism and Christianity. However, everyone is missing the point and the moral of this big story.

The moral of the story is how God tested Abraham, how harsh and gut-wrenching that test was, and how Abraham submitted to Him despite the resistance of every particle in his body. When Abraham passed the test, God then brought the rams out of no-

GOD TESTING YOU

where for him!

2:124
And remember when Abraham was tested by his Lord with commands and he fulfilled them. God said, "Indeed, I will make you a leader for the people." Abraham said, "And of my descendants?" God said, "My covenant does not include the wrongdoers."

And that's the lesson. When you pass God's test and stay in faith, no matter how hard you are hit with whatever has struck you, He will deliver "your ram" to you, out of nowhere!

Here are a few verses about God testing us:

2:155
We will surely test you through some fear, hunger, and loss of money, lives, and crops. Give good news to the people who have patient.

5:48
*Then we revealed to you this scripture, truthfully, confirming previous scriptures, and superseding them. You shall rule among them in accordance with **GOD**'s revelations, and do not follow their wishes if they differ from the truth that came to you. For each of you, we have decreed laws and different rites. Had **GOD** willed, He could have made you one nation (united in religion). But He thus puts you to the test through the revelations He has given each of you. You shall compete in righteousness. To **GOD** is your final destiny—all of you—then He will inform you of everything you had disputed.*

6:42
We have sent (messengers) to communities before you, and we put them to the test through adversity and hardship, that they may implore.

6:165
And it is He who has made you successors upon the earth and has raised some of you above others in degrees [of rank] that He may test you through what He has given you. Indeed, your Lord is swift in penalty; but indeed, He is Forgiving and Merciful.

9:16
*Did you think that you will be left alone without **GOD** distinguishing those among you who strive, and never ally themselves with **GOD**'s enemies, or the enemies of His messenger, or the enemies of the believers? **GOD** is All-Knowing of everything you do.*

11:7

And it is He who created the heavens and the earth in six days - and His Throne had been upon water - that He might test you as to which of you is best in deed. But if you say, "Indeed, you are resurrected after death," those who disbelieve will surely say, "This is not but obvious magic."

18:7

We have adorned everything on earth, in order to test them, and thus distinguish those among them who work righteousness.

20:85
God said, "We have put your people (Children of Israel) to the test after you left, but the Samarian misled them."

22:53
He would make Satan's temptations a trial for those whose hearts are hard and sick. The wrong-doers are far away from the Lord,

38:34
We tested Solomon by (causing death to his son) and leaving his body on Solomon's chair. Then he turned to Us in repentance

38:41
Remember our servant Job: he called upon his Lord, "The devil has afflicted me with hardship and pain."

72:17
We will surely test them all. As for him who disregards the message of his Lord, He will direct him to ever increasing retribution.

Fear of God

In Islam God is feared and is feared fiercely, but at the same time He is the Most Kind and Most Forgiving. The lesson learned from the Quran is, He is **just**, and do not get on the wrong side of God or, simply put, you will pay for it—if not in this life, definitely in the afterlife.

In our daily prayer, we do ask God to, **"Guide us to the right path, the path of those who you bestowed your blessings, not those who earned your anger and not those who went astray" (1:6,7).**

In this chapter, I go over most of the verses describing God, as there are many of them. In Islam, God is absolute, all powerful, and just. He is kind and rewards behavior. He is just. If you do wrong, you are not going to get away with it. We love Him, we respect Him, and we also fear Him. As He is all-seeing, all-knowing of what we do.

God is absolute and is feared in Islam, similar to in Judaism.

In Christianity, God, the creator of universe, has been put in the background. Jesus is believed to be His son, God of the universe and the savior in the day of judgment. "Jesus owns it all," as the TV preachers say all the time. Everything happens through Jesus. Christianity keeps the religion very sweet. You hardly hear any Christian preacher talk about fear of God. In Christianity they believe you can do no wrong, and even if you do, in the end you are saved and forgiven by Jesus. Christians believe Jesus died on the cross for them, so their sins are then forgiven on Judgment Day.

Every religion is respected, but our views in Islam differ from those of Christianity. In Islam, God is feared and feared fiercely.

You pay for everything you do, right or wrong. At the end your actions are tallied up. Your good deeds are measured against your bad deeds. You are judged by God the Almighty, and there is no savior or intermediary for anybody in any religion according to the Quran and Islam. If you escape the penalty of your wrongdoings in this life, you will definitely pay for them in the afterlife!

As the Quran says, "God is a good accountant" (21:47). He won't miss your good and bad deeds.

21:47
And We place the scales of justice for the Day of Resurrection, so no soul will be treated unjustly at all. And if there is [even] the weight of a mustard seed, We will bring it forth. And sufficient are We as accountant

Here are a few verses regarding your relationship with God and fear:

16:51
And God has said, "Do not take for yourselves two deities. He is but one God, so fear only Me."

5:7
Remember God's favors to you and the firm covenant that He has made with you. You said because of this covenant, "We have heard (the words of the Lord) and have obeyed Him." Have fear of God; He knows well all that the hearts contain.

8:2
Believers are those who when God is mentioned they feel fear (out of respect) in their heart and when his verses are recited to them, their faith strengthens. In God alone do they trust.

FEAR OF GOD

2:150
And from wherever you start forth (for prayer) turn your face in the direction of Al- Masjid Al Haram (kabah). And wherever you are turn your face towards it, so that people will not have any argument against you except the wrongdoers among them, so do not fear them but fear Me, so that I may complete My favor upon you, perhaps you may be guided.

9:18
The masjids of God will maintain only by those who believe in God and the final day and establish the prayer and gives zakah (charity) and they do not fear anyone except God. Those are the guided ones.

30:31
Turn in repentance to Him. Have fear of Him. Be steadfast in your prayer. Do not be of those who associate others with God.

3:120
If any good touches you, it grieves them; and if any misfortune strikes you, they rejoice at it. And if you are patient and fear God, their plot will not harm you at all. Indeed God (knows) all-about of what they do.

[3:175] It is the devil's system to instill fear into his subjects. Do not fear them and fear Me instead, if you are believers

12:90
They said," Are you indeed Joseph? He said" I am joseph, and this is my brother. God has certainly favored us. Indeed, he who fears God and is patient, then indeed, God does not allow to be lost the reward of those who do good".

7:96
And if the people of the cities had believed and feared God, we would have surely opened the blessings from the heaven and the earth, but they denied, so we held them from their earnings.

[59:16]
They are like Satan who said to people, "Reject the faith," but when the people rejected the faith he said, "I have nothing to do with you. I fear the Lord of the Universe".

Satan

Satan and his associates are very real in Islam, and we are constantly reminded in the Quran to stand against Satan and his associates. We are instructed to stand against Satan and his associates and their promises of the wealth and glitter of this earthly life, in exchange for our soul. We are constantly reminded of how temporary this life is and how at the end it will pass, as if it was just a few days or just hours.

As the Quran describes it, Satan woos you with the glitter of this life, and then sits back and watches you as you step in at your own will. When he is done with your soul, he will leave you in this life and in the afterlife, and you will have no support. What is anybody without their soul?

14:22
When the judgment of God is issued, Satan will say, "God's promise to you was true, but I, too, made a promise to you and disregarded it. I had no authority over you. I invited you and you responded to me. Do not blame me but blame yourselves. I cannot help you and you cannot help me. I did not agree with your belief that I was equal to God." The unjust will face a painful punishment

2:102
They pursued what the devils taught concerning Solomon's kingdom. Solomon, however, was not a disbeliever, but the devils were disbelievers. They taught the people sorcery, and that which was sent down through the two angels of Babel, Haroot and Maroot. These two did not divulge such knowledge without pointing out:

"This is a test. You shall not abuse such knowledge." But the people used it in such evil schemes as the breaking up of marriages. They can never harm anyone against the will of GOD. They thus learn what hurts them, not what benefits them, and they know full well that whoever practices witchcraft will have no share in the Hereafter. Miserable indeed is what they sell their souls for, if they only knew.

The Quran teaches you to achieve happiness within your soul. The earthly possessions come and go. There are many people who attain wealth but are not happy. This life is too short and is nothing but child's play. The final destination is the afterlife. The good deeds we do today save us for the afterlife. We all die one day and leave this place. God is the only thing that remains!

10:62-64
The friends of God will certainly have nothing to fear, nor will they be grieved.
Those who believe and live a righteous life.
will receive glad news both in this life and in the life hereafter. The words of God do not change. This alone is the supreme triumph

We constantly seek refuge in God from Satan and his associates in our daily prayer—at least five times! In 113:03, some translate this as seeking refuge "from evil when it comes out at night."

113.00
In the name of most kind and forgiving God
I seek refuge to the Lord of the dawn
From Evils of what He has created
From the evil of darkness when it spreads (113.03)
Form people who commit sorcery
And from the envier who envies

The word-by-word translation of (113:03) is, "And from the evil of darkness when it spreads." It can also be translated as "from the evil of overtaking darkness."

The real meaning of "darkness" comes out in the next verse, so we understand the Quran is simply talking about the darkness of the night or the darkness of dark forces and evil when they spread and take over. The next verse is, "From people who commit sorcery." The word by word of 113:04 is, "And from the evil of the blowers in ties (loops)." At the time of Muhammad, this was one of the ways the sorcerers would do their magic spells. I imagine there are various techniques by which the sorcerers were practicing their witchcraft in those days and in the present.

Those who do sorcery seek the help of Satan. Which gives a clearer meaning of the previous verse, 113:03, and an interpretation of "from the evil of overtaking darkness."

What can we use as an example of how the "overtaking forces of darkness" would feel or look?

In the Middle East it could be ISIS, Al-Qaeda, or the Taliban overtaking a town or a village. Or if a foreign country or enemy takes over or invades your country.

An example of "overtaking forces of darkness" in the US would be the spread of perversion among the young and children. It appears as if a demonic force or a satanic cult or secret society or whatever you want to call it is pushing this agenda and other issues. Most people don't even know about it or can escape from it.

58:10
Holding secret counsels for (evil purposes) is a work of Satan to cause grief to the believers, but he can do no harm to them except by the will of God. Let the believers trust in God.

7:30
Some He guided, while others are committed to straying. They have taken the devils as their masters, instead of GOD, yet they believe that they are guided.

One of the examples of perversion within this group and spreading these ideas among the young is the so-called "experimentation," where members of the same sex experience having sex with each other. Some of the famous singers and celebrities have been doing it and talking about or putting it in their songs as well as selling their soul to the devil. Some kids look at these celebs as role models. If only young people knew not to follow these celebs or exchange their soul for anything and stay with God, it would be great.

In my opinion, kids should stay away from any song, singer, actor, actress, or performer who is related to any message about such activities. Parents should talk to their kids at a much younger age, or this satanic group will do it before them with their cartoons!

If you see homosexuality has grown here in the West, it is not by accident, nor have more homosexuals come out of the closet. Homosexuality can be a learned behavior. They are emasculating American young men more and more every day. From the way they dress to the way they act. The ultimate goal of this satanic cult is to make every man behave and dress like a woman, and every woman behave and dress like a man and alter God's creation.

Unfortunately, the Christian preachers here in the US have made the religion so sweet and without any sacrifice, that at times like this they cannot tell people the reality. They are too busy competing with each other for TV ratings and market share, and they fear giving stern news may scare off their flock!

There is not one charismatic Christian leader who can raise people against this Evil!

Whoever is promoting this vision of a future one-world government and religion is simply doing so for their own benefit and to enforce their own agendas. It is against God's will. God wants the Abrahamic faiths to stay separate and compete with each other.

5:48
*Then we revealed to you this scripture, truthfully, confirming previous scriptures, and superseding them. You shall rule among them in accordance with **GOD**'s revelations, and do not follow their wishes if they differ from the truth that came to you. For each of you, we have decreed laws and different rites. Had **GOD** willed, He could have made you one nation (united in religion). But He thus puts you to the test through the revelations He has given each of you. You shall compete in righteousness. To **GOD** is your final destiny—all of you—then He will inform you of everything you had disputed.*

For now, the best way to protect ourselves against this Evil is through religion, no matter what religion one practices.

In the Quran, we learn that as long as you are calling on God and you are under His shadow and protection, Satan cannot touch you.

16:99
He (Satan) has no power over those who believe and trust in their Lord.

But when you stay away from God you are fair game, and Satan will invite you in, unless you call on God and believe in Him. Satan constantly tries to bring you out of God's shadow with temptations. Satan will try to entice you with forbidden physical gains, wealth, glitter, gold, and any shining object that can attract your attention to the pleasures of this life. Satan will try to make these worldly things attractive and irresistible to you. Satan whispers in your heart and invites you in, and then he withdraws and watches you step in, as you step in at your own will!

Muslims, Christians, and Jews all have to hold onto their Scriptures, as dearly as possible, because this is all the protection we have. Our daily prayers and seeking God's protection is our only shield against this menace. In order to survive in the US, you have to have a strong belief in God no matter what religion you practice.

2:256
There is no persuasion in religion. Certainly, right has become clearly distinct from wrong. Whoever rejects the devil and believes in God has firmly taken hold of a strong handle that never breaks. God is All-hearing and knowing.

2:257
God is the Guardian of the believers and it is He who takes them out of darkness into light. The Devil is the guardian of those who deny the Truth and he leads them from light to darkness. These are the dwellers of hell wherein they will live forever.

9:111
GOD has bought from the believers their lives and their money in exchange for Paradise. Thus, they fight in the cause of GOD, willing to kill and get killed. Such is His truthful pledge in the Torah, the Gospel, and the Quran-and who fulfills His pledge better than GOD? You shall rejoice in making such an exchange. This is the greatest triumph.

16:99
He (Satan) has no power over those who believe and trust in their Lord.

SATAN

We Muslims have to keep our traditions, our beliefs, and our religion, and keep away from what gets preached to the masses here in the US as trendy and stylish. We Muslims are often criticized for not assimilating. We are assimilating, but with caution. We pick and choose. We should assimilate mostly with other people of faith. We do not necessarily give in to the fads and styles of today. We have to pick and choose which values are good American values and which are not and are being spread among the young and old by this Satanic cult in America. Let non-believers follow what is preached to them by the media. Let them criticize us Muslims for not being hip or assimilating to their ways of living or perversions or homosexual agendas. They cannot see themselves, but we are looking at them from the other side of the window! We are building and living in our own arks here in the US!

God is the light of the world; without Him we would be empty. We light up with how much of Him we have inside. Without Him, it's nothing but darkness. If you are not under His shadow, you are not protected against Satan.

We pray and seek refuge to God from Evil at least five times a day in our daily prayers. Perhaps one of the reasons the dark forces of this world, who control most of the countries and media outlets, hate Islam is the strong stand it takes against Satan.

113.00
In the name of most kind and forgiving God
I seek refuge to the Lord of the dawn
From Evils of what He has created
From the evil of overtaking darkness
Form people who commit sorcery
And from the envier who envies

114:00
In the name of most kind and forgiving God
I seek refuge to the Lord of the mankind
The king of the mankind
The Lord of the mankind
From the evil whisperer who whispers in the heart of people and withdraws
From evil and mankind

Here are some verses regarding Satan:

20:117
So We said, "O Adam, indeed this is an enemy to you and to your wife. Then let him not remove you from Paradise so you would suffer.

2:34
When we said to the angels, "Fall prostrate before Adam," they fell prostrate, except Satan; he refused, was too arrogant, and a disbeliever.

2:168
O mankind, eat from whatever is on earth [that is] lawful and good and do not follow the footsteps of Satan. Indeed, he is to you a clear enemy.

2:208
Believers, submit yourselves to the will of God as a whole. Do not follow the footsteps of Satan; he is your sworn enemy.

[2:256]
There is no persuasion in religion. Certainly, right has become clearly distinct from wrong. Whoever rejects the devil and believes in God has firmly taken hold of a strong handle that never breaks. God is All-hearing and knowing

SATAN

3:175
It is the devil's system to instill fear into his subjects. Do not fear them and fear Me instead, if you are believers

4:76
Those who believe are fighting for the cause of GOD, while those who disbelieve are fighting for the cause of tyranny. Therefore, you shall fight the devil's allies; the devil's power is nil.

4:118 -119 (cloning)
God condemned Satan when he said, «I will certainly take my revenge from Your servants

And I will mislead them, and I will arouse in them [sinful] desires, and I will command them so they will slit the ears of cattle, and I will command them so they will change the creation of God.» And whoever takes Satan as his guardian instead of God has certainly sustained a clear loss upon himself.

6:142
And of the grazing livestock are carriers [of burdens] and those [too] small. Eat of what God has provided for you and do not follow the footsteps of Satan. Indeed, he is to you a clear enemy

7:11
We created and shaped you, then told the angels to prostrate themselves before Adam. All the angels obeyed except Satan who did not

9-111
God has purchased the souls and property of the believers in exchange for Paradise. They fight for the cause of God to destroy His enemies and to sacrifice themselves. This is a true promise which He has revealed in the Torah, the Gospel, and the Quran. No one

is more true to His promise than God. Let this bargain be glad news for them. This is indeed the supreme triumph.

2:208
Believers, submit yourselves to the will of God as a whole. Do not follow the footsteps of Satan; he is your sworn enemy.

16:98
*When you read the Quran, you shall seek refuge in **GOD** from Satan the rejected.*

17:61
When we said to the angels, "Fall prostrate before Adam," they fell prostrate, except Satan. He said, "Shall I prostrate to one You created from mud?"

18:50
When We told the angels to prostrate before Adam they all obeyed except Iblis. He was a jinn and he sinned against the command of his Lord. Why do you (people) obey him and his offspring instead of Me, even though they are your enemies? How terrible will be the recompense that the wrong doers will receive!

23:97
Say, "My Lord, I seek refuge in You from the whispers of the devils.

24:21
O you who have believed, do not follow the footsteps of Satan. And whoever follows the footsteps of Satan - indeed, he enjoins immorality and wrongdoing. And if not for the favor of God upon you and His mercy, not one of you would have been pure, ever, but God purifies whom He wills, and God is Hearing and Knowing

SATAN

*[2:102] They pursued what the devils taught concerning Solomon's kingdom. Solomon, however, was not a disbeliever, but the devils were disbelievers. They taught the people sorcery, and that which was sent down through the two angels of Babel, Haroot and Maroot. These two did not divulge such knowledge without pointing out: "This is a test. You shall not abuse such knowledge." But the people used it in such evil schemes as the breaking up of marriages. They can never harm anyone against the will of **GOD**. They thus learn what hurts them, not what benefits them, and they know full well that whoever practices witchcraft will have no share in the Hereafter. Miserable indeed is what they sell their souls for, if they only knew.*

*[2:256] There shall be no compulsion in religion: the right way is now distinct from the wrong way. Anyone who denounces the devil and believes in **GOD** has grasped the strongest bond; one that never breaks. **GOD** is All-Hearing and Knowing.*

2:268
Satan threatens you with poverty and commands you to commit sin. God promises you forgiveness and favors. God is All-Encompassing and All-knowing

3:175
It is the devil's system to instill fear into his subjects. Do not fear them and fear Me instead, if you are believers.

4:38
*They give money to charity only to show off, while disbelieving in **GOD** and the Last Day. If one's companion is the devil, that is the worst companion.*

4:60
(Muhammad), have you seen those who think that they have faith in what is revealed to you and to others before you, yet choose to take their affairs to Satan for judgment even though they are commanded to deny him. Satan wants to lead them far away from the right path

4:76
*Those who believe are fighting for the cause of **GOD**, while those who disbelieve are fighting for the cause of tyranny. Therefore, you shall fight the devil's allies; the devil's power is nil.*

4:120
Satan promises them and entices them; what the Satan promises is no more than an illusion.

5:90
Believers, wine, gambling, the (sacrificing to) stone altars (to other than God) and arrows (that the pagans associate with certain divine characters) are all abominable acts associated with satanic activities. Avoid them so that you may have everlasting happiness.

5:91
*The devil wants to provoke animosity and hatred among you through intoxicants and gambling, and to distract you from remembering **GOD**, and from observing the Contact Prayers (Salat). Will you then refrain?*

6:68
If you see those who mock our revelations, you shall avoid them until they delve into another subject. If the devil causes you to forget, then, as soon as you remember, do not sit with such evil people.

SATAN

6:71
Say to them, "Should we, instead of asking for God's help, seek help from that which can neither benefit nor harm us, but would only turn us back to disbelief after God had granted us guidance? To do so would be to act like (those who have been) seduced by Satan, leaving them wandering aimlessly here and there, even though their friends call them, 'Come to the right guidance that has come to us.' " Say, "God's guidance is the only true guidance and we are commanded to submit ourselves to the Lord of the Universe

[7:20]
Satan tempted them to reveal that which was kept private from them and said, "Your Lord has not prohibited you (to eat the fruits of this tree) unless you want to be angels or immortal."

[7:22]
Thus, he deceitfully showed them (the tree). When they had tasted (fruits) from the tree, their private parts became revealed to them and they began to cover their private parts with leaves from the garden. Their Lord then called out to them saying, "Did I not forbid you to eat (fruits) from the tree and tell you that Satan was your sworn enemy?"

*[7:30] Some He guided, while others are committed to straying. They have taken the devils as their masters, instead of **GOD**, yet they believe that they are guided.*

[7:175] Recite for them the news of one who was given our proofs, but chose to disregard them. Consequently, the devil pursued him, until he went astray.

*[7:200] When the devil whispers to you any whisper, seek refuge in **GOD**; He is All-hearing All seeing..*

[7:201]
Indeed, those who fear God - when an impulse touches them from Satan, they remember [Him] and at once they have insight

8:11
Remember] when He overwhelmed you with drowsiness [giving] security from Him and sent down upon you from the sky, rain by which to purify you and remove from you the evil [suggestions] of Satan and to make steadfast your hearts and plant firmly thereby your feet

12:5
He said, "My son, do not tell your brothers about your dream, lest they plot and scheme against you. Surely, the devil is man's worst enemy.

12:42
And he said to the one whom he knew would go free, "Mention me before your master." But Satan made him forget the mention [to] his master, and Joseph remained in prison several years.

20:120
But the devil whispered to him, saying, "O Adam, let me show you the tree of eternity and unending kingship."

23:97
Say, "My Lord, I seek refuge in You from the whispers of the devils.

25:29
He led me away from the true guidance after it had come to us. Satan is a traitor to people

29:38
How the people of Ad and Thamud were destroyed is evident to you from their homes. Satan made their deeds seem attractive to

them and prevented them from the right path, even though they had visions.

31:33
O' people, fear your Lord and fear the Day that a father cannot help his son and a son cannot help his father. Indeed, the promise of God is truth, so let not deceive you the worldly life and let not the deceiver (Satan) deceive you about God.

35:6
The devil is your enemy, so treat him as an enemy. He only invites his party to be the dwellers of Hell.

36:60
Did I not covenant with you, O Children of Adam, that you shall not worship the devil? That he is your most ardent enemy?

41:36
*When the devil whispers an idea to you, you shall seek refuge in **GOD**. He is the All-Hearing and Seeing*

47:25
Surely, those who slide back, after the guidance has been manifested to them, the devil has enticed them and led them on.

58:10
Holding secret counsels for (evil purposes) is a work of Satan to cause grief to the believers, but he can do no harm to them except by the will of God. Let the believers trust in God

Repent

❖

Asking for forgiveness from God and starting over with a clean slate is a prominent part of many religions.

By asking God for forgiveness, we are acknowledging our guilt in front of the Highest Judge in the universe. We are showing our remorse and asking to be forgiven. We are asking God to give us another chance so we can replace what we did wrong.

In Islam, we believe by doing good we can wipe out some of our previous sins and bad deeds.

25:70
But only those who repent and believe and act righteously will have their sins replaced by good deeds; God is All-forgiving and All-merciful

29:7
Those who believe and lead a righteous life, we will certainly remit their sins, and will certainly reward them generously for their righteous works.

39:35
That God will remove for them their worst bad deed and reward them their due for the best of what they used to do.

9:102
Some of them have already confessed their sins and have mixed virtuous deeds with sinful ones. Perhaps God will forgive them. God is All-forgiving and All-merciful

In our daily prayer, every time after the first prostration, one of the common phrases we say is, "O' Lord, forgive my sins," as we ask for forgiveness from the Most High God.

We also learn that God delays our punishment for a sin for a specified time, giving us a chance to make up for it. (71:4) As when the judgement day comes He is a good account keeper. (21:47)

71:4
God will forgive you of your sins and delay you for a specified term. Indeed, the time [set by] God, when it comes, will not be delayed, if you only knew.' "

21:47
And We place the scales of justice for the Day of Resurrection, so no soul will be treated unjustly at all. And if there is [even] the weight of a mustard seed, We will bring it forth. And sufficient are We as accountant.

All broken up have come to Your Gate cause the healer
Prescribed a potion of Your Love with the address of Your Gate

Hafez, Persian poet 14th century
Translation and Rhyme
Faramarz F, Davati

The following are some of the verses emphasizing repentance:

110:03
Then Glorify and praise your Lord and ask for forgiveness. Indeed He is ever accepting of repentance.

2:160
Except for those who repent and correct themselves and make evident [what they concealed]. Those - I will accept their repentance, and I am the Accepting of repentance, the Merciful.

REPENT

2:286
God never burdens a soul beyond its means: to its credit is what it earns, and against it is what it commits. "Our Lord, do not condemn us if we forget or make mistakes. Our Lord, and protect us from blaspheming against You, like those before us have done. Our Lord, protect us from sinning until it becomes too late for us to repent. Pardon us and forgive us. You are our Lord and Master. Grant us victory over the disbelieving people.

3:89
Except for those who repent after that and correct themselves. For indeed, God is Forgiving and Merciful.

3:90
Those who disbelieve after believing, then plunge deeper into disbelief, their repentance will not be accepted from them; they are the ones astray

4:16
The couple who commits adultery shall be punished.* If they repent and reform, you shall leave them alone. God is Redeemer, Most Merciful.

4:17
God will only accept the repentance of those who commit evil in ignorance, if they repent immediately. God is All-knowing and All-wise

4:18
Not acceptable is the repentance of those who commit sins until death comes to them, then say, "Now I repent." Nor is it acceptable from those who die as disbelievers. For these, we have prepared a painful retribution.

4:48
God does not forgive the sin of considering others equal to Him, but He may choose to forgive other sins. Whoever believes in other Gods besides Him has indulged in a great sin.

4:146
Except for those who repent, correct themselves, hold fast to God, and are sincere in their religion for God, for those will be with the believers. And God is going to give the believers a great reward

5:34
*Exempted are those who repent before you overcome them. You should know that **GOD** is Forgiver, Most Merciful.*

5:39
If one repents after committing this crime, and reforms, God redeems him. God is Forgiver, Most Merciful.

5:74
Would they not repent to God, and ask His forgiveness? God is Forgiver, Most Merciful.

6:54
When the faithful come to you, say to them, "Peace be upon you. Your Lord has decreed for Himself to be All-merciful. Anyone of you who commits a sin out of ignorance, then repents, and reforms himself will find that God is All-forgiving and All-merciful.

7:153
To those who commit bad deeds, but, then, repent and believe (in God), Your Lord will certainly be All-forgiving and All-merciful.

9:3
This Announcement from God and His Messenger is to be made to the people on the day of the great Pilgrimage; God and His Mes-

REPENT

senger have declared no amnesty for the pagans. If you (pagans) repent, it would be better for you, but if you turn away (from God), know that you cannot make God helpless. (Muhammad) tell the unbelievers that a painful punishment has been prepared for them

11:3
Seek forgiveness from your Lord and turn to Him in repentance for your sins. He will provide you good sustenance for an appointed time and will reward everyone according to his merits. I am afraid that you will suffer torment on the great Day (of Judgment) if you turn away (from God).

11:52
O my people, seek forgiveness from your Lord, then repent to Him. He will then shower you with provisions from the sky, and augment your strength. Do not turn back into wrongdoers

11:61
To Thamud We sent their brother Salih who told them, "My people, worship God; He is your only Lord. It is He who has created you from the earth and has settled you therein. Seek forgiveness from Him and turn to Him in repentance. My Lord is certainly close to everyone and He hears all prayers.

11:90
Seek forgiveness from your Lord and turn to Him in repentance. My Lord is certainly All-merciful and Loving

11:112
(Muhammad), be steadfast (in your faith) just as you have been commanded. Those who have turned to God in repentance with you, should also be steadfast in their faith. Do not indulge in rebellion. God is certainly aware of what you do.

16:119
Then, indeed your Lord, to those who have done wrong out of ignorance and then repent after that and correct themselves- indeed, your Lord, thereafter, is Forgiving and Merciful.

17:25
Your Lord knows what is in your souls. If you would be righteous, know that He is All-forgiving to those who turn to Him in repentance

19:60
Only those who repent, believe, and lead a righteous life will enter Paradise, without the least injustice.

20:82
I am surely Forgiving for those who repent, believe, lead a righteous life, and steadfastly remain guided.

24:5
except that of those who afterwards repent and reform themselves; God is All-forgiving and All-merciful

25:70
But only those who repent and believe and act righteously will have their sins replaced by virtue; God is All-forgiving and All-merciful

25:71
Those who repent and lead a righteous life, God redeems them; a complete redemption.

28:67
But as for one who had repented, believed, and done righteousness, it is promised by God that he will be among the successful.

REPENT

39:35
That God will remove for them their worst bad deed and reward them their due for the best if what they used to do.

40:3
The forgiver of sin, acceptor of repentance, severe in punishment, owner of abundance. There is no God except Him; to Him is the ultimate destination.

40:7
Those who serve the throne and all those around it glorify and praise their Lord, and believe in Him. And they ask forgiveness for those who believe: "Our Lord, Your mercy and Your knowledge encompass all things. Forgive those who repent and follow Your path, and spare them the retribution of Hell.

42:25
It is He who accepts the repentance of His servants, forgives their evil deeds and knows all about what you do

49:11
O you who have believed, let not a people ridicule [another] people; perhaps they may be better than them; nor let women ridicule [other] women; perhaps they may be better than them. And do not insult one another and do not call each other by [offensive] nicknames. Wretched is the name of disobedience after [one's] faith. And whoever does not repent - then it is those who are the wrongdoers

66:8
Believers, turn to God in repentance with the intention of never repeating the same sin. Perhaps your Lord will expiate your evil deeds and admit you to Paradise wherein streams flow. On the

Day of Judgment, God will not disgrace the Prophet and those who have believed in him. Their lights will shine in front of them and to their right. They will say, "Our Lord, perfect our light for us and forgive our sins. You have power over all things".

101:6-11
God says in the Quran that our deeds will be measured or weighed, and whosoever has more good deeds will enter the Gardens of Paradise and whose evil deeds weigh more than the good ones will be entered into the Hell fire.

110:03
Then Glorify and praise your Lord and ask for forgiveness. Indeed He is ever accepting of repentance.

Path of God

The general meaning of *walking in the path of God* is that someone is righteous, follows the fundamentals and teachings of a certain religion, is observant and a believer in that religion and its teachings, and follows its path for salvation.

To ask God to put the *right* path in front of you means to ask God to put you on the path of life He has designed specifically for you, in order to receive his blessings. This path of life will lead you to the right job, business, and people He has in mind for you to meet or come across.

We Muslims ask God at least fourteen times a day during our daily prayers, "Guide us to the straight path" (1:6), which is interpreted as being pious, righteous, doing good and the right thing, saying prayers, fasting for Ramadan, helping others, paying religious taxes, giving charity, helping the needy, and any other good deeds we can think of.

I personally believe that it can also mean asking God to put the right path, that He had in mind, in front of us. The verse that follows it (1:7) explains it a little more:
So we have:

1:6-7
6- Guide us to the straight path,
7- The path of those who you gave your blessings, not those who earned your anger and not those who go astray.

Verse 1:7 is the combination of both. The first part, "the path of those who you gave your blessings," is the path of life that He will put in front of us, to earn a living and bring in His blessings. Then the second part, "not those who earned your anger," is the righteous path, the believer's path of praying and praising him, and not doing anything bad to anger Him. "And not those who go astray" would mean not to putting us on the path of the disbeliever and leaving us on our own, like those who wander around aimlessly in life without any plan, direction, or destination.

So, when I say my prayer, I personally say it with the intention of God to put me on the right path that He has designed for me!

2:255
God exists. There is no God but He, the Everlasting and the Guardian of life. Drowsiness or sleep do not seize him. To Him belongs all that is in the heavens and the earth. No one can intercede with Him for others except by His permission. He knows about people's present and past. No one can grasp anything from His knowledge besides what He has permitted them to grasp. The heavens and the earth are under His dominion. He does not experience fatigue in preserving them both. He is the Highest and the Greatest.

He knows my whole life history, good and bad. He knows my background, and my future, better than I or anybody else. He knows my strengths and my weaknesses. He knows what I can be good at, and what I am not suited for. So I ask Him to put the right path in front of me to fulfill my destiny that He has in mind for me.

I believe He has a plan for each and every one of us. If you let Him guide you, He will put you on the right path, the one especially designed for you and what He had in mind when He created you.

We are all His subjects, although we are free and have freedom of choice. Some of us are lucky and tap into what He had in mind for us to do; others may not be so lucky and follow a routine way of life.

If you believe in Him strongly and create that connection we talked about earlier, He will make things fall into your lap, with the right path, right job, right business, and right people in front of you.

I personally believe that is the way verses 1:6-7 are interpreted. What better way to serve God than to ask Him to put us on the path He had in mind for us when He created us?

When I am in any situation where I need His help and support, I say my prayers out loud. I ask Him to put the right path or right situation in front of me, as He can see a lot further down the road than I can. He has always helped me in the past and has never disappointed me. That's where our trust in Him comes in; remembering how He has always come to our aid in the past and knowing He will do it again. So I am asking Him one more time, to reach out and help me, as His hand is above all hands and He is in full control of all affairs as I trust-in Him and move forward.

- God's hand is above all hands.
- Everything is possible through God.
- God strongly and very capably is in control over everything.

For those who believe in Him, it is amazing when you see your prayer answered. For me, it is always an "awe" moment, a confirmation. It's a moment when you literally sit back, enjoy, and soak in the greatness of that moment.

When you receive or come across the exact thing you had in mind or prayed for, large or small, that is God answering your call and putting the right situation, right path, or right person in front of you.

Here are a few verses from the Quran regarding the path of God:

29:69
We shall certainly guide those who strive for Our cause to Our path. God is certainly with the righteous ones.

6:39
And those who rejected our verses are deaf and dumb and are in darkness. Whoever God wants he wills him go astray and whoever He wills, He places him on the straight path.

6:87
And from their father and descendants and their brothers, we chose them and we guided them to the straight path.

6:153
And more over this is my path which is the straight path, so follow it. And do not follow other path, as it will separate you from his path. That he has instructed you, so that you may become righteous.

6:161
Say, "indeed as for me, my Lord has guided me to a straight path- a right religion- the religion of Abraham, a true monotheist. And he was not of those who associated partners with God.

10:25
And God calls (invites) to the home of peace and guide whom He wills, in the right path.

11:56
Indeed, I put my trust upon God, my Lord and your Lord. There is no creature but he has a hold on its forelock (life). Indeed my Lord is on a straight path.

PATH OF GOD

16:121
He was grateful for his blessings. And God chose him and guided him to a straight path.

22:12
They worship things instead of God which can neither harm them nor benefit them. This is indeed to stray far away from the right path.

42:52
Thus, We have revealed to you an inspiration of Our command, (Muhammad). Before, you did not even know what a Book or Faith was, but We have made the Quran as a light by which We guide whichever of Our servants We want. You certainly guide (people) to the right path.

42:53
The path of God, to whom belongs whatever is in the heavens and whatever is on the earth. Unquestionably, all affairs reach to God.

4:175
Those who believe in GOD, and hold fast to Him, He will admit them into mercy from Him, and grace, and will guide them to Him in a straight path.

48:20
GOD has promised you many spoils that you will gain. He thus advanced some benefits for you in this life, and He has withheld the people's hands of aggression against you, and has rendered this a sign for the believers. He thus guides you in a straight path.

Forgiveness

God is a forgiving God. He does encourage us in the Quran to ask for forgiveness. It is then up to Him if He grants it or not. But we have to ask for it, the same way we ask for blessings and His help.

He has created us in His own image, so He also expects and encourages us to be forgiving toward others.

The Quran advises it is better to forgive someone who has done us wrong, than get revenge or get even, despite the fact that it is our right and we are entitled to it.

In forgiving someone, we cease to carry that hurt inside. It is the hurt and hate inside that causes stress and poisons our health. Some may say, "Where do you draw the line in confronting evil and forgiving?" That's a tough one, and I believe it's personal.

God tells us always to stand up to evil of any kind. Otherwise, not only it will try to overtake us, but it will hurt others as well. It is my personal opinion that you forgive people in personal relationships, minor disputes, and accidents of any type when it was unintentional. But someone who purposely tries to hurt you in any way or walk all over you, you have to stand up and defend and protect yourself. The Quran agrees that an eye for any eye and tooth for a tooth is justice. But the Quran also encourages forgiveness.

[5:45]
And we commanded for them in it that (Torah): the life for the life, the eye for the eye, the nose for the nose, the ear for the ear, the

tooth for the tooth, and an equivalent injury for any injury. If one forfeits what is due to him as a charity, it will compensate for his sins. Those who do not rule in accordance with GOD's revelations are the unjust.

Choosing Your Friends

Here in the US we Muslims have our share of friends and enemies. Our friends are people we have been associating with professionally and casually for years. We have known them and they have known us based on their friendship with us, not by what is preached in the media. They have already seen and heard all the negative images and news the US media constantly broadcasts about us. They know us and know who owns the media, and can make a decision about their friendship with us.

Having good friends is very important for us and the young Muslim children, as your friends will rub off on you whether you like it or not. The Quran reminds us of that when it tells of when Noah's son started hanging out with the non-believers and became like them.

11:42
When the Ark sailed on with them amid the mountainous waves, Noah called out to his son who kept away from them, "My son, get on board with us. Do not stay with the unbelievers."

11:43
His son replied, "I shall climb up a mountain and this will save me from the flood." Noah said, "No one can escape on this day from God's command except those on whom He has mercy." The waves separated Noah from his son who was then drowned with the rest (of the unbelievers)

There is an old Persian poem for this event:

Noah's son hung out with the wrong crowd in the neighborhood
Lost his life and family line of prophethood

Our best friends are other people of faith of all religions, people we meet at school, work, sports or civic activities.

49:10
The believers are members of one family; you shall keep the peace within your family and reverence GOD, that you may attain mercy.

The following are some of the verses regarding choosing your friends:

20:130
(Muhammad), have patience with what they say, glorify your Lord, and always praise Him before sunrise, sunset, in some hours of the night and at both the beginning and end of the day, so that you may become content (get what you want).

5:57
Oh you who believe do not take those who ridicule and make fun of your religion as friend, regardless if they are from the people of the Book or disbelievers. And fear God if you are a believer.

60:5-9
They prayed, "Lord, we have trust in You, turned to You in repentance, and to You we shall all return. Lord, save us from the evil intentions of the disbelievers. Our Lord, forgives us. You are Majestic and All-wise"

They are the best examples for those who have hope in God and the Day of Judgment. Whoever turn away should know that God is Self-sufficient and Praiseworthy

CHOOSING YOUR FRIENDS

God will perhaps bring about love between you and those of the disbelievers with whom you were enemies. God is All-powerful, All-merciful, and All-forgiving

God does not forbid you to deal kindly and justly with those who have not fought against you about the religion or expelled you from your homes. God does not love the unjust people.

He only forbids you to be friends with those who have fought against you about the religion, expelled you from your homes or supported others in expelling you. Whoever loves these people are unjust.

60:13
Believers, do not establish friendship with the people who have become subject to the wrath of God. They do not have any hope in the afterlife, they are just as hopeless as the disbelievers who are already in the graves.

Hope

Hope goes hand in hand with expectations for God. Your hope and expectations for God are strengthened by your faith in God. When we ask something from God, we should have the expectancy of receiving it from him.

26:82
It is He whom I expect to forgive my sins on the Day of Judgment.
Here I have left six translations for comparison on this subject.
http://corpus.quran.com/translation.jsp?chapter=26&verse=82

26:82
Sahih International: And who I aspire that He will forgive me my sin on the Day of Recompense."

Pickthall: And Who, I ardently hope, will forgive me my sin on the Day of Judgment.

Yusuf Ali: "And who, I hope, will forgive me my faults on the day of Judgment.

Shakir: And Who, I hope, will forgive me my mistakes on the day of judgment.

Muhammad Sarwar: It is He whom I expect to forgive my sins on the Day of Judgment.

Mohsin Khan: "And Who, I hope will forgive me my faults on the Day of Recompense, (the Day of Resurrection),"

So whatever we hope for from God, we should have the expectancy of receiving it, to make it happen.

No one disappointed, ever turned from You
Anyone who had a hope, and came to see You.

Araghi, Persian poet 13th century
Translation and Rhyme
Faramarz F, Davati

And no matter how bad we are hurt, we can always seek refuge in Him and ask for His help to recover, as His hand is above all hands and He is in control of everything. <u>As mentioned earlier:</u>

All broken up have come to Your Gate, cause the healer
Prescribed a potion of Your Love, with the address of Your Gate

Hafez, Persian poet 14th century
Translation and Rhyme
Faramarz F, Davati

Here are some verses about *hope*:

7:170
And those who cling (refuge) to the Book and establish the prayer,
We indeed will not let the reward of the reformers go to waste. (We will not disappoint them)

18:46
Wealth and children are [but] adornment of the worldly life. But the enduring good deeds are better to your Lord for reward and better for [one's] hope.

26:51
Indeed, we hope that our Lord will forgive us our sins because we were the first of the believers."

HOPE

5:84
Why should we not believe in God and the Truth that has come to us and hope that the Lord will admit us into the company of the righteous people?"

32:16
Their sides give-up rest in beds in order to pray before their Lord in fear and hope. They spend for the cause of God out of what we have given them.

Miracles

You believe in Me (God), and I will show you a miracle in your life.

Indeed we make clear miracles for those who firmly believe (2:118).

Prophets and their miracles are perhaps one of the most important factors of each religion, as they prove to their believers the connection between the prophet and the divine.

Growing up in Tehran, Iran, I remember we lived on a street with many people of other religious minorities besides the dominant Shia Islam that is the official religion of the country. We had a few Christians, a few Jewish people, some Zoroastrians, and one or two Baha'is.

As children, in our mind, we thought the Christian kids had it best, as they would get New Year's presents twice a year, at the Persian New Year and Christian New Year, and the rest of us would get New Year's presents only once a year!

Since I was six or seven years old, every now and then me and my playmates would talk about religion and our differences. With wrestling being big in Iran, I remember we were so young that we would argue if Muhammad, Jesus, or Moses would wrestle who would win!?

I grew up with a big question, why Muhammad did not do any miracles. I know the Quran is a miracle, but what I mean is big, instant, earth-shattering miracles like Moses and Jesus did.

My parents explained to me many times how the Quran was Muhammad's miracle. How he was not an educated man, but yet all these verses were revealed to him by the angel Gabriel. But I was a kid, and I wanted to see a Superman hero with Superman actions and miracles. This is especially around the time when the famous movie, The Ten Commandments, starring Charlton Hesston as Moses came to the widescreen cinema. After seeing that, I really wanted to see Muhammad open the Red Sea or do something similar to confirm my beliefs. I know some Muslims talk about this hadith or that hadith, or splitting the moon and all that, but I am talking about a real earth-shattering verifiable miracle. Not just some hadith that someone made up in order to match the Christians or Jews, claiming it was verified by Al Bukhari[6]. That would be as bad as the "Nicaea Council[7]". I am talking about something verifiable that everyone saw, talked about, and wrote about. Even in the Quran there are verses that say people complained, asking why Muhammad did not do any miracles like his predecessors. Then there are other verses mentioning that God sends miracles when he wants, and that you wait and Muhammad waits along with you for these miracles to occur. 6:109, 29:50, 2:118

6:109

They swore by GOD, solemnly, that if a miracle came to them, they would surely believe. Say, "Miracles come only from GOD." For all

---

[6] *Imam al-Bukhari or Imam Bukhari was a Persian Islamic scholar who was born in Bukhara (the capital of the Bukhara Region [viloyat] of Uzbekistan). He authored the hadith collection known as Sahih al-Bukhari, regarded by Sunni Muslims as one of the most authentic (sahih) hadith collections. He also wrote other books such as Al-Adab al-Mufrad. Wikipedia*

[7] *The First Council of Nicaea was the first ecumenical council of the Church. Most significantly, it resulted in the first uniform Christian doctrine, called the Nicene Creed. With the creation of the creed, a precedent was established for subsequent local and regional councils of Bishops (Synods) to create statements of belief and canons of doctrinal orthodoxy—the intent being to define unity of beliefs for the whole of Christendom. Wikipedia*

you know, if a miracle did come to them, they would continue to disbelieve

29:50
They say, "Why a miracle is not sent to him from his Lord." Say, "Miracles are in the hands of God. I am simply a warner."

Although, I was a believer in Islam, God, and the Quran, this question of why Muhammad did not perform earth-shattering miracles like Moses and Jesus stayed with me all through my adulthood.

Years back, when I decided to write this book, I had a moment of clarity regarding the "miracle" issue I had.

They say if you ask yourself smart questions, you will get back smart answers!

I asked myself, "Who are prophets of God who either had extraordinary powers or came with visible earth-shattering miracles?" The major ones that are in the Quran and come to my mind are:

David

Solomon

Moses

Jesus

I know there are others, but for now let's talk about these major ones. David had a gift of speaking with and understanding the animals, birds, and insects. Solomon had extraordinary and supernatural powers, not just on elements such as wind, but also on demons.

And then we come to Moses. You name it, God sent miracles for it.

He was at the presence of God at the burning bush on top of the mountain. He is the only one who has ever literally spoken to God. We Muslims call him "Mosa Kaleem–ul-Allah" (the one who talked to God).

1- He is the one that went with his brother, Aaron, to the pharaoh and threw his staff. His staff turned into a snake. Pharaoh's magicians also threw their magic that turned into snakes. Moses's snake overtook Pharaoh's magicians' snakes.

2- Then the plague came to Egypt.

3- The Nile turned red.

4- Frogs and insects overtook Egypt.

5- The Red Sea opened and gave passage to the Jews, and then closed, killing all the Egyptians who were pursuing them.

6- Moses went to the mountain and received the Ten Commandments tablets from God Himself.

7- God sent food in the desert for the Jews he brought out of Egypt.

8- God told Moses to hit the rock in the desert to open up fountains of water for different tribes of Israel.

Is there anything else, besides flying, that Moses could have done in front of the children of Israel to convince his people that he was for real and was a prophet of God? I don't think so.

Then we come to Jesus, who we Muslims know as a prophet of God. According to our Quran,
Mary was a virgin when she gave birth to Jesus.

1- God blew from his own spirit into Jesus.

2- God equipped Jesus with the Holy Spirit.

3- Jesus could speak in the cradle.

4- He would make clay birds in childhood and blow in them, and they would fly away like a bird.

5- He raised the dead.

6- He cured the blind and leprous.

7- And according to our Quran, Jesus is the only prophet that comes back on the final day (43:61).

Among all these prophets of God, I cannot find a prophet with more visible, spectacular, verifiable, earth-shattering miracles than Moses. The Quran confirms that God gave Moses nine miracles. My listings may be slightly different in order from the way you will find them in the Quran.

17:101
And We had certainly given Moses nine evident signs, so ask the Children of Israel [about] when he came to them and Pharaoh said to him, "Indeed I think, O Moses, that you are affected by magic."

So if having the highest number of spectacular miracles was as important as I thought or some people argue, then why the majority of the people on earth aren't Jewish? Why have'nt most of the world grown to Judaism, despite all the verifiable miracles of

Moses? Instead, in most countries around the world except Israel, Jews are among the minorities.

2:211
Ask the Children of Israel how many profound miracles have we shown them! For those who disregard the blessings bestowed upon them by God, God is most strict in retribution.

So why is it that God does not give an earth-shattering miracle to his last prophet on earth, Muhammad? Why instead of miracles did God send a series of structured instructions to be performed over and over again along with some very strict rules for the "lost" descendants of Ishmael in Arabia. He sent these instructions as a "cure" through one of their own people, who knew their language and customs very well.

41:44
*And if We had made it a non-Arabic Qur'an, they would have said, "Why are its verses not explained in detail [in our language]? Is it a foreign [recitation] and an Arab [messenger]?" Say, "It is, for those who believe, a guidance and **cure**." And those who do not believe - in their ears is deafness, and it is upon them blindness. Those are being called from a distant place.*

God sent the Quran as an instructional book, simply because these people, by their own admission, were going through what they call an "ignorant period" and needed some clear, simple instructions to follow every moment, every day, over and over repetitiously, till they became habit and directed them to the right path. They were stuck in a pit and could not get out on their own and needed help.

Imagine if you were to come across a tribe or village in the middle of the jungles of Africa, or a rainforest with indigenous people who had not seen civilization. You would not do a magic show in front of them or they would start worshipping you as God. This is what followers of Jesus did, as his miracles were coming from him, versus Moses, whose miracles were external. For these "lost" people, you would give them a series of instructions in order to live better.

27:13
When our miracles were presented to them, clear and profound, they said, "This is obviously magic."

54:2
Then they saw a miracle; but they turned away and said, "Old magic."

When the American Peace Corps goes around the world to different villages in third-world countries to help them out, they give instructions of how to live better to local villagers. They do not do a magic show!

It's the fundamentals of Islam—the instructions, believing in One God, the habits of praying every day at least five times, praising God throughout the day (they were pagans before Muhammad) as you count your blessings, giving charity, and fasting once a year–that one could adopt regardless of if he or she is Muslim or not. These fundamentals, along with a strong and unshakable belief in God, will lead you to a better life.

Simply put, the Quran teaches you how by believing firmly in God and practicing what the Quran teaches, you can create your own miracles (2:118)!

2:118
And those who do not know say, why God does not speak to us or send us a miracle? And there were others who said the same before them. Their hearts are alike. Indeed we make clear miracles for those who firmly believe.

If God had sent Muhammad miracles, then the "lost" people would have started worshiping Muhammad like a God, like the followers of Jesus did.

Islam was needed at that time in that part of the world. Bedouin people were idol worshipers. The way they would talk to their idols was they had a bag that contained wooden chips with "yes" and "no" written on them. They would talk to their idols and ask a question. Then they would reach inside the bag and pull out one of the chips, and that was their answer from their Idol.

Islam changed all that. Islam brought in a much-needed structured monotheist religion with the Quran as a recorded text for generations to follow. Islam taught them who the One and Only God is and who he is not. Islam taught the Bedouins how to communicate with God through prayers and taught them the habits of giving charity, doing good deeds, being righteous, and helping or giving refuge to the needy, orphans, destitute travelers, and those who have fallen. Islam encouraged learning how to read and write, a privilege that was earlier blocked by the Zoroastrians and was only given to certain classes of the society. Islam abolished the class system.

Islam is a miracle of its own in the way it can changes one's life. Its instructions on developing the habits of praying throughout the day, praising God, giving charity, doing good deeds, counting your blessings, and being righteous, along with many other instructions one can find in its pages, can be used to improve one's life, regardless of if he or she is a Muslim or not.

Here are a few verses about miracles:

2:60
When Moses prayed for rain, We told him to strike the rock with his staff. Thereupon twelve fountains gushed out of the rock and each tribe knew their drinking place. The Lord told them, "Eat and drink

MIRACLES

from God's bounties and do not abuse the earth with corruption."

2:87
And We did certainly give Moses the Torah and followed up after him with messengers. And We gave Jesus, the son of Mary, clear proofs and supported him with the Holy Spirit. But is it [not] that every time a messenger came to you, [O Children of Israel], with what your souls did not desire, you were arrogant? And a party [of messengers] you denied and another party you killed

2:92
And Moses had certainly brought you clear proofs. Then you took the calf [in worship] after that, while you were wrongdoers.

2:118
And those who do not know say, why God does not speak to us or send us a miracle? And there were others who said the same before them. Their hearts are alike. Indeed we make clear miracles for those who firmly believe.

2:145
And if you brought to those who were given the Scripture every miracle, they would not follow your qiblah (direction of prayer). Nor will you be a follower of their qiblah. Nor would they be followers of one another's qiblah. So if you were to follow their desires after what has come to you of knowledge, indeed, you would then be among the wrongdoers.

2:211
Ask the Children of Israel how many profound miracles have we shown them! For those who disregard the blessings bestowed upon them by God, God is most strict in retribution.

2:253
*These messengers; we blessed some of them more than others. For example, **GOD** spoke to one, and we raised some of them to higher ranks. And we gave Jesus, son of Mary, profound miracles and supported him with the Holy Spirit. Had **GOD** willed, their followers would not have fought with each other, after the clear proofs had come to them. Instead, they disputed among themselves; some of them believed, and some disbelieved. Had **GOD** willed, they would not have fought. Everything is in accordance with **GOD**'s will.*

4:153 The people of the scripture challenge you to bring down to them a book from the sky! They have asked Moses for more than that, saying, "Show us God, physically." Consequently, the lightning struck them, as a consequence of their audacity. Additionally, they worshiped the calf, after all the miracles they had seen. Yet, we pardoned all this. We supported Moses with profound miracles.

5:110
God will say, "O Jesus, son of Mary, remember My blessings upon you and your mother. I supported you with the Holy Spirit, to enable you to speak to the people from the crib, as well as an adult. I taught you the scripture, wisdom, the Torah, and the Gospel. Recall that you created from clay the shape of a bird by My leave, then blew into it, and it became a live bird by My leave. You healed the blind and the leprous by My leave, and revived the dead by My leave. Recall that I protected you from the Children of Israel who wanted to hurt you, despite the profound miracles you had shown them. The disbelievers among them said, 'This is obviously magic.'

6:35
If their rejection gets to be too much for you, you should know that even if you dug a tunnel through the earth, or climbed a ladder into the sky, and produced a miracle for them (they still would not be-

MIRACLES

lieve). Had GOD willed, He could have guided them, unanimously. Therefore, do not behave like the ignorant ones.

6:109
They swore by GOD, solemnly, that if a miracle came to them, they would surely believe. Say, "Miracles come only from GOD." For all you know, if a miracle did come to them, they would continue to disbelieve.

[7:203]
If you do not produce a miracle that they demand, they say, "Why not ask for it?" Say, "I simply follow what is revealed to me from my Lord." These are enlightenments from your Lord, and guidance, and mercy for people who believe.

10:20
They say, "How come no miracle came down to him from his Lord?" Say, "The future belongs to God; so wait, and I am waiting along with you."

13:7
Those who disbelieved say, "If only a miracle could come down to him from his Lord (we will then believe)." You are simply a warner— every community receives a guiding teacher.

13:27
Those who disbelieve would say, "If only a miracle could come down to him from his Lord (we would believe)." Say, "God sends astray whomever He wills, and guides to Him only those who obey."

14:5
Thus, we sent Moses with our miracles, saying, "Lead your people out of darkness into the light, and remind them of the days of God." These are lessons for every steadfast, appreciative person.

17:101
We supported Moses with nine profound miracles—ask the Children of Israel. When he went to them, Pharaoh said to him, "I think that you, Moses, are bewitched."

20:133
They said, "If he could only show us a miracle from his Lord!" Did they not receive sufficient miracles with the previous messages?

21:5
They even said, "Hallucinations," "He made it up," and, "He is a poet. Let him show us a miracle like those of the previous messengers."

26:154
"You are no more than a human like us. Produce a miracle, if you are truthful."

27:12
"Put your hand in your pocket; it will come out white, without a blemish. These are among nine miracles to Pharaoh and his people, for they are wicked people."

27:13
When our miracles were presented to them, clear and profound, they said, "This is obviously magic."

28:35
He said, "We will strengthen you with your brother, and we will provide you both with manifest authority. Thus, they will not be able to touch either one of you. With our miracles, the two of you, together with those who follow you, will be the victors."

MIRACLES

29:50
They said, "If only miracles could come down to him from his Lord!" Say, "All miracles come only from God; I am no more than a manifest warner."

29:51
Is it not enough of a miracle that we sent down to you this book, being recited to them? This is indeed a mercy and a reminder for people who believe.

40:78
*We have sent messengers before you—some of them we mentioned to you, and some we did not mention to you. No messenger can produce any miracle without **GOD**'s authorization.* Once **GOD**'s judgment is issued, the truth dominates, and the falsifiers are exposed and humiliated.*

Karma in Islam

The concept of karma[8] has been believed and described in different ways in different religions and cultures. I always associated karma with Eastern religions that believe in the rebirth of the spirit in future lives. This is something we Muslims do not believe.

In Islam it has been simply explained and believed that whatever you do, you do it to yourself, whatever good or bad you do.

45:15
Whoever does a good deed - it is for himself; and whoever does evil - it is against the self. Then to your Lord you will be returned

Here is a poem by Nasir Khusraw on karma:

Just because you have a blade, it's not for killing
God doesn't forget the ones, who do the killing

Steel is not forged, just for making blades
And grapes aren't crushed, just for making wine

---

8 *Karma means action, work or deed; it also refers to the spiritual principle of cause and effect where intent and actions of an individual (cause) influence the future of that individual (effect). Good intent and good deed contribute to good karma and future happiness, while bad intent and bad deed contribute to bad karma and future suffering. Karma is closely associated with the idea of rebirth in many schools of Asian religions. In these schools, karma in the present affects one's future in the current life, as well as the nature and quality of future lives.*
With origins in ancient India, karma is a key concept in Hinduism, Buddhism, Jainism, Sikhism, and Taoism. Wikipedia

ALCHEMY OF THE QURAN

Jesus saw a dead man who was lying on the ground
Jesus was dismayed and asked in puzzle

Who have you ever slain? Get slayed this bizarre?
And who will slay the one, who slew you now?

Don't you lay finger, in hurting a soul
So you don't hurt too, when God throws a punch

> Nasir Khosrow, Persian poet, 11 century
> Translation and Rhyme
> Faramarz Davati

Here are a few verses regarding karma:

17:7
(We told you), "If you do good, it will be for your own benefit, but if you do bad, it will be against your souls. When the prophecy of your second wrong doing will come to pass, sadness will cover your faces. They (your enemies) will enter the mosque as they did the first time to bring about utter destruction.

41:46
Whoever acts righteously does so for his own good and whoever commits evil does so against his soul. Your Lord is not unjust to His servants

42:30
Whatever hardship befalls you is the result of your own deeds. God pardons many of your sins

42:30
The recompense for evil will be equivalent to the deed. He who pardons (the evil done to him) and reforms himself, will receive his reward from God. God certainly does not love the unjust.

52:21

The offspring of the believers will also follow them to Paradise. So shall We join their offspring to them because of their faith. We shall reduce nothing from their deeds. Everyone will be responsible for his own actions

3:195

Their Lord answered their prayers saying, "I do not neglect anyone's labor whether the laborer be male or female. You are all related to one another. Those who migrated from Mecca, those who were expelled from their homes, those who were tortured for My cause, and those who fought and were killed for My cause will find their sins expiated by Me and I will admit them into the gardens wherein streams flow. It will be their reward from God Who grants the best rewards."

4:123

Believers and People of the Book, wishes alone can never provide you with salvation. Whoever commits evil will be punished accordingly and no one besides God will be his guardian or helper.

Revenge

When someone mistreats us or crosses our boundaries, we naturally want to defend ourselves and retaliate against that person.

Sometimes you can take legal action, and sometimes you may not be able to fight legally. These could be things like a bad neighbor, a bad coworker who gossip behind you at work, or having a bad boss. These things you are to leave to God. You do not need to waste your time or emotion or lose your joy. Instead let God fight your battle for you. Ask God to vindicate you and serve justice to them. Then continue with your life and do not lose your joy over what they have done to you, as the kind of redemption God takes for you is ten times worse than what you could do to them. What was that old saying? "God's hammer of redemption may not make a sound, but when it hits, there is no cure for it."

The Quran instruct us to fight the enemy when we are attacked, but not to be the aggressor.

33:48
And do not obey the disbelievers and the hypocrites but do not harm them (try to get even with them in revenge), and rely upon God. And sufficient is God as Disposer of affairs.

Leave those difficult people to God, and ask God for your redemption. The key is in not trying to get revenge yourself, because in doing evil to someone else, you are hurting yourself as well. Just let God take care of it. As 33:48 says, "Rely upon God, and He is sufficient to take care of the affair."

When a snake bites you, the bite does not kill you. It's the venom that the snake injects inside you that kills you. Do not allow the serpents around you, no matter who they are, to create that venom inside you. Keep God in first place, ask God to vindicate you against your enemies and their families, the same way they have been unjust to you and your family. Move forward and only fear God.

I heard a good Christian pastor on TV who was talking about this very same subject. He said a very interesting phrase, which I am going to use and pass on to you: "**Drop it, leave it, and let it go**," meaning once you drop it, leave it, and do not go back days, months, or years later to try to settle the score. Do not carry that hurt or poison inside so that one day you get a chance to settle the score. Just let it go, continue on with what time you have left in this life, and enjoy it.

Whatever number of minutes, hours, weeks, months, and years you spend on getting even with or getting revenge on someone, the same amount of time you have lost in having fun and enjoying this life. As the Quran constantly remind us, this life is too short and is nothing but child's play (47:36, 57:20). In 57:20 it mentions, "The worldly life is the enjoyment of an Illusion."

The Quran tell us, when we are in the afterlife it feels as if we were in this life for no more than just a few hours.

When someone does the unjust to me, I add the Surat al-Kawthar (108) to my daily prayers and ask God to vindicate me, and I let it go. I ask God to vindicate me and cut off my enemy's blessings.

108 (kothar):
Indeed we have granted you the fountain of blessings
So pray to your Lord and give charity
Indeed your enemy is the one who will be cut off (from blessings).

REVENGE

This is when God tells you to leave it to Him. It is when at the end of your daily prayers you ask God to settle the score with your enemy. Just leave it in His hands, drop it, and let it go.

All you have to do is stay in faith, do your prayers, and let him settle the score for you. God's Hand is above all hands.

67:1
Blessed is He in Whose hand is the kingdom, and He has power over all things,

Here are some of the verses about dealing with enemies:

8:45
O you who have believed, when you encounter a company of enemy forces, be firm and remember God much that you may be successful.

33:48
And do not obey the disbelievers and the hypocrites but do not harm them (try to get even with them in revenge), and rely upon God. And sufficient is God as Disposer of affairs.

41:34
Virtue and evil are not equal. If you replace evil habits by virtuous ones, you will certainly find that your enemies will become your intimate friends.

42:30
The recompense for evil will be equivalent to the deed. He who pardons (the evil done to him) and reforms himself, will receive his reward from God. God certainly does not love the unjust.

Life, Death, and the Afterlife

No other holy book talks about how temporary this earthly life is and how we should invest by doing good for the afterlife. The afterlife is the destination, as we will be there forever. The Quran specifically describes the Judgment Day and how you will be judged. There will be no intermediary regardless of what religion you practice, and your results are based on what you have done in this earthly life, good and bad. As it says, God is a good account holder for your good deeds as well as the bad deeds. (21:47)

21:47
And We place the scales of justice for the Day of Resurrection, so no soul will be treated unjustly at all. And if there is [even] the weight of a mustard seed, We will bring it forth. And sufficient are We as accountant

It is mentioned over and over in the Quran that our earthly life is nothing but a game and passes very quickly. Therefore, do not be concerned with the ornaments of this life. It is the afterlife that is important. By doing good in this life, we make savings for the afterlife. This life is like a farm as we plant for the afterlife. The reward for those who do good is living well in Paradise, and for those who do bad the reward is simply hell.

47:36
The worldly life is only a play and amusement. And if you believe and fear God, He will grant your rewards and will not ask you to pay for them.

57:20
Know that the worldly life is only a game, a temporary attraction, a means of boastfulness among yourselves and a place for multiplying your wealth and children. It is like the rain which produces plants that are attractive to the unbelievers. These plants flourish, turn yellow, and then become crushed bits of straw. In the life hereafter there will be severe torment or forgiveness and mercy from God. The worldly life is the enjoyment of an illusion.

57:21
Compete with one another to achieve forgiveness from your Lord and to reach Paradise, which is as vast as the heavens and the earth, and is prepared for those who believe in God and His Messenger. This is the blessing of God and He grants it to whomever He wants. The blessings of God are great.

The concept of Paradise and how you get there is not the same in every Abrahamic faith. In Judaism there is no Paradise. Most liberal Christians believe they all go to heaven and their sins will all be forgiven, regardless of what they have done in this life, because Jesus died on the cross for them. More conservative Christians believe you also have to have your sins forgiven and not have mortal sins to go to heaven, even if you have been "saved." And some believe you have to do good works as well. The help that Muslim refugees are getting in Europe is a prime example of that. For us Muslims, there is no intermediary. As God mentions to Muhammad in the Quran, Abraham could not ask for forgiveness for his father. Noah could not ask for forgiveness and the saving of his son! For everything good or bad we do, we pay. If not in this life, definitely in the afterlife!

The Quran also constantly reminds us of how temporary this life is. And it passes very quickly. At the end we only feel that we were here on this earth for an hour.

LIFE, DEATH, AND THE AFTERLIFE

10:45
On the day when He summons all of them, they will feel as if they lasted in this world one hour of the day, during which they met. Losers indeed are those who disbelieved in meeting GOD; and chose to be misguided.

Asked a Guru a picture of life to draw
A bubble next to an ocean he drew!

> Ostad Shahriar, Persian poet 20th century
> Translation and Rhyme
> Faramarz F, Davati

The Quran teaches us that for this short time on earth, it is far better to fight the devil and his temptation than to join him. Do not listen to him when he whispers in your ear and entices you with the ornaments of this life. Do not sell your soul to the devil and take him as a friend, as he is a halfway friend and will leave you by yourself on Judgment Day.

Instead, do good and add up your good points for your afterlife. We Muslims believe everyone will get his report of his life's deeds, listing all the good deeds and the bad deeds.

39:35
That God will remove for them their worst bad deed and reward them their due for the best of what they used to do.

So build up your good deeds as God overwrites your bad deeds and gives you a chance to repair the damage (39:35). We Muslims believe it is our good deeds that will be our savior on Judgment Day, not Moses, Jesus, or Muhammad.

The Quran teaches us that this life is way too short. The more good deeds we do, the more savings we have put away for our afterlife.

Rumi, the great Persian poet and philosopher, compares our life with the life of a silkworm: After it has made its silk cocoon, the silkworm sheds off his dead silkworm body, and its life continues as it transforms into a butterfly. It flies out of its nest to its next life as a butterfly.

As humans we also shed our earthly bodies after our death, and our life continues through our soul as it ascends to the afterlife.

When it comes to how temporary this life is, Abu Saeed describes it this way:

Asked a Guru, "What's the secret of the life?"
Said to me it's either wind, or daydream, or fairy tale

Asked him, tell me the secrets of my life
Said to me it's either lightning, candlelight, or a monarch

Asked him, and those who are in love with it?
Said to me, must be drunk, or a blind or gone mad

Abu Saeed, Persian poet 11th century
Translation and Rhyme
Faramarz F, Davati

Life

This life is our testing ground for the afterlife. This life is our field of agriculture for our afterlife, as each and every one of us plant our seeds and nurture our crops in this life, and reap what we have sown in the afterlife. This is the time and place that God tests all of us through adversaries, loss of income, jobs, health, and other challenging matters to test our belief in Him.

This is where God sees if we are the type of believers that only ask for blessings during the good times but as soon as we are struck with grief, we completely change and forget about Him and question His existence and where is He now that we need Him. We don't want to be those types of believers. We want to be committed and persistent, with our eyes, our prayers, and our patience all toward Him. We need to be persistent and steadfast in our prayers and believe in Him as we patiently expect to receive from Him. No matter what goes on with our life, we need only ask Him for help, as He is the eternal refuge.

In the following verses, I have tried to separate the verses related to life, death, and afterlife, though some of the verses relate to all three topics.

2:212
The worldly life is made to seem attractive to the disbelievers who scoff at the faithful, but the pious, in the life hereafter, will have a position far above them. God grants sustenance (without account) to anyone He wants.

3:14
It is beautified for mankind the love of things that he desires, such as woman, sons, heaps of stored up gold and silver, fine branded horses and cattle and cultivated land these are the enjoyments of worldly life. But the best destination is toward God.

3:145
And no one dies, except with a permission from God and it is a judgment that has been predetermined, Whoever wants reward from this world we will give him, and whoever wants reward for after life we will give him. And we will reward the ones who are grateful.

4:134
Whoever desires the reward of this life, with God, he gets the reward of this life and the afterlife. And God is All –hearing and All-seeing.

6:32
And this life and this world is nothing but play and amusement, but the home in the afterlife is important for those who are God conscious. Don't you think?

7:158
Say, 'O' man kind! Indeed I am the messenger of God to you all, the one for who rules the heavens and the earth. There is no God except him. He gives life and causes death so believe in God and his Messenger, the unschooled prophet the one who believes in God, and His Words, and follow him, so that you may be guided.

9:116
Indeed God is the ruler of earth and skies. He gives life and he cause death. And you do not seek any protector or helper beside him.

LIFE

10:07
Indeed there are who do not expect a meeting with Us and are pleased with the worldly life and feel satisfied with it. And there are those who are neglectful (thoughtless) of our Signs.

10:23
When We saved you, you started to rebel unjustly in the land. People, your rebellion will only harm yourselves. You may enjoy the worldly life but to Us you will all return and We will let you know all that you had done.

10:56
He gives life and causes death and to Him you will be returned.

10:64
For them there is good news in this life and the Hereafter. There is no change in God's word. That is the great success.

10:88
Moses said, "Lord, You have given the Pharaoh and his people great riches and splendor in this life and this makes them stray from Your path. Lord, destroy their wealth and harden their hearts in disbelief so that they will suffer the most painful torment".

11:56
I trust God who is my Lord as well as yours. It is God who controls the destiny of all living creatures. It is my Lord who knows the right path.

13:26
God gives abundant sustenance to whomever He wants and determines everyone's destiny. Some people are very happy with the worldly life. Compared to the life to come it is only a temporary means.

13:34
The unbelievers will face torment in this world and their punishment in the life hereafter will be even greater. No one can save them from the wrath of God

14:27
And God keeps firm those who believe with the firm word in the life of the world and in the Hereafter. And God lets the wrong doers go astray. And God does what He wills.

16:30
The righteous ones will be asked, "What did your Lord reveal to you?" They will reply," He revealed only Good." The share of the righteous ones is virtue in this world and greater virtue in the afterlife. How blessed will be the home of the righteous ones.

16:97
Whoever does righteousness, whether male or female, while he is a believer we will surely grant him a blessed happy life and we shall pay them certainly a reward proportion to their action (in the hereafter).

17:21
Look how we have favored (in blessing) some of them over others (in this life). But the Hereafter will be greater in degrees and greater in preference.

18:46
Wealth and children are (but) adornment of the worldly life. But the enduring good deeds are better to your Lord for reward and better for (one's) hope.

20:72
They (the magicians) said, "We would never prefer you to the miracles that we have seen or to our Creator. Do what you want. This life is only for a short time.

LIFE

20:97
Moses said, "Go away! Throughout your life you will not be able to let anyone touch you. This will be your punishment in this life. The time for your final punishment is inevitable. You will never be able to avoid it. Look at your God which you have been worshipping. We will burn it in the fire and scatter its ashes into the sea.

21:111
And I do not know, perhaps it (this life) is a trial for you and enjoyment for a time.

22:06
That is because God is the Supreme Truth who gives life to the dead and who has power over all things.

22:11
Some people worship God to achieve worldly gains. They are confident when they are prosperous, but when they face hardships they turn away from (worship). They are lost in this life and will be lost in the life to come. Such loss is indeed destructive.

24: 10
And if not for the favor of God upon you and His mercy...(your life would have been in chaos) and because God is Accepting of repentance and Wise.

29:64
And this worldly life is not but play and amusement. And indeed, the home of the Hereafter is the real (eternal) life, if only they knew this.

31:33
O' people, fear your Lord and fear the Day that a father cannot help his son and a son cannot help his father. Indeed, the promise of God is truth, so let not deceive you the worldly life and let not the deceiver (Satan) deceive you about God.

40:68
He is the one who gives life and causes death and when He decrees a matter then only He says it, "Be" and it is.

42:36
So whatever thing you have been given – it is but [for] enjoyment of the worldly life. But what is with God is better and more lasting for those who have believed and trust upon their Lord.

47:36
This worldly life is only an amusement. If you have faith and piety, He will give you your rewards and will not ask you for your possessions.

50:43
Indeed, it is We who give life and cause death, and to Us is the destination

53:29
So turn away from whoever turns his back on Our message and desires not except the worldly life.

91:01
By the sun and its brightness

91:02
And by the moon when it follows it

92:05
As, for he who gives and fear God

92:06
And believes in the best (reward)

LIFE

92:07
Then we will ease him toward ease (easy life)

92:13
Indeed the Hereafter and this life belong to US.

Death

The Quran teaches us that our life is not over after we die, and we continue in the afterlife either in Paradise or in hell. After death the return of all of us is to Him.

21:35
Every soul will taste death. And We test you with evil and with good as trial; and to Us you will be returned.

6:61
And He is the captor of His subjects, and He sends over you guardian-angels until, when death comes to one of you, Our messengers take him, and they do not fail (in their duties).

7:158
Say, 'O' mankind! Indeed I am the messenger of God to you all, the one for who rules the heavens and the earth. There is no God except him. He gives life and causes death So believe in God and his Messenger, the unschooled prophet the one who believes in God, and His Words, and follow him, so that you may be guided.

9:116
To God belongs the Kingdom of the heavens and the earth. He grants life and causes death. God is your only Guardian and Helper.

10:56
He gives life and causes death and to Him you will be returned.

21:35
Every soul will taste death. And we test you with the bad and the good as trial, and to Us you will return.

23:99
Until the death comes to one of them and he says My Lord, send me back

29:57
Every soul will taste death. Then to US you will be returned.

32:11
Say, the angle of death, the one who has been put in charge of you will take your soul. Then you will be returned to your Lord.

40:68
He is the one who gives life and causes death and when He decrees a matter then only He says it, "Be" and it is.

----------------*50:19-23 secrets of death and Final Day* ----------------

50:19-23
And the intoxication of death will bring the truth; that is what you were trying to avoid

The Horn will certainly be sounded. This will be the day (about which you) were threatened

Every soul will be accompanied (by an angel) behind him and another as a witness

(He will be told), "You were completely heedless of this day. We have removed the veil from your eyes and your vision will now be sharp and strong"

DEATH

His (angelic) companion will say, "(Lord), the record of his deeds is with me and is all ready".

50:43
Indeed, it is We who give life and cause death, and to Us is the destination

63:10
And spend [in the way of God] from what We have provided you before death approaches one of you and he says, "My Lord, if only You would delay me for a brief term so I would give charity and be among the righteous.

Afterlife

The Quran always emphasizes how temporary and short this life is. We should strive and save for the afterlife. Never give into Satan and his associates in any way or form, and always stand against him.

73:20
Your Lord knows that you and a group of those who are with you get up for prayer sometimes for less than two-thirds of the night, sometimes half and sometimes one-third of it. God determines the duration of the night and day. He knew that it would be hard for you to keep an exact account of the timing of the night prayers, so He turned to you with forgiveness. Thus, recite from the Quran as much as possible. He knew that some of you would be sick, others would travel in the land to seek God's favors, and still others would fight for the cause of God. Thus, recite from the Quran as much as possible, be steadfast in prayer, pay the zakat, and give virtuous loans to God. Whatever good deeds you save for the next life, you will certainly find them with God. This is the best investment, and for this you will find the greatest reward. Ask forgiveness from God. God is All-forgiving and All-merciful

29:19-20
Have they not seen how GOD initiates the creation, then repeats it? This is easy for GOD to do.

(Muhammad), say to them, "Travel through the land and see how He has begun the creation and how He will invent the next life. God has power over all things

29:22
You cannot challenge God in the heavens or in the earth. No one besides God is your guardian or helper.

29:23
Those who have rejected God's revelations have no hope in receiving His mercy. They will face a painful torment

2:04
And those who have faith in what has been revealed to you and others before you and have strong faith in the life hereafter.

2:114
And who are more unjust than those who prevent the name of God from being mentioned in his masjid and strive for their destruction? (As for) those, it is not for them that they enter them (i.e., masjid) except in fear. For them, there is disgrace in this world and a great punishment in the hereafter.

7:156
"Grant us well-being in this life and in the life hereafter for we have turned ourselves to You." The Lord replied, "My torment only afflicts those whom I want to punish, but My mercy encompasses all things. I shall grant mercy to those who maintain piety, pay their religious tax, and those who have faith in Our revelations."

11:19
Those who averted people from the way of God and sought to make it look deviant and they don't believe in the Hereafter.

12:57
The reward in the next life is certainly better for the faithful ones who have observed piety in this life.

AFTERLIFE

13:26
God gives abundant sustenance to whomever He wants and determines everyone's destiny. Some people are very happy with the worldly life. Compared to the life to come it is only a temporary means

14:27
And God keeps firm those who believe with the firm word in the life of the world and in the Hereafter. And God lets the wrong doers go astray. And God does what He wills.

16:60
For those who do not believe in the Hereafter, are similarity to evil. God is the similarity of the Highest. And He is the Al-mighty and All-wise.

Those who do not believe in the afterlife to come are evil examples. To God belongs the highest attributes; He is the Majestic and the All-wise.

16:122
And We gave him Good in this world and indeed, in the hereafter, he will surely be among the righteous.

17:19
The effort of one who faithfully strives hard for the (happiness) of the afterlife to come will be appreciated (by God)

17:13
We have made every person's action cling to his neck. On the day of Judgment, We will bring forth the record of his actions in the form of a wide open book.

17:21
Look how we have favored (in blessing) some of them over others (in this life). But the Hereafter will be greater in degrees and greater in preference.

27:3
Those who establish the prayer and give zakah and they certainly believe in the Hereafter.

29:64
And this worldly life is not but play and amusement. And indeed, the home of the Hereafter is the real (eternal) life, if only they knew this.

31:04
Those who establish the prayer and give Charity and they believe firmly in the hereafter.

92:13
Indeed the Hereafter and this life belong to US.

Paradise

In general Muslims and Christians do believe in Paradise, while Jewish people do not have or believe in Paradise. We believe in the afterlife. If your good deeds outweigh your bad deeds you go to heaven. And if your bad deeds outweigh your good deeds you go to hell.

101:6-11
God says in the Quran that our deeds will be measured or weighed, and whosoever has more good deeds will enter the Gardens of Paradise and whose evil deeds weigh more than the good ones will be entered into the Hell fire.

That is why the Quran encourages you throughout its pages to do good deeds, to give charity, to feed the hungry, to help out the homeless and the orphan kids. Adopt them if you can. We believe your good deeds can wash away your bad deeds.

39:35
That God will remove for them their worst bad deed and reward them their due for the best of what they have done.

We also emphasize that your bad deeds do not go unpunished and God keeps the records. So for all those who do not pay for their bad deeds in this life, they will definitely pay for them in the afterlife.

There are some false assumptions about Paradise in Islam. There is a famous falsehood that we hear in the media or even among some Muslims, that every man that dies as a Muslim will get seventy virgins in heaven! There is no place in the Quran saying anything like this. My assumption is someone probably tried to encourage Muslim men to be good and refrain from having sex out of marriage, by promising them all these girls in heaven. Somehow I do not understand how they came up with the number seventy!

The Quran emphasizes that everyone who is righteous, regardless of his or her religion, goes to heaven and does not have to worry (2:62). And all those who say only the people of their religion go to heaven are baseless (2:111).

Here are a few verses about Paradise:

(Quran 2:62, 5:69)
Surely, those who believe, those who are Jewish, Sabeans (people of the land of Sheba, today's Yemen) the Christians, and anyone who believes in GOD, and believes in the Last Day, and leads a righteous life, will receive their recompense from their Lord. They have nothing to fear, nor will they grieve.

2:111
And they say, None will enter Paradise except one who is a Jew or a Christian, that is their wishful thinking. Say bring your proof if you are truthful.

4:124
And those who are believers and do righteous deeds from man and woman will enter the paradise and they will not be wronged, even as little as the specks curve on a date's seed.

3:142
Do you think that you enter the paradise without making a hard attempt and showing commitment?

PARADISE

4:124
Any believer, male or female, who acts righteously, will enter Paradise and will not suffer the least bit of injustice

6:127
They will live in peace with God. God protects them as a reward for their deeds; He is their Guardian

7:42
But those who believe and do good deeds, we do not burden their soul above their capacity. Those are the ones who will be in paradise and will be there forever.

9-111
God has purchased the souls and property of the believers in exchange for Paradise. They fight for the cause of God to destroy His enemies and to sacrifice themselves. This is a true promise which He has revealed in the Torah, the Gospel, and the Quran. No one is more true to His promise than God. Let this bargain be glad news for them. This is indeed the supreme triumph.

11:23
Indeed those who believe and do good deeds and humble themselves before their God, those are the companions of paradise and they will abide there forever.

13:35
The example of paradise, which the righteous have been promised, is [that] beneath it rivers flow. Its fruit is lasting and its shade. That is the end result of the righteous and the end result of disbelievers is the Fire.

19:76
God further enlightens those who seek guidance. To those who charitable deeds which produce continuing benefits, your Lord will give a better reward and a better place in Paradise.

23:8-11
Those who are true to their trust
To their promise
And who are steadfast in their prayer
These are the heirs of Paradise wherein they will live forever.

25:75
Those will be rewarded with the highest place (in Paradise) because of their patience. Therein they shall be met with greetings and the word of peace.

29:58
And those who have believed and done righteous deeds - We will surely assign to them of Paradise [elevated] chambers beneath which rivers flow, wherein they abide eternally. Excellent is the reward of the [righteous] workers

54:54
Indeed the righteous will be among the gardens and rivers (of Paradise)

57:12
On the Day of Judgment you will see the believers with their light shining in front of them and to their right. They will be told, "Paradise wherein streams flow is the glad news for you today. You will live therein forever. This is the greatest triumph"

PARADISE

57:21
Compete with one another to achieve forgiveness from your Lord and to reach Paradise, which is as vast as the heavens and the earth, and is prepared for those who believe in God and His Messenger. This is the blessing of God and He grants it to whomever He wants. God is the possessor of Great Blessings.

64:09
On the day when We shall gather you all together (for the Day of Judgment), all cheating will be exposed. Those who believe in God and act righteously will receive forgiveness for their sins. They will be admitted into Paradise wherein streams flow and they will live forever. This certainly is the greatest triumph

66:08
Believers, turn to God in repentance with the intention of never repeating the same sin. Perhaps your Lord will expiate your evil deeds and admit you to Paradise wherein streams flow. On the Day of Judgment, God will not disgrace the Prophet and those who have believed in him. Their lights will shine in front of them and to their right. They will say, "Our Lord, perfect our light for us and forgive our sins. You have power over all things"

22:14
GOD admits those who believe and lead a righteous life into gardens with flowing streams. Everything is in accordance with GOD's will.

God's Pick for His Plans

7:144
God said, "O Moses, I have chosen you over the people with My messages and My words [to you]. So take what I have given you and be among the grateful."

What God has planned for us in life may be completely different than what we may have in mind. Many times we see people doing very different things when they follow their heart or talent instead of their formal training or what they had in mind in the early part of their career. I personally believe God has a specific plan for each and every one of us. If someone had told me twenty years ago that one day I would attempt a book like this, I would have laughed. I think God realizes everyone's talent and tries to point him or her in that direction. It's up to individuals to listen to their heart and get those hints from above.

Sometimes God picks specific people for what He has in mind, big or small. One thing I believe He looks for is perseverance, the ability not to quit, no matter how hard the situation gets. The people God chooses may have flaws or imperfections, but God completely overlooks that. The important things is that the people he chooses are committed and able to persevere. Almost all God's prophets had flaws or weaknesses. But their monumental tasks ahead of them outweighed those imperfections.

In 20:115 God shows His disappointment with Adam for his lack of determination.

20:115
We had commanded Adam (certain matters). He forgot Our commandment and We did not find in him the determination to fulfil Our commandments.

Somehow there is a general expectancy among people that God's prophets have to be perfect human beings, immaculate, complete, all-righteous, all-wise, all-kind, all-pure, all-flawless, perfect specimens of goodness in all walks of life, who pray and fast for God 24/7, and that is why God chose them to be His messenger. This is not true. Most of the prophets of God had to practically scream that they were just a messenger from Him. They ate, slept, and had needs just like everyone else.

I believe God simply picks the right men for the job. He picks the kind of men that can get the job done and deliver the message the way He wants. No matter who they are. As simple as that!

They may have flaws or questionable characters in the eyes of the men, but it appears God overlooks that, due to the enormous task that He gives them to do. I believe He looks inside a man or woman for a task that He has in mind, and He thinks they can get it done.

In Islam, Umar was a staunch enemy of Muslims and Islam and wanted to kill Muhammad in the beginning. When he heard his sister and her husband had turned Muslim, he headed to her house to kill her. When he reached his sister's house, he heard the sound of prayer inside. After entering the house angrily and scuffling with his sister's husband and her, he decided to read what they were reading, which was the beginning of Sura Ta-Ha (20). When he realized how beautiful it was, he then decided to convert to Islam. Later on, Umar, this man who was the enemy of Muhammad and Islam at the beginning, became one of the most influential companions of Muhammad and was the second calif of Islam after Muhammad's death.

GOD'S PICK FOR HIS PLANS

When we study other religions, we see similar situations. Moses killed an Egyptian when he saw he was whipping a Hebrew, before he was anointed as a prophet.

28:15
Once he entered the city unexpectedly, without being recognized by the people. He found two men fighting; one was (a Hebrew) from his people, and the other was (an Egyptian) from his enemies. The one from his people called on him for help against his enemy. Moses punched him, killing him. He said, "This is the work of the devil; he is a real enemy, and a profound misleader."

Moses also stuttered when he talked. You would think of all the people God would choose as a prophet, he would be a good public speaker in order to influence the people better. At least that is the way we humans think. But God looks at other qualities.

God chose Moses because He knew he could deliver no matter what. God did not see the twist in his tongue, but the will in his heart, even if he wandered in the desert for forty years! Moses never gave up. He is one of the most beloved prophets in the Quran, as he endured so much for so long, especially the last part of his journey.

Speaking of imperfections of prophets and men of God, how about Jacob? We Muslims believe in Jacob and his twelve sons (2:136). However, the Quran gives limited information about Jacob and his sons.

According to the Old Testament, Jacob compelled his brother Esau to give him his birthright (Genesis 25:29-34). One day when Esau came from the field famished he saw Jacob had a pot of stew. He begged Jacob for a bowl of stew. Jacob offered to give him a bowl of stew in exchange for his birthright, and Esau agreed. Later on Jacob, with the help of their mother, Rebecca, who favored Jacob over Esau, tricked their father, Isaac, into giving his blessing to Jacob instead of Esau. Esau was the first-born son, and he was the favorite of Isaac.

As some may not be familiar with the story, Isaac was going blind in his old age. He asked Esau to hunt for him and prepare a meal for him the way he liked it, so then he could give his blessings to Esau. Rebecca heard that and told Jacob to bring two baby goats. She prepared a stew the way Isaac liked. Esau was a hairy individual, versus Isaac, who had smooth skin. Then their mother, Rebecca, asked Jacob to wear Esau's clothes so he would smell like him, and put goat skin that was hairy on his arm and neck, so when Isaac touched him to give his blessing he would think he was Esau. Esau took stew and wine to Isaac. Isaac became suspicious, as Jacob smelled like Esau but sounded like Jacob. So Isaac asked him, "Are you Esau?" Jacob responded, "Yes." Isaac reportedly ate the stew and drank the wine and asked Jacob to come close so he could kiss him and give him his blessing. When Jacob came close, he smelled like Esau, and Isaac thought he was Esau and gave Jacob the blessing that he meant for Esau According to the Old Testament the blessing was this (Genesis 27:28-29):

Therefore God give thee of the dew of heavens, and the fatness of the earth, and plenty of corn and wine: Let people serve thee: be lord over thy brethren, and let thy mother's sons bow down to thee: cursed be every one that curseth thee, and blessed be he that blesseth thee.

Now there is nothing good and honorable about what Jacob did, as he tricked his father into giving him the blessing meant for his brother, yet later on we see God chose Jacob as the patriarch of the Israelis, and we Muslims also believe in him and his twelve sons (*asbat*) as prophets of God (2:136).

According to another story in the Old Testament, Abraham was living in Gerar, a place in the land of Philistine, and he had to introduce his wife, Sarah, as his sister so King Abimelech, who was ruling the region, would not kill him to take his wife, Sarah. King Abimelech took Sarah, but did not lay a hand on her. That night he had a dream that God told him he had taken a married woman and should return her to Abraham, which he did.

And how about David, who saw the naked body of his neighbor's wife when she was bathing? He sent her husband on a very dangerous mission that he knew he would not return from, so he could have his wife. And God did punish him for that!

And how about Jesus? He has been criticized for having an enigmatic personality, as he is difficult to interpret or understand. There are some passages in the Bible in which he said strange things, from things about eating his flesh to drinking his blood!

For the record, doesn't he call himself "son of man"? (Matt 8:20, John 6:62, 6:53).

Here are a few passages from the Bible:
http://biblehub.com/john/6-53.htm

Matthew 8:20
Jesus replied, "Foxes have dens, and birds of the air have nests, but the Son of Man has no place to lay His head."

Matt 8:22
"Let the dead bury their own dead"

Mark 9:43
"If your hand causes you to stumble, cut it off"

John 6:51
I am the living bread that came down from heaven. If anyone eats of this bread, he will live forever. And this bread, which I will give for the life of the world, is My flesh."

John 6:62
Then what will happen if you see the Son of Man ascend to where He was before?

John 6:53
Truly, truly, I say to you, unless you eat the flesh of the Son of Man and drink his blood, you have no life in you.

So what this tells us is that despite our imperfections, God looks for different qualities in different people when He chooses them for certain tasks, big or small. We create our own prejudice against others based on our own limitations. God looks at all of us equally as His creation and simply picks the right man or woman for the job.

What seems to us like imperfections pales against the monumental task God had put in front of the prophets to achieve. I believe He has a certain task for everyone, that suits his or her background. The Quran teaches us, God never overburdens a person with a task He knows he or she cannot handle (23:62).

If God decides to choose a person as a prophet, despite what we may consider a flaw, who are we to criticize or to judge? God makes the choice as He knows best. He does what He wants.

Some of the critics of Islam and Muslims, who try to find flaws with our religion without looking at their own first, often criticize Muhammad for having multiple wives, as they do not know about other cultures. For the record, according to the Bible, Solomon had seven hundred wives and three hundred concubines (1 Kings 11:1).

Having a number of wives in Arabia is part of their current and past culture and is customary and ordinary. Muhammad was simply a man of his time and the place he grew up. Not only Muhammad, but his companions and later leaders of Islam all had multiple wives as a way of their life and culture. So it was not something just for him. Muhammad was the right man for the job in that culture, and God chose him to lead his nation out of the bad period of time they were going through. He brought Islam and monotheism to that part of the world, as they had become pagan people. He made the Arabian people give up idol worshipping and united them under One God.

And to Muhammad and the Quran's testament, he is the last prophet God chose, and up to this day, there has not been another prophet sent and will not be another one till the end of time.

Here are a few verses from the Quran:

14:01
Alif, Lam, Ra. [This is] a book which We have revealed to you, [O Muhammad], that you might bring mankind out of darkness into the light by permission of their lord to the path of Almighty, the praiseworthy.

2:257
God is the Guardian of the believers and it is He who takes them out of darkness into light. The Devil is the guardian of those who deny the Truth and he leads them from light to darkness. These are the dwellers of hell wherein they will live forever.

5:16
With it, God guides those who seek His approval. He guides them to the paths of peace, leads them out of darkness into the light by His leave, and guides them to the right path.

57:28
Believers, have fear of God and believe in His Messenger. God will grant you a double share of mercy, a light by which you can walk, and forgive your sins. God is All-forgiving and All-merciful

65:03
And He will provide for him from where he does not expect. And whoever puts his trust upon God, then God is sufficient for him. Indeed God will accomplish His purpose. God has set a measure for everything.

6:91
And they did not appraise God with true appraisal when they said, " God did not reveal to a human being anything." Say, "Who revealed the Scripture that Moses brought as light and guidance to the people? You [Jews] make it into pages, disclosing [some of] it and concealing much. And you were taught that which you knew not - neither you nor your fathers." Say, " God [revealed it]." Then leave them in their useless debate

6:122
Is someone who was dead (depressed) and we gave him life and showed him the light so he could walk among people (in its illumines) similar to someone who is in darkness and cannot come out of it? The deeds of the unbelievers are made to seem attractive to them.

66:08
Believers, turn to God in repentance with the intention of never repeating the same sin. Perhaps your Lord will expiate your evil deeds and admit you to Paradise wherein streams flow. On the Day of Judgment, God will not disgrace the Prophet and those who have believed in him. Their lights will shine in front of them and to

their right. They will say, "Our Lord, perfect our light for us and forgive our sins. You have power over all things"

5:15
Oh people of the book, our messenger has come to you making clear of what you have concealed from the Scriptures and overlooking many. Surely there has come to you a light from God and a clear Book.

[9:48] They sought to spread confusion among you in the past, and confounded the matters for you. However, the truth ultimately prevails, and God's plan is carried out, in spite of them.

Competition between Religions

There has always been competition between the three Abrahamic faiths' followers, as to which one is the true faith of God, as the follower of each faith tries to be triumphant in proving to be the right faith.

In 5:48 in the Quran, God says the followers of the three religions should try to compete with each other in doing good deeds. I personally think this is one of the most beautiful verses of the Quran, as it sets the bar on what to strive for, for all three religions, instead of arguing who is the true religion of God. It has been mentioned in the Quran in many places that the most important good deed is helping other human beings in need: the fallen ones, the poor, the orphans, and the woman and children without protectors.

I am putting four separate translations of the verse that tells us to compete between the three religions, so you get a chance to see all of them (Corpus.quran.com):

5:48

Sahih International: *And We have revealed to you, [O Muhammad], the Book in truth, confirming that which preceded it of the Scripture and as a criterion over it. So judge between them by what God has revealed and do not follow their inclinations away from what has come to you of the truth. To each of you We prescribed a law and a method. Had God willed, He would have made you one nation [united in religion], but [He intended] to test you in what He has given you; so race to [all that is] good. To God is your return all* *together, and He will [then] inform you concerning that over which you used to differ.*

Yusuf Ali: *To thee We sent the Scripture in truth, confirming the scripture that came before it, and guarding it in safety: so judge between them by what God hath revealed, and follow not their vain desires, diverging from the Truth that hath come to thee. To each among you have we prescribed a law and an open way. If God had so willed, He would have made you a single people, but (His plan is) to test you in what He hath given you: so strive as in a race in all virtues. The goal of you all is to God; it is He that will show you the truth of the matters in which ye dispute*

Muhammad Sarwar: *We have revealed the Book to you (Muhammad) in all Truth. It confirms the (original) Bible and has the authority to preserve or abrogate what the Bible contains. Judge among them by what God has revealed to you and do not follow their desires instead of the Truth which has come to you. We have given a law and a way of life to each of you. Had God wanted, He could have made you into one nation, but He wanted to see who are the more pious ones among you. Compete with each other in righteousness. All of you will return to God who will tell you the truth in the matter of your differences.*

*[5:48] Then we revealed to you this scripture, truthfully, confirming previous scriptures, and superseding them. You shall rule among them in accordance with **GOD**'s revelations, and do not follow their wishes if they differ from the truth that came to you. For each of you, we have decreed laws and different rites. Had **GOD** willed, He could have made you one nation (united in religion). But He thus puts you to the test through the revelations He has given each of you. You shall compete in righteousness. To **GOD** is your final destiny—all of you—then He will inform you of everything you had disputed.*

COMPETITION BETWEEN RELIGIONS

To be fair, Christians seem to be ahead of everyone else so far, as they help others without being prejudiced against others' religion or race.

Muslims have their plate full. Most Muslim countries in the Middle East, regardless if they are friendly or non-friendly to the West, are constantly under attack or getting undermined by the West. They have no other choice than to resort to some kind of fundamentalism in order to survive. The latest military coup in Turkey allegedly made by the US is a prime example. Turkey has been a friend to the US for many, many years. According to Turkish newspapers and news, the US was planning to replace Erdogan with Fethullah Gulen, an anti-Iranian, anti-Shiite clergyman who lives in Pennsylvania, to reportedly start a Shiite-Sunni war between Turkey and Iran. The shift to fundamentalism for survival against the United States, Israel, and England has caused many social and cultural issues in those countries. Currently many Muslim countries have to deal with refugees left behind from US attacks in Afghanistan, Iraq, Libya and Syria. In addition, they are dealing with all kinds of sanctions put on them by the US and their allies. So when it comes to helping others while trying to survive, their plates are truly full. I have explained this further in chapter 39, "Dealing with our enemies"

The majority of the charitable acts by the Jews are toward the State of Israel.

With the current refugee crisis coming mainly from Syria and other parts of the Muslim world to Europe, Christians have shown they are doing good deeds and being patient. They are acting more Muslim (according to the Quran) than some of the capable Muslim countries. The capable Muslim countries could do more for refugees instead of shouldering out of it. If they have their differences with certain regimes politically, I am sure they have nothing against ordinary Muslims, despite the fact they are from different sects. Muhammad predicted that his religion would have more branches than Judaism and Christianity.

Christians have a famous saying: "What would Jesus do?" I wish the more capable Muslim countries would do what "Muhammad would do" at a time like this.

In 2:17 God insists that helping destitute people is a prayer by itself and is being righteous.

2:177
Righteousness is not determined by facing East or West during prayer. Righteousness consists of the belief in God, the Day of Judgment, the angels, the Books of God, His Prophets; to give money for the love of Him to relatives, orphans, the destitute, and those who are on a journey and in urgent need of money, beggars; to set free slaves and to be steadfast in prayer, to pay the religious tax (zakah) to fulfill one's promises, and to exercise patience in poverty, in distress, and in times of war. Such people who do these are truly righteous and pious.

Parallels with Science

At the beginning of the book, I mentioned some of the verses that are parallel with science, and these facts of science were not yet discovered at that time. What is fascinating is who is saying it and from what part of the world this voice is coming!

Muhammad was illiterate. I am sure he could count and had some knowledge of numbers and probably very basic letters, since he was a merchant. But to come up with a book which is like poetry, that also reveals some of the secrets and knowledge of the universe, now that is indeed a miracle and a revelation from above.

I do not know of any other religious book that says life starts from the sea, warns us about cloning, or tells us that the universe is expanding, God created a dome above the earth to protect us (atmosphere), water was brought to earth from the sky (universe), we have placed mountains as firm anchors on earth, the earth and moon run smoothly in their orbit, day and night should not overtake each other, or He has released the two oceans (sea) to meet side by side but there is a barrier between them and they do not merge together, at the beginning the earth was covered with water (and His throne had been upon the water) (11:7). Here is a man, walking in the desert of Arabia! What does he know about all these facts!

All of these were in the Quran before they were discovered by modern science later on. Scientists have always been baffled where all the water on earth came from to begin with, and they still do not know how or where. Some give the possibility that the water came from colliding with an ice comet, but they still do not know.

And finally, last but not least, recently I have seen comments on the Internet and some Muslim websites regarding cloning and verse 4:119 in the Quran. They have never told us what the reason and purpose for cloning are, which makes it more suspicious. As I was reading the information regarding different techniques of cloning, several articles mentioned that cloning cows is easier compared to other animals and was explaining how they take an ear cell from a healthy adult cow and use it to create a new clone.

Here is the verse that warns against cloning and altering God's creation:

4:118-119
(118) God condemned Satan when he said, "I will certainly take my revenge from Your servants."

(119) And I will mislead them, and I will arouse in them [sinful] desires, and I will command them so they will slit the ears of cattle, and I will command them so they will change the creation of God." And whoever takes Satan as an ally instead of God has certainly sustained a clear loss.

So for all those who say Muhammad wrote the Quran or invented it, what would Muhammad know about cloning?

2:23
Should you have any doubt about what We have revealed to Our servant, (Muhammad) present one chapter (Surah) comparable to it and call all your supporters, besides God, if your claim is true.

Here are some of the verses at the introduction and more:

24:45
"God created every animal from water"

PARALLELS WITH SCIENCE

51:47
The universe, We have built it with power, Verily We are expanding it.

21:32
And we made the sky a protected ceiling, but yet they turn away from its sign.

21:30
Have those who disbelieved not considered that the heavens and the earth were a joined entity, and We separated them and made from water every living thing? Then will they not believe?

13:2
It is God who erected the heavens (universe) without pillars that you [can] see; then He established Himself above the Throne and made subject the sun and the moon, each running [its course] for a specified term. He arranges [each] matter; He details the signs that you may, of the meeting with your Lord, be certain.

31:29
Have you not seen that God causes the night to enter into the day and the day into the night. He has made the sun and moon subservient (to Himself). Each running (its course) for an appointed time. God is certainly All-aware of what you do

39:5
He created the heavens and earth in truth. He wraps the night over the day and wraps the day over the night and has subjected the sun and the moon, each running [its course] for a specified term. Unquestionably, He is the Majestic and All-Forgiving

36:38
And the sun runs its course steadily, and that is the determination of the Majestic, all Knowing God

86:1-3
By the sky and the knocker (loud one). And how will you [Muhammad] know what the knocker is? (loud one is?) The star that piercing (loud, deafening puncturing)

It is verses like these and many others like them that give validity to the Quran as God's words, as they had not yet been discovered when the Quran was revealed to Muhammad. The Quran clearly says, "Before you, there were other humans and animals on earth. We wiped them off and started with new, see how they do" (10:13,14). An idea or a statement that other religions have a hard time accepting is that there were other people and animals on this earth before us.

10:13,14
We destroyed certain generations who lived before you because of their injustice. Our Messengers came to them and showed them miracles, but they would not believe. Thus do We punish the criminals. We have made you their successors in the land so that We could see how you behaved.

The Quran does say Adam was created from clay, and God blew from his spirit to it, but it also says humans and animals came from the water. This is way before modern science. What would Muhammad, this forty-plus-year-old Bedouin man, walking in the deserts of Arabia know about the atmosphere protecting the earth like a shield (21:32)! Or every living thing coming from water (24:45, 21:30)!

6:125 (decreasing oxygen with altitude)
God will open the hearts of whomever He wants to guide to Islam, but He will tighten the chest of one whom He has led astray, as though he was ascending high up into the sky. Thus, God places wickedness on those who do not accept the faith.

PARALLELS WITH SCIENCE

*(79:30-33) And the mountains He set firmly
After this, He spread out the earth,
produced water and grass therefrom,
then set-up firmly the mountains
As provision for you and your grazing livestock*

*78-7
And the mountains as pegs (to anchor the earth)?*

*50-7
(Have they not seen) how We have spread out the earth, placed on it firm mountains and have made all kinds of flourishing pairs of plants grow?*

*21-31
And We placed within the earth firmly set mountains, so it would not shift with them, and We made therein [mountain] passes [as] roads that they might be guided.*

Barrier between the Two Oceans

*27:61
Is He [not best] who made the earth a stable ground and placed within it rivers and made for it firmly set mountains and placed between the two seas a barrier? Is there a deity with God? [No], but most of them do not know.*

*55:19-20
He has let released the two seas, meeting (side by side), between them is a barrier so they will not merge together.*

*11:7
And it is He who created the heavens and the earth in six days - and His Throne had been on water - that He might test you as to*

which of you is best in deed. But if you say, "Indeed, you are resurrected after death," those who disbelieve will surely say, "This is not but obvious magic."

Parallels with Other Religions

(Quran 2:62, 5:69)
Surely, those who believe, those who are Jewish, the Christians, and the converts; anyone who believes in GOD, and believes in the Last Day, and leads a righteous life, will receive their recompense from their Lord. They have nothing to fear, nor will they grieve.

The Lord reminds us that the act of being righteous and doing good deeds is universal and does not depend on our religion. Although we may look different in our appearances and manners, the act of doing good deeds and helping others is just that and has no boundary and does not belong to any particular religion or manner. Anyone who believes and acts in such a way will be recompensed. And these people have nothing to worry about or have fear from.

There are many parallels in Islam with the Old Testament and other religions. Especially Moses and the children of Israel. Although, throughout the Quran it has been emphasized in many places that the Quran reads with its predecessors and previous revelations (Torah) and Bibles, but there are some differences. Many people around the world simply do not know that Islam worships the same God of Abraham and Moses.

Some try to mislead people or the public out of their ignorance, saying that Muslims worship a black cube in the desert because they have seen the ceremony of Hajj on TV.

According to the Quran we accept Abraham, Ishmael, Isaac, and Jacob and his twelve sons. Jacob is known as a prophet in Islam. Jacob is also known as the patriarch of Israelites, and Muslims believe in the teachings of him and his twelve sons, as each one became a father of one of the twelve tribes of Israel (3:84).

3:84
Say, "We believe in GOD, and in what was sent down to us, and in what was sent down to Abraham, Ismail, Isaac, Jacob, and the Patriarchs (12 sons of Jacob), and in what was given to Moses, Jesus, and the prophets from their Lord. We make no distinction among any of them. To Him alone we are submitters."

Most of the parallels found are with the Old Testament. The Quran has parallels with the story of Adam and Eve, Paradise, Satan, the expulsion of Adam and Eve from Paradise, Enoch, Noah, The Flood; Scrolls of Abraham, Isaac, Jacob and his twelve sons; Joseph, Scrolls of Moses, miracles of Moses and exodus, scrolls of David, Psalms, scrolls of Solomon, Zachariah, and Yahya (John the Baptist).

The parallels with Christianity are, Mary and the virgin birth of Jesus, the Holy Ghost, curing the blind and leprous, raising the dead, bringing food to his disciples (5:112-114), and Jesus returning on Judgment Day. *(43:61, "And indeed, Jesus will be [a sign for] knowledge of the Hour, so be not in doubt of it, and follow Me. This is a straight path.")* There are also miracles involving Jesus that are not mentioned in Christianity. According to the Quran, Jesus could talk in the cradle and in childhood made birds with clay, which he would blow in, and they would become alive and fly away.

Jesus has a special stature compared to others in Islam. Jesus is viewed as similar to Adam, as God blew from his own soul into Jesus and God calls his birth a miracle of its own.

21:91
Into the woman who maintained her chastity We breathed Our Spirit and made her and her son a miracle for all people

2:87
We gave the Book to Moses and made the Messengers follow in his path. To Jesus, the son of Mary, We gave the miracles and supported him by the Holy Spirit. Why do you arrogantly belie some Messengers and murder others whenever they have brought you messages that you dislike?

Here are a few more verses about Jesus in the Quran.

5:112
(Recall) when the disciples said, "Jesus, son of Mary, can your Lord send us a table full of food from heaven?" and you replied, "Have fear of God if you are true believers"

5:113
They said, "We only wish to eat therefrom to comfort our hearts, to know that you have spoken the Truth to us, and to bear witness to it along with the others.

5:114
When Jesus prayed, "Lord, send us a table full of food from heaven so that it will make a feast for us and for those who are yet to come in this world and an evidence from You. Give us sustenance, for You are the best Provider,"

5:115
God replied, "I am sending it to you, but if anyone of you turns back to disbelief, I will make him suffer a torment that no one has ever suffered."

3:46
He will speak to the people while in his cradle and preach to them when he will be a man. He will be one of the righteous ones.

19:30
[Jesus] said, "Indeed, I am the servant of God. He has given me the Scripture and made me a prophet

19:31
He has blessed me no matter where I dwell, commanded me to worship Him and pay the religious tax for as long as I live.

19:32
He has commanded me to be good to my parents and has not made me an arrogant rebellious person.

19:33
I was born with peace and I shall die and be brought to life again with peace.

3:49
He will be a Messenger of God to the Israelites to whom he will say, "I have brought you a miracle from your Lord. I can create for you something from clay in the form of a bird. When I blow into it, it will become a real bird, by the permission of God. I can heal the blind and the lepers and bring the dead back to life, by the permission of God. I can tell you about what you eat and what you store in your homes. This is a miracle for you if you want to have faith.

---------------Parallel with Bible ----------------

Mark 6:5
He could not do any miracles there, except lay his hands on a few sick people and heal them.

Acts 2:22
A man attested to you by God with miracles and wonders and signs which God performed through him in your midst.

PARALLELS WITH OTHER RELIGIONS

Islam considers all the previous prophets as Muslim, meaning they have submitted to God and there is no difference between them. Moses has been repeated over 140 times in the Quran. Mary has a complete chapter for herself. Most of the Quran is stories of the past and lessons learned from them or where they went wrong. The teachings of Islam are embedded among and in the stories.

The following are some of the verses that have similarity with other holy books. In the following chapters, I have included verses about Noah, Abraham, Moses, Jesus, and Mary, as these are questioned by people of other faiths out of their curiosity.

(Deuteronomy 6:4-5, Mark 12:29-30, Quran 3:18)
Hear, O Israel! The Lord our God is One God! Therefore you shall adore the Lord your God with all your heart, with all your soul, with all your mind, and with all your strength.

Quran 3:18
God Himself testifies that He is the only Lord. The angels and the men of knowledge and justice testify that God is the only Lord, the Majestic, and All-wise.

(Quran 2:62, 5:69)
Surely, those who believe, those who are Jewish, the Christians, and the converts; anyone who believes in GOD, and believes in the Last Day, and leads a righteous life, will receive their recompense from their Lord. They have nothing to fear, nor will they grieve.

Noah

Noah has been mentioned in the Quran in many places. He is the symbol of trust in God and God guiding him to safe passage after all the turbulence. He followed the step-by-step instructions of God, despite all the ridicule and laughter he received from the people. He is another symbol of total submission to God and leaving everything in God's hands and He will deliver you. His total trust-in God with comfort, has been exemplary and symbolized around the world. He submitted to God completely, listened to God, followed God's steps and instructions, and at the end, he and his family survived while the sinners and wrongdoers drowned in the big flood. He is revered in all three religions and spoke highly of in the Quran.

3:33
God chose (and gave distinction to) Adam, Noah, the family of Abraham, and Imran over all the people of the world.

4:163.
(Muhammad), We have sent revelations to you just as were sent to Noah and the Prophets who lived after him and to Abraham, Ishmael, Isaac, Jacob, his descendants, Jesus, Job, Jonah, Aaron, and Solomon. We gave the Psalms to David.

6:84
We gave (Abraham) Isaac and Jacob. Both had received Our guidance. Noah received Our guidance before Abraham and so did his descendants: David, Solomon, Job, Joseph, Moses, and Aaron. Thus is the reward for the righteous people

7:59
We sent Noah to his people. He told them, "Worship God for He is your only Lord. I am afraid of the punishment that you might suffer on the great Day (of Judgment)".

[7:69]
Does it seem strange to you that a reminder from your Lord should be sent to a man among you so that He may warn you? Recall when God appointed you as successors of the people of Noah and increased your power over other people. Give thanks to God for His blessings so that perhaps you will have everlasting happiness."

9:70
Have they not heard the stories of the people of Noah, the tribe of Ad, Thamud, the people of Abraham, the dwellers of the city of Midian, and the evildoers (of Sodom and Gomorrah)? God's Messengers came to each of them with miracles. God did not do any injustice to them, but they wronged themselves.

10:71
(Muhammad), tell them the story of Noah who told his people, "Even if my belief and my preaching of the revelation of God seem strange to you, I put my trust in Him. Unite yourselves and seek help from your idols. You should not regret what you want to do, but should execute your plans against me without delay

11:25
We sent Noah to his people, saying, "I come to you as a clear warner.

11:32
They said, "Noah, you have argued with us a great deal. Bring down on us whatever torment with which you have been threatening us if what you say is true".

NOAH

11:36
It was revealed to Noah that besides those who had already accepted his faith, no one from his people would ever believe him. He was told not to be disappointed about what his people had done

11:40
When at last Our decree was fulfilled, water gushed forth from the Oven (in Noah's house). We told him to carry in the Ark a pair (male and female) from every species, his family - except those who were destined to perish - and the believers. No one believed in him, except a few.

11:41
(Noah) said, "Embark in it. It will sail in the name of God, in His Name it will sail and in His Name it will cast anchor. My Lord is All-forgiving and All-merciful"

11:42
When the Ark sailed on with them amid the mountainous waves, Noah called out to his son who kept away from them, "My son, embark with us. Do not stay with the unbelievers."

11:43
His son replied, "I shall climb up a mountain and this will save me from the flood." Noah said, "No one can escape on this day from God's command except those on whom He has mercy." The waves separated Noah from his son who was then drowned with the rest (of the unbelievers)

11:44
Then the earth was told to swallow-up its water and the sky was ordered to stop raining. The water abated and God's command had been fulfilled. The Ark came to rest on Mount Judi. A voice said, "The unjust people are far away from the mercy of God."

[11:45]
Noah prayed to his Lord saying, "Lord, my son is a member of my family. Your promise is always true and you are the best Judge"

11:46
He said, "O Noah, he is not of your family. It is unrighteous to ask Me for something you do not know. I advise you not to become an ignorant person

11:48
Noah was told, "Get down from the Ark. Your Lord's peace and blessings are upon you and your followers. Your Lord will grant favors to other nations and then afflict them with a painful torment."

14:9
Have you (believers) ever heard the news about those who lived before you, like the people of Noah, Ad, Thamud, and those who lived after them? No one knows about them except God. Messengers were sent to them with miracles, but they put their hands to their mouths and said, "We do not believe in whatever you preach and we are also doubtful and uncertain about that to which you invite us."

17:3
(We made it a guide for) the offspring of those whom We carried in the Ark with Noah, a thankful servant (of God).

19:58
These were the Prophets from the offspring of Adam, from those who embarked with Noah and from the offspring of Abraham and Israel. God guided them and chose them for His favor. Whenever they would hear the revelations of the Beneficent God they would bow down in prostration with tears.

NOAH

21:76
We answered the prayer of Noah who had prayed to Us before and saved him and his followers from the great disaster

22:42
And if they deny you, [O Muhammad] - so, before them, did the people of Noah and 'Aad and Thamud deny [their prophets]

23:23
We sent Noah to his people, saying, "O my people, worship God. You have no other God beside Him. Would you not be righteous?"

[23:27]
We then inspired him: "Make the watercraft* under our watchful eyes, and in accordance with our inspiration. When our command comes, and the atmosphere boils up, put on it a pair of every kind (of your domesticated animals), and your family, except those condemned to be doomed. Do not speak to Me on behalf of those who transgressed; they will be drowned.

25:37
We drowned the people of Noah because of their rejection of the Messengers and made them evidence of the Truth for mankind. We have prepared a painful torment for the unjust ones

26:105
The people of Noah denied the messengers

29:14
And We certainly sent Noah to his people, and he remained among them a thousand years minus fifty years, and the flood seized them while they were wrongdoers.

33:7
And [mention, O Muhammad], when We took from the prophets their covenant and from you and from Noah and Abraham and Moses and Jesus, the son of Mary; and We took from them a solemn covenant

37:75
Noah called for help. How blessed was the answer which he received

38:12
Disbelieving before them were the people of Noah, 'Ãd, and the mighty Pharaoh.

40:5
The people of Noah denied before them and the [disbelieving] factions after them, and every nation intended [a plot] for their messenger to seize him, and they disputed by [using] falsehood to [attempt to] invalidate thereby the truth. So I seized them, and how [terrible] was My penalty.

51:46
The people of Noah who lived before them were also evil doing people.

53:52
and the people of Noah; they were the most unjust and rebellious people.

54:9
The people of Noah denied before them, and they denied Our servant and said, «A madman,» and he was repelled.

NOAH

57:26
We sent Noah and Abraham, and we granted their descendants prophethood and the scripture. Some of them were guided, while many were wicked.

66:10
God has told the disbelievers the story of the wives of Noah and Lot as a parable. They were married to two of Our righteous servants but were unfaithful to them. Nothing could protect them from the (wrath) of God and they were told to enter hell fire with the others

71:1
We sent Noah to his people telling him, «Warn your people before a painful torment approaches them».

71:21
Noah said, «My Lord, indeed they have disobeyed me and followed him whose wealth and children will not increase him except in loss.

71:26
Noah also said, «My Lord, do not leave a single disbeliever on earth.

5:20

The sun, moon and stars are by my command their best instruments, and the sole possessors of them were just, while they were warm.

25:10

God has for these reasons his mercy on the Israelites of Noah's ark, and therefore, they were reduced to two of our righteous sons, and as a universal to them. Nothing could protect them from the power of God, and they were told to enter the Ark with... more...

We such faith in the Lord, sharing humble, harmonious brook, room, a gift of torment or disputes from a.

12:27

aforesaid, what of the Lord, in God, they have in store godful and followed in his name, wealth, and of children will not lose the him of them in case...

Faith and self-knowledge: by a cup of honey unutterable, one eager...

Abraham

Abraham is known as one of God's most important prophets in Islam. His two offspring, Ishmael and Isaac, became fathers of two nations. Abraham took a stand against paganism in the famous story of him breaking the idols. The Quran also talks about how Abraham was saved from the burning fire after he broke the Idols.

Abraham built Kaaba with Ishmael as the house of God for prayers (2:124-127). It is known that Abraham started the Hajj ritual (22:27-30), which continues up to this day.

Abraham is the model citizen in Islam. His devotion and complete obedience and submission to God, by following God's order to sacrifice his son for Him, passed the ultimate test. As mentioned earlier it is irrelevant which son was asked to sacrifice. The moral of the story is, if you submit to God, He rescues you and does not disappoint you, and at the end he always delivers to you "your ram" or what is better for you.

The story is perhaps an example to the rest of the world of what is meant by *total submission* to God and how it looks. If you completely submit to God, He will deliver.

In our daily prayers, in the last part, when we are sitting on the ground and finishing the prayer, after we testify that there is no God but one God and He does not take any partner and we testify that Muhammad is His messenger and His subject, then we ask God if he will elevate and bless us, like Abraham and his followers:

Oh Lord, raise Muhammad and his people, the same way you raised Abraham and his people. Indeed you are full of Glory full of Majesty.

Oh Lord, bless Muhammad and his people, the same way you blessed Abraham and his people.

Indeed you are full of Glory, full of Majesty.

Here are some of the verses in which Abraham has been mentioned in the Quran.

29:24

(Abraham's) people had no answer except suggesting, "Kill him or burn him." But God saved him from the fire. In this there is evidence (of truth) for the believing people.

2:124

When his Lord tested Abraham's faith, (by His words) and he satisfied the test, He said, "I am appointing you as the leader of mankind." Abraham asked, "Will this leadership also continue through my descendants?" The Lord replied, "The unjust do not have the right to exercise My authority."

2:125

We made the house (in Mecca) as a place of refuge and sanctuary for men. Adopt the place where Abraham stood as a place for prayer. We advised Abraham and Ishmael to keep My house clean for the pilgrims, the worshippers and for those who bow down and prostrate themselves in worship

2:126

When Abraham prayed to the Lord saying, "Lord, make this town a place of security and provide those in the town who believe in God and the Day of Judgement, with plenty," God replied, "I shall allow

ABRAHAM

those who hide the truth to enjoy themselves for a while. Then I shall drive them into the torment of hell fire, a terrible destination!"

2:127
While Abraham and Ishmael were raising the foundation of the house, they prayed, "Lord, accept our labor. You are All-hearing and All-knowing

.... Abraham starting the Hajj ritual ....

22:26
When We prepared for Abraham the place to build the Sacred House, We told him not to consider anything equal to Me and to keep the House clean for those walking around it, those standing, bowing down, and prostrating in prayer.

22:27
(We commanded Abraham), "Call people for hajj - an act of worship accomplished by visiting the sacred sites in Mecca." They will come on foot and on lean camels from all the distant quarters

22:28
To see their benefits, commemorate the name of God during the appointed days, and offer the sacrifice of the cattle that God has given them. They themselves should consume part of the sacrificial flesh and give the rest to the destitute and needy people.

22:29
Let the pilgrims then neatly dress themselves, fulfil their vows, and walk seven times around the Kabah.

....

2:130

And who turns away from the religion of Ibrahim (Abraham) (i.e. Islamic Monotheism) except him who befools himself? Truly, We chose him in this world and verily, in the Hereafter he will be among the righteous.

2:131

When God commanded Abraham to submit, he replied, "I have submitted myself to the Will of the Lord of the universe."

2:132

Abraham left this legacy to his sons and, in turn, so did Jacob saying, "God has chosen this religion for you. You must not leave this world unless you are a Muslim (submitted to the will of the Lord of the Universe)."

2:133

Had you witnessed Jacob on his death bed; he said to his children, "What will you worship after I die?" They said, "We will worship your God; the God of your fathers Abraham, Ismail, and Isaac; the one God. To Him we are submitters."

2:135

The Jews and the Christians have asked the Muslims to accept their faith to have the right guidance. (Muhammad) tell them, "We would rather follow the upright religion of Abraham who was not a pagan".

2:136

(Muslims), say, "We believe in God and what He has revealed to us and to Abraham, Ishmael, Isaac, and their descendants, and what was revealed to Moses, Jesus, and the Prophets from their Lord. We make no distinction among them and to God we have submitted ourselves."

ABRAHAM

2:140
Or do you say that Abraham and Ishmael and Isaac and Jacob and the Descendants were Jews or Christians? Say, "Are you more knowing or is God?" And who is more unjust than one who conceals a "testify" he has from God? And God is not unaware of what you do.

2:258
(Muhammad), have you heard about the one who argued with Abraham about his Lord for His granting him authority? Abraham said, "It is only my Lord who gives life and causes things to die." His opponent said, "I also can give life and make things die." Abraham said, "God causes the sun to come up from the East. You make it come from the West." Thus the unbeliever was confounded. God does not guide the unjust people

2:260
Abraham said, "My Lord, show me how You revive the dead." He said, "Do you not believe?" He said, "Yes, but I wish to reassure my heart." He said, "Take four birds, study their marks, place a piece of each bird on top of a hill, then call them to you. They will come to you in a hurry. You should know that God is Almighty, Most Wise."

3:33
God chose (and gave distinction to) Adam, Noah, the family of Abraham, and Imran over all the people of the world.

3:65
Ask the People of the Book, "Why do you argue about Abraham? The Torah and Gospel were revealed only after him. Why do you not understand?

3:67
Abraham was not a Jew or a Christian. He was an upright person who had submitted himself to the will of God. Abraham was not a pagan.

3:68
The nearest people to Abraham, among mankind, are those who followed him, this Prophet (Muhammad) and the true believers. God is the Guardian of the true believers

3:84
(Muhammad), say, "We believe in God and in that which has been revealed to us and in that which was revealed to Abraham, Ishmael, Isaac, Jacob, and their descendants. We believe in that which was given to Moses, Jesus, and the Prophets by their Lord. We make no distinction between them and we have submitted ourselves to the will of God".

3:95
(Muhammad), say, "God has spoken the Truth. Follow the upright tradition of Abraham who was not an idolater."

3:97
In (Kaaba), there are many clear signs (evidence of the existence of God). Among them is the spot where Abraham stood. Whoever seeks refuge therein will be protected by the laws of amnesty. Those who have the means and ability have a duty to God to visit the House and perform the hajj (pilgrimage) rituals. The unbelievers should know that God is Independent of all creatures.

4:54
Are they jealous of the favors that God has done to some people? We have given to the family of Abraham the Book, Wisdom, and a great Kingdom

ABRAHAM

4:125
*Who is better guided in his religion than one who submits totally to **GOD**, leads a righteous life, according to the creed of Abraham: monotheism? **GOD** has chosen Abraham as a beloved friend.*

4:163
Indeed, We have revealed to you, [O Muhammad], as We revealed to Noah and the prophets after him. And we revealed to Abraham, Ishmael, Isaac, Jacob, the Descendants, Jesus, Job, Jonah, Aaron, and Solomon, and to David We gave the book [of Psalms]

6:74
Consider when Abraham asked his father, Azar, "Why do you believe idols to be your Gods? I find you and your people in absolute error".

6:75
Also, We showed (Abraham) the kingdom of the heavens and the earth to strengthen his faith.

6:83
Such was our argument, with which we supported Abraham against his people. We exalt whomever we will to higher ranks. Your Lord is Most Wise, Omniscient.

6:84
And We gave to Abraham, Isaac and Jacob - all [of them] We guided. And Noah, We guided before; and among his descendants, David and Solomon and Job and Joseph and Moses and Aaron. Thus do We reward the doers of good.

6:161
Say, "Indeed, my Lord has guided me to a straight path - a correct religion - the way of Abraham, inclining toward truth. And he was not among those who associated others with God."

9:70
Have they not learned anything from the previous generations; the people of Noah, 'Ād, Thamûd, the people of Abraham, the dwellers of Midyan, and the evildoers (of Sodom and Gomorrah)? Their messengers went to them with clear proofs. God never wronged them; they are the ones who wronged their own souls.

9:114
The only reason Abraham asked forgiveness for his father was that he had promised him to do so. But as soon as he realized that he was an enemy of God, he disowned him. Abraham was extremely kind, clement.

11:69
When our messengers went to Abraham with good news, they said, "Peace." He said, "Peace," and soon brought a roasted calf.

11:74
When Abraham had controlled his fear and received the glad news, he started to plead with Us for the people of Lot

11:75
Indeed, Abraham was pleasant, extremely kind, and obedient.

11:76
(The angels said), "O Abraham, give up this [plea]. Indeed, the command of your Lord has come, and indeed, there will reach them a punishment that cannot be repelled."

12:6
Thus, your Lord will select you, teach you the interpretation of dreams, and grant His favors to you and the family of Jacob, just as He granted His favors to your fathers, Abraham and Isaac. Your Lord is certainly All-knowing and All-wise."

ABRAHAM

[12:38] and I have embraced the religion of my fathers, Abraham, Isaac, and Jacob. And it was not for us to partner anything with God. This is part of God's blessing to us and the people, but most people are not grateful.

14:35
Recall that Abraham said, "My Lord, make this a peaceful land, and protect me and my children from worshiping idols.

16:120
Indeed, Abraham was a [comprehensive] leader, devoutly obedient to God, inclining toward truth, and he was not of those who associate others with God

16:123
Then we inspired you (Muhammad) to follow the religion of Abraham, the monotheist; he was not of those who associates with God.

19:41
And mention in the Book [the story of] Abraham. Indeed, he was a man of truth and a prophet

19:58
These were the Prophets from the offspring of Adam, from those who embarked with Noah and from the offspring of Abraham and Israel. God guided them and chose them for His favor. Whenever they would hear the revelations of the Beneficent God they would bow down in prostration with tears.

21:51
To Abraham We gave the right guidance and We knew him very well.

21:60-63
Some of them said, "We heard a youth called Abraham speaking against the idols"
They said, "Then bring him before the eyes of the people that they may testify."
They said, "Have you done this to our Gods, O Abraham?"
He said, "Rather, this - the largest of them - did it, so ask them, if they should [be able to] speak."

21:69
We said, "O fire, be cool and safe for Abraham."

21:73
And We made them leaders guiding by Our command. And We inspired to them the doing of good deeds, establishment of prayer, and giving of zakah; and they were worshippers of Us.

22:78
Strive steadfastly for the Cause of God. He has chosen you but has not imposed on you hardship in your religion, the noble religion of your father, Abraham. God named you Muslims (submitters) before and in this Book, so that the Messenger will witness (your actions) and will be the witness over mankind. Be steadfast in your prayer, pay the religious tax, and seek protection from God; He is your Guardian, a gracious Guardian and Helper

29:16
Abraham told his people, "Worship God and have fear of Him. It is better for you if only you knew it.

29:31
And when Our messengers came to Abraham with the good tidings, they said, "Indeed, we will destroy the people of that Lot's city. Indeed, its people have been wrongdoers."

ABRAHAM

33:7
And [mention, O Muhammad], when We took from the prophets their covenant and from you and from Noah and Abraham and Moses and Jesus, the son of Mary; and We took from them a solemn covenant

38:45
Remember also our servants Abraham, Isaac, and Jacob. They were resourceful, and possessed vision.

42:13
He has plainly clarified the religion which is revealed to you and that which Noah, Abraham, Moses, and Jesus were commanded to follow (He has explained it) so that you would be steadfast and united in your religion. What you call the pagans to is extremely grave for them. God attracts to (the religion) whomever He wants and guides to it whoever turns to Him in repentance

43:26
When Abraham said to his father and his people, "I boldly renounce what you worship

43:28
God made (belief in one God) an everlasting task for his successors, so that perhaps they would return (to Him).

57:26
We sent Noah and Abraham, and we granted their descendants prophethood and the scripture. Some of them were guided, while many were wicked.

60:4
Abraham and those with him are the best examples for you to follow. They told the people, "We have nothing to do with you and with

those whom you worship besides God. We have rejected you. Enmity and hatred will separate us forever unless you believe in One God." Abraham told his father, "I shall ask forgiveness for you only, but I shall not be of the least help to you before God".

Children of Israel

The children of Israel have been mentioned in the Quran many times. The verses are mixed. Sometimes they are reminded of the blessings they have received, sometimes they are warned about their wrongdoings. They have been criticized for killing prophets of God, worshiping the golden calf, and other mischief. Some of the verses are about the history of the children of Israel, and some can be interpreted as events to come after the gathering of the children of Israel, when the great height of arrogance and the return of Jesus is a sign of Doomsday (43:61).

The following verse is about blessings they have received:

45:16
We have given the Children of Israel the scripture, wisdom, and prophethood, and provided them with good provisions; we bestowed upon them more blessings than any other people.

The following verse warns against their wrongdoings:

2:211
Ask the children of Israel about how many visible miracles We had shown them. God is certainly stern in His retribution to those who change the bounty of God (His revelation), after having received His guidance.

They were criticized and were reminded about worshiping the golden calf, and this is the reprimand they received from God:

2:93
We made a covenant with you, as we raised Mount Sinai above you, saying, "You shall uphold the commandments we have given you, strongly, and listen." They said, "We hear, but we disobey." Their hearts became filled with adoration for the calf, due to their disbelief. Say, "Miserable indeed is what your faith dictates upon you, if you do have any faith."

[2:87]
We gave the Book to Moses and made the Messengers follow in his path. To Jesus, the son of Mary, We gave the miracles and supported him by the Holy Spirit. Why do you arrogantly belie some Messengers and murder others whenever they have brought you messages that you dislike?

7:148
In Moses's absence, his people manufactured a hollow sounding calf out of their ornaments. Could they not see that it could not speak to them or provide them with any guidance? They gained only evil by worshipping the calf.

7:152
"Those who worshipped the calf will be afflicted by the wrath of their Lord and disgraced in their worldly life. Thus, We will recompense those who invent falsehood."

20:88
Then the Samiri forged the body of a motionless calf which gave out a hollow sound. The people said, "This is your Lord and the Lord of Moses whom he (Moses) forgot to mention."

20:97
Moses said, "Go away! Throughout your life you will not be able to let anyone touch you. This will be your punishment in this life. The

time for your final punishment is inevitable. You will never be able to avoid it. Look at your God which you have been worshipping. We will burn it in the fire and scatter its ashes into the sea."

Some of the verses talk about the children of Israel's history and past:

7:141
Recall that we delivered you from Pharaoh's people, who inflicted the worst persecution upon you, killing your sons and sparing your daughters. That was an exacting trial for you from your Lord.

7:105
It is incumbent upon me that I do not say about GOD except the truth. I come to you with a sign from your Lord; let the Children of Israel go.

7:134
Whenever a plague afflicted them, they said, "O Moses, implore your Lord—you are close to Him. If you relieve this plague, we will believe with you, and will send the Children of Israel with you."

7:138
We delivered the Children of Israel across the sea. When they passed by people who were worshiping statues, they said, "O Moses, make a God for us, like the Gods they have." He said, "Indeed, you are ignorant people."

10:90
We delivered the Children of Israel across the sea. Pharaoh and his troops pursued them, aggressively and sinfully. When drowning became a reality for him, he said, "I believe that there is no God except the One in whom the Children of Israel have believed; I am a submitter."

And some, like the ones below, are interpreted as events to come, especially with the current affairs of Zionism overtaking and dissolving Judaism around the world.

17:4
We addressed the Children of Israel in the scripture: "You will commit gross evil on earth, twice. You are destined to fall into great heights of arrogance."

17:104
And we said to the Children of Israel afterward, "Go live in this land. When the final prophecy comes to pass, we will summon you all in one group."

Zionism has become the image and identity of the Jews around the world. There is a difference between Judaism and Zionism. Not all pious Jews agree with Zionism. A Jew lives his life according to the laws and rituals of the Torah. Zionism is a political movement. They believe in their exclusivity as Jews, their right to Jerusalem and ownership of all the other lands they believe once belonged to them that are currently owned by others. Every Zionist "thinks" he is a Jew, but not every Jew is a Zionist.

With Zionism overtaking the image of Judaism, some of the good deeds the Jews do are not recognized or get buried under the bad reputation they have inherited from Zionism. As an example, within hours after Trump declared the Muslim ban, a mosque in the small town of Victoria, Texas, was burned to the ground. The rabbi from the B'nai Israel Temple gave the keys to their synagogue to the Muslim community so they would have a place to worship.

This is the difference between Judaism and Zionism. If a Zionist could come up with a story that the land underneath that mosque was inhibited by Jews 4,000 years ago, he would do whatever he could to claim the land underneath instead of helping them. This problem and story has been playing out in the Middle East as long as I can remember. Would America give up their land to the Native Americans because they owned it approximately 250 years ago? No. But somehow they expect others to do so, as the US, Israel, and England have been trying to redraw the maps of the Middle East since 2006 by false "springs," "different color revolutions," and wars.

Mr. Elliott Richard Freidman, the famous Bible scholar, in his books *Who Wrote the Bible?* and *The Bible with Sources Revealed*, mentions that the first five book of Moses were written by different people, giving the possibility of people who had altered the Bible depending on their motivation or purpose. Originally everyone thought the books of Moses were written by Moses. The Quran does warn against people who intentionally altered what God gave to Moses.

2:75
Do you hope, that they will believe you while indeed a group among them used to hear the words of God and then distort the Torah, after they understood it, while they (did that) knowingly?

2:79
Woe to those who write the Book themselves and say, "This is from God," so that they may sell it for a small price! Woe unto them for what they have done and for what they have gained!

Freidman in *The Bible with Sources Revealed*, page 19 writes, *"God promises Abraham the land 'from the river of Egypt to the great river, the river Euphrates' (Gen 15:18). This matches the borders attributed to David. First king of Judah."*

As a matter of fact these are the borders of King David and King Solomon.

2 Chr 9:26
He (Solomon) ruled over all the kings from the Euphrates River to the land of the Philistines, as far as the border of Egypt.

1 King 4:21
And Solomon ruled over all the kingdoms from the Euphrates River to the land of the Philistines, as far as the border of Egypt. These countries brought tribute and were Solomon's subjects all his life.

Joshua 21:43-45
So the Lord gave Israel all the land he had sworn to give their ancestors, and they took possession of it and settled there. The Lord gave them rest on every side, just as he had sworn to their ancestors. Not one of their enemies withstood them; the Lord gave all their enemies into their hands. **Not one of all the Lord's good promises to Israel failed; every one was fulfilled.**

God's promise has already been fulfilled according to Bible and was carried out during the time of David and Solomon. There is no promise in the Bible of the Jews coming back and repossessing that land again. If every country, nation, or religion in the world wanted to claim what their borders were once before, hundreds or thousands of years ago, the whole world would be at war.

To use one line from the Old Testament as an excuse to kill and uproot thousands of people to steal their land makes the Zionists no better than ISIS.

Zionism tries to champion itself as the identity of the Jewish people and a defender of their rights in appearance, but their actions, arrogance, and greed speak louder than words. According to BBC, there is a difference between Anti-Zionism and Anti-Semitism: "Israeli government and its supporters are deliberately confusing anti-Zionism with anti-Semitism to avoid criticism."

http://www.bbc.com/news/magazine-36160928

CHILDREN OF ISRAEL

Zionism has kidnapped Judaism for their own ambitions and control. Zionism has become the new "golden calf" for most Jews, and they are sacrificing their identity and core beliefs for it, despite the fact that it's against half of their Ten Commandments.

The seduction of the new "golden calf" has made most of them a worshiper of the "calf" more than what Moses brought them. They are projecting a negative image on Jews and Judaism around the world, the same way ISIS projects a negative image of Muslims and Islam around the world. Hollywood and the global media have almost completely dissolved Judaism into Zionism, and they try to force people around the world to drink this bitter juice they have created. They have injected their message through their controlling media and shoved it down people's throat, whether they like it or not, since they own the media. They cannot force people to like Zionism or the Zionists, as they have shown their true colors through their actions, not their words.

This has resulted in backlash on the Jews. The current rise in anti-Semitism in the US, Canada, and Europe, despite all the promotions of Zionism worldwide, is a good example of it. If they blame the anti-Semitism here in the US on Trump supporters, what about friendly Canada!

Ironically, they pretend they don't know what is causing the new anti-Semitism around the world, and question it in the media!

They saw the light of Moses, gathered around Moses
*Korah eclipsed, they gathered around Korah

Ascending souls reach for the Isa (Jesus)
Pharaonic souls reach for the Korah

Rumi, Persian poet 13th century
Translation and Rhyme
Faramarz F. Davati

*Korah= Qaru'n, 28:76-82 in Quran

Korah = https://en.wikipedia.org/wiki/Korah15

One of my best friends is half Jewish, my attorney for several years is Jewish, some of my doctors are Jewish, and they are some of the nicest people I have ever met and gotten to know here in the US. If they are the ambassadors of their faith, I certainly see no reason for anti-Semitism. I have never seen any of them display any arrogance as I see from the Zionist figures in the US and what comes out of the government of Israel. One has to differentiate a normal Jewish person who practices Judaism from a Zionist here in the US or abroad.

For the record, so you can see for yourself how the Zionists are breaking their own laws, the following is a list of the Ten Commandments we talked about earlier:

http://www.the-ten-commandments.org/the-ten-commandments.html

The Ten Commandments (Exodus 20:2-17) New King James Version:

1. I am the Lord your God, who brought you out of the land of Egypt, out of the house of bondage. You shall have no other Gods before Me.

2. You shall not make for yourself a carved image, or any likeness of anything that is in heaven above, or that is in the earth beneath, or that is in the water under the earth; you shall not bow down to them nor serve them. For I, the Lord your God, am a jealous God, visiting the iniquity of the fathers on the children to the third and fourth generations of those who hate Me, but showing mercy to thousands, to those who love Me and keep My Commandments.

3. You shall not take the name of the Lord your God in vain, for the Lord will not hold him guiltless who takes His name in vain.

4. Remember the Sabbath day, to keep it holy. Six days you shall labor and do all your work, but the seventh day is the Sabbath of the Lord your God. In it you shall do no work: you, nor your son, nor your daughter, nor your male servant, nor your female servant, nor your cattle, nor your stranger who is within your gates. For in six days the Lord made the heavens and the earth, the sea, and all that is in them, and rested the seventh day. Therefore the Lord blessed the Sabbath day and hallowed it.

5. Honor your father and your mother, that your days may be long upon the land which the Lord your God is giving you.

6. You shall not murder.

7. You shall not commit adultery.

8. You shall not steal.

9. You shall not bear false witness against your neighbor.

10. You shall not covet *(desire)* your neighbor's house; you shall not covet your neighbor's wife, nor his male servant, nor his female servant, nor his ox, nor his donkey, nor anything that is your neighbor's.

And for those who say the Ten Commandments only applies to Jews and not their non-Jew neighbors, here are some verses from the Bible to counter that claim.

(Dt. 24:17-18) Do not deprive the foreigner or the fatherless of justice, or take the garment of the widow as collateral for a loan. Remember that you were slaves in Egypt and the LORD YOUR GOD REDEEMED YOU FROM THERE. THAT IS WHY I COMMAND YOU TO DO THIS.

(Exod. 22:21) Do not mistreat or oppress a foreigner, for you were foreigners in Egypt.

(Exod. 12:49) The same law applies both to the native-born and to the foreigner residing among you.

Here are a few verses from the Quran on the subject of the Children of Israel:

2:211
Ask the Children of Israel how many profound miracles have we shown them! For those who disregard the blessings bestowed upon them by God, God is most strict in retribution.

4:153
the People of the Book ask you to make a Book descend to them from the heavens. However, they had asked Moses for things much harder to do than this, by saying, "Show us God in person." Thunder and lightning struck them because of their unjust demands. Despite all the evidence that had come to them, they started to worship the calf, but We forgave them for their sins and gave Moses clear authority

14:35
Recall that Abraham said, "My Lord, make this a peaceful land, and protect me and my children from worshiping idols.

5:110
God will say, "O Jesus, son of Mary, remember My blessings upon you and your mother. I supported you with the Holy Spirit, to en-

CHILDREN OF ISRAEL

able you to speak to the people from the crib, as well as an adult. I taught you the scripture, wisdom, the Torah, and the Gospel. Recall that you created from clay the shape of a bird by My leave, then blew into it, and it became a live bird by My leave. You healed the blind and the leprous by My leave, and revived the dead by My leave. Recall that I protected you from the Children of Israel who wanted to hurt you, despite the profound miracles you had shown them. The disbelievers among them said, 'This is obviously magic.

10:93
We have endowed the Children of Israel with a position of honor, and blessed them with good provisions. Yet, they disputed when this knowledge came to them. Your Lord will judge them on the Day of Resurrection regarding everything they disputed.

17:2

To Moses We gave the Book and made it a guide for the children of Israel, so that they would not have any one as their guardian other than Me

17:04
And we conveyed for the children of Israel in the Book, Surely you will cause corruption in the earth twice and surely your will reach arrogance.

17:104
And We said after Pharaoh to the Children of Israel, "Dwell in the land, and when there comes the promise of the Hereafter, We will bring you forth in [one] gathering."

20:47
So go to him and say, 'Indeed, we are messengers of your Lord, so send with us the Children of Israel and do not torment them. We

have come to you with a sign from your Lord. And peace will be upon he who follows the guidance

26:17
"'Let the Children of Israel go.'"

40:53
We have given Moses the guidance, and made the Children of Israel inherit the scripture.

44:30
And We certainly saved the Children of Israel from the humiliating torment

45:16
And We did certainly give the Children of Israel the Scripture and judgement and prophethood, and We provided them with good things and preferred them over the worlds

[61:14]
O you who have believed, be supporters of God, as when Jesus, the son of Mary, said to the disciples, "Who are my supporters for God?" The disciples said, "We are supporters of God." And a faction of the Children of Israel believed and a faction disbelieved. So We supported those who believed against their enemy, and they became dominant

2:67
Moses said to his people, God commands you to sacrifice a heifer." They said, "Are you mocking us?" He said, "I seek refuge in God from being among the ignorant."

[2:70]
They said, "Call upon your Lord to show us which one. The heifers look alike to us and, God willing, we will be guided."

In Entering the Canaan

5:24

They said O, indeed we will never enter it as long as they are in it. So you and your God, you both go and fight. Indeed we are sitting here.

5:25

(Moses) Said, Oh God, I do not have authority except over myself and my brother. So make a separation between us and this defiantly disobedient people.

5:26

(God) said, then indeed it is forbidden to them for forty years (in which), they will wander in the earth. Do not grieve over the defiantly disobedient people.

Moses

20:39
'Put him into the chest and cast it into the river, and the river will throw it onto the bank; there will take him an enemy to Me and an enemy to him.' And I bestowed upon you love from Me that you would be brought up under My eye.

Moses is perhaps the most beloved prophet in the Quran, as his name is mentioned over 140 times. Most of the stories are about him. The Quran says God loved him (20:39). He is among the favorites in Persian poetry, perhaps because he went through so much and endured for so long that everyone admires him and loves him. He is a symbol of endurance. His stories and events are the most epic stories compared to other prophets. Perhaps the closest another prophet comes to him is Noah and the building of the ark. After him, it's the stories and events of Joseph, Abraham, Jacob, Solomon, and David. But no one is as spectacular as Moses.

The Quran contains many dialogs between Moses and God. In Islam Moses is given the title "Kalimullah," meaning "The one who talked to God."

Although there are some differences between the stories in the Quran and the Torah, I like to look at them as similarities between the two religions, as they worship the same God as we Muslims do. They also believe in One God.

The following are the verses in which Moses's names have been mentioned in the Quran. You can read the verses before and after it, to become more familiar with any particular event.

Mentioning *all* the verses before and after here would have made it a very large chapter.

2:51
Then We called Moses for an appointment of forty nights. You began to worship the calf in his absence, doing wrong to yourselves.

2:53
We gave Moses the Book and the criteria (of discerning right from wrong) so that perhaps you would be rightly guided.

[2:54]
Moses said to his people, "My people, you have done wrong to yourselves by worshipping the calf. Seek pardon from your Lord and slay yourselves." He told them that it would be best for them in the sight of their Lord, Who would forgive them, for He is All-forgiving and All-merciful.

2:55
When you argued with Moses, saying that you were not going to believe him unless you could see God with your own eyes, the swift wind struck you and you could do nothing but watch

2:60
When Moses prayed for rain, We told him to strike the rock with his staff. Thereupon twelve fountains gushed out of the rock and each tribe knew their drinking place. The Lord told them, "Eat and drink from God's bounties and do not abuse the earth with corruption."

[2:61] Recall that you said, "O Moses, we can no longer tolerate one kind of food. Call upon your Lord to produce for us such earthly crops as beans, cucumbers, garlic, lentils, and onions." He said, "Do you wish to substitute that which is inferior for that which is

good? Go down to Egypt, where you can find what you asked for." They have incurred condemnation, humiliation, and disgrace, and brought upon themselves wrath from God. This is because they rejected God's revelations, and killed the prophets unjustly. This is because they disobeyed and transgressed.

[2:67] Moses said to his people, "God commands you to sacrifice a heifer." They said, "Are you mocking us?" He said, "God forbid, that I should behave like the ignorant ones."

2:87
We gave the Book to Moses and made the Messengers follow in his path. To Jesus, the son of Mary, We gave the miracles and supported him by the Holy Spirit. Why do you arrogantly belie some Messengers and murder others whenever they have brought you messages that you dislike?

2:92
And Moses had certainly brought you clear proofs. Then you took the calf [in worship] after that, while you were wrongdoers.

2:108
Do you want to address the Prophet in the same manner in which Moses was addressed? Anyone who exchanges belief for disbelief has certainly gone down the wrong path

2:136
Say, "We believe in GOD, and in what was sent down to us, and in what was sent down to Abraham, Ismail, Isaac, Jacob, and the Patriarchs; and in what was given to Moses and Jesus, and all the prophets from their Lord. We make no distinction among any of them. To Him alone we are submitters."

2:248
And their prophet said to them, "Indeed, a sign of his kingship is that the chest will come to you in which is assurance from your Lord and a remnant of what the family of Moses and the family of Aaron had left, carried by the angels. Indeed in that is a sign for you, if you are believers."

3:84
Say, "We believe in God, and in what was sent down to us, and in what was sent down to Abraham, Ismail, Isaac, Jacob, and the Patriarchs, and in what was given to Moses, Jesus, and the prophets from their Lord. We make no distinction among any of them. To Him alone we are submitters."

4:153
(Muhammad), the People of the Book ask you to make a Book descend to them from the heavens. However, they had asked Moses for things much harder to do than this, by saying, "Show us God in person." Thunder and lightning struck them because of their unjust demands. Despite all the evidence that had come to them, they started to worship the calf, but We forgave them for that and gave Moses clear authority.

4:164
And [We sent] messengers about whom We have related [their stories] to you before and messengers about whom We have not related to you. And God spoke to Moses directly.

5:20
Recall that Moses said to his people, "O my people, remember God's blessings upon you: He appointed prophets from among you, made you kings (out of your own), and granted you what He never granted any other people.

MOSES

5:22
They said, "O Moses, there are powerful people in it, and we will not enter it, unless they get out of it. If they get out, we are entering."

5:24
They said, "O Moses, indeed we will not enter it, ever, as long as they are within it; so go, you and your Lord, and fight. Indeed, we are remaining right here."

[5:44] We have sent down the Torah,* containing guidance and light. Ruling in accordance with it were the Jewish prophets, as well as the rabbis and the priests, as dictated to them in God's scripture, and as witnessed by them. Therefore, do not fear human beings; you shall fear Me instead. And do not trade away My revelations for a cheap price. Those who do not rule in accordance with God's revelations, are the disbelievers.

6:84
And We gave to Abraham, Isaac and Jacob - all [of them] We guided. And Noah, We guided before; and among his descendants, David and Solomon and Job and Joseph and Moses and Aaron. Thus do We reward the doers of good.

6:91
And they did not appraise God with true appraisal when they said, " God did not reveal to a human being anything." Say, "Who revealed the Scripture that Moses brought as light and guidance to the people? You [Jews] make it into pages, disclosing [some of] it and concealing much. And you were taught that which you knew not - neither you nor your fathers." Say, " God [revealed it]." Then leave them in their useless debate

6:154
We gave Moses the Book to complete (Our favor) for the righteous ones, the Book that contained a detailed explanation of all things, a guide and a mercy so that perhaps they would have faith in the Day of Judgment.

7:134
Whenever a plague afflicted them, they said, "O Moses, implore your Lord-you are close to Him. If you relieve this plague, we will believe with you, and will send the Children of Israel with you."

And when the punishment descended upon them (Egyptians), they said, "O Moses, pray for us your Lord by what He has promised you. If you [can] remove the punishment from us, we will surely believe you, and we will send with you the Children of Israel."

7:143
When Moses came at our appointed time, and his Lord spoke with him, he said, "My Lord, let me look and see You." He said, "You cannot see Me. Look at that mountain; if it stays in its place, then you can see Me." Then, his Lord manifested Himself to the mountain, and this caused it to crumble. Moses fell unconscious. When he came to, he said, "Be You glorified. I repent to You, and I am the most convinced believe."

7:103
After the time of those people, We sent Moses with Our miracles to Pharaoh and his people, but they too rejected Our miracles. Consider, how terrible the end of the evil-doers is!

7:104
Moses told the Pharaoh, "I am a Messengers from the Lord of the Universe.

MOSES

7:115-117
They said, "O Moses, either you throw [your staff], or we will be the ones to throw [first]."

He replied, "Throw yours first." Their great magic bewitched people's eyes and terrified them.

We inspired Moses to throw his staff, and suddenly it began to swallow-up all that the magicians had (falsely) invented

[7:127]
Some of the Pharaohs people said, "Will you let Moses and his people destroy the land and disregard you and your Gods?" The Pharaoh said, "We will kill their sons and leave their women alive; they are under our domination."

7:128
Moses told his people to seek help from God and exercise patience. The earth belongs to Him and He has made it the heritage of whichever of His servants He chooses. The final victory is for the pious ones.

7:131
When good faith came their way, they said, "We have deserved this," but when a hardship afflicted them, they blamed Moses and those with him. In fact, their faith are decided only by God, but most of them do not know.

7:134
And when the punishment descended upon them, they said, "O Moses, invoke for us your Lord by what He has promised you. If you [can] remove the punishment from us, we will surely believe you, and we will send with you the Children of Israel."

7:138
We delivered the Children of Israel across the sea. When they passed by people who were worshiping statues, they said, "O Moses, make a God for us, like the Gods they have." He said, "Indeed, you are ignorant people.

7:142
We summoned Moses for thirty nights, and completed them by adding ten. Thus, the audience with his Lord lasted forty nights. Moses said to his brother Aaron, "Stay here with my people, maintain righteousness, and do not follow the ways of the corruptors."

7:143
When Moses came at our appointed time, and his Lord spoke with him, he said, "My Lord, let me look and see You." He said, "You cannot see Me. Look at that mountain; if it stays in its place, then you can see Me." Then, his Lord manifested Himself to the mountain, and this caused it to crumble. Moses fell unconscious. When he came to, he said, "Be You glorified. I repent to You, and I am the most convinced believer."

7:144
God said, "O Moses, I have chosen you over the people with My messages and My words [to you]. So take what I have given you and be among the grateful."

7:148
In Moses' absence, his people manufactured a hollow sounding calf out of their ornaments. Could they not see that it could not speak to them or provide them with any guidance? They gained only evil by worshipping the calf

MOSES

7:150
When Moses returned to his people with anger and sorrow, he said, "What you have done in my absence is certainly evil. Why were you hasty about the commandments of your Lord?" He threw away the Tablets (which contained the commandments of God), grabbed his brother and started to pull him to himself. His brother begged him saying, "Son of my mother, the people suppressed me and almost killed me. Do not humiliate me before the enemies or call me unjust".

7:151
(Moses) said, "My Lord, forgive me and my brother, and admit us into Your mercy. Of all the merciful ones, You are the Most Merciful."

7:154
And when the anger subsided in Moses, he took up the tablets; and in their inscription was guidance and mercy for those who are fearful of their Lord

7:155
And Moses chose from his people seventy men for Our appointment. And when the earthquake seized them, he said, "My Lord, if You had willed, You could have destroyed them before and me [as well]. Would You destroy us for what the foolish among us have done? This is not but Your trial by which You send astray whom You will and guide whom You will. You are our Protector, so forgive us and have mercy upon us; and You are the best of forgivers.

7:159
Among the people of Moses are some whose guidance and Judgment are based on the Truth.

7:160
We divided the descendants of Israel into twelve tribes and told Moses to strike the rock with his staff to let twelve fountains gush out therefrom; his people had asked him to supply them with water. The twelve flowing springs were divided among them (a spring for each tribe) and each tribe knew its drinking place well. We provided them with shade from the clouds, sent down manna and quails to them for food, and told them to eat the pure things which We had given them. They did not do injustice to Us but they wronged themselves.

10:75
Then We sent after them Moses and Aaron to Pharaoh and his establishment with Our signs, but they behaved arrogantly and were a criminal people

10:77
Moses said, "Do you say [thus] about the truth when it has come to you? Is this magic? But magicians will not succeed."

10:80
When the magicians came, Moses said to them, "Throw whatever you are going to throw."

10:81
When the magicians had thrown theirs, Moses said, "What you have performed is magic. God will certainly prove it to be false; He will not make the deeds of the corrupt people righteous.

10:83
None believed with Moses except a few of his people, while fearing the tyranny of Pharaoh and his elders. Surely, Pharaoh was much too arrogant on earth, and a real tyrant.

MOSES

10:84
Moses said, "O my people, if you have really believed in GOD, then put your trust in Him, if you are really submitters."

10:87
We inspired Moses and his brother. "Maintain your homes in Egypt for the time being, turn your homes into synagogues, and maintain the Contact Prayers (Salat). Give good news to the believers."

10:88
Moses said, "Our Lord, You have given Pharaoh and his elders luxuries and wealth in this world. Our Lord, they only use them to repulse others from Your path. Our Lord, wipe out their wealth, and harden their hearts to prevent them from believing, until they see the painful retribution."

10:89
God said, "Your prayer has been answered (O Moses and Aaron), so be steadfast on the right course, and do not follow the ways of those who do not know."

10:90
We delivered the Children of Israel across the sea. Pharaoh and his troops pursued them, aggressively and sinfully. When drowning became a reality for him, he said, "I believe that there is no God except the One in whom the Children of Israel have believed; I am a submitter."

11:17
Should they be compared with those whose Lord has given them a guidance which is testified by a witness from among their own people and by the Book of Moses, a guide and a mercy. Such people do believe in this guidance (in the Quran). Those who disbelieve

(in the Quran) will have hell as their dwelling place. Thus, (Muhammad), have no doubt about it (the Quran). It is certainly the truth from your Lord, yet many people do not have faith

11:96
And We did certainly send Moses with Our signs and a clear authority

11:110
We gave the Book to Moses but people had different views about it. Had the Word of your Lord not been already ordained, He would have settled their differences (there and then). They are still in doubt about this.

14:5
We sent Moses and gave him miracles in order to lead his people from darkness into light and to remind them of the days of God. In this there is evidence (of the truth) for those who exercise patience and give thanks.

14:6
Moses told his people, "Remember the favors that God granted you when He saved you from the people of the Pharaoh who had punished you in the worst manner by murdering your sons and keeping your women alive. It was a great trial for you from your Lord

14:8
Moses told his people, "If you and everyone on the earth turn to disbelief, know that God is Self-sufficient and Praiseworthy."

17:2
(Similarly) To Moses We gave the Book and made it a guide for the children of Israel, so that they would not have any one as their guardian other than Me

MOSES

17:101
And We had certainly given Moses nine evident signs, so ask the Children of Israel [about] when he came to them and Pharaoh said to him, "Indeed I think, O Moses, that you are affected by magic.

18:60-82 (Moses meeting Khidr)
(Consider) when Moses said to his young companion, "I shall continue travelling until I reach the junction of the two seas or have travelled for many years".
When they reached the junction of the two seas they found out that they had forgotten all about the fish (which they had carried for food). The fish found its way into the sea.
Moses asked his young companion when they crossed this point, "Bring us our food; the journey has made us tired."
His companion replied, "Do you remember the rock on which we took rest? Satan made me forget to mention to you the story of the fish and how it miraculously made its way into the sea
Moses said, "That is exactly what we are seeking. They followed their own foot prints back (to the rock).
There they met one of Our servants who had received blessings and knowledge from Us
Moses asked him, "Can I follow you so that you would teach me the guidance that you have received?"
He (Khidr) replied, "You will not be able to have patience with me.
"How can you remain patient with that which you do not fully understand?"
Moses said, "If God wishes, you will find me patient and I shall not disobey any of your orders."
He said to Moses, "If you will follow me, do not ask me about anything until I tell you the story about it."
They started their journey and some time latter they embarked in a boat in which he made a hole. Moses asked him, "Did you make the

hole to drown the people on board? This is certainly very strange"
He said, "Did I not tell you that you would not be able to remain patient with me?"
Moses said, "Please, forgive my forgetfulness. Do not oblige me with what is difficult for me to endure."
They continued on their journey until they met a young boy whom he killed. Moses said, "How could you murder an innocent soul? This is certainly a horrible act".
He responded, "Did I not tell you that you will not be able to remain patient with me?"
Moses said, "If I ask you such questions again, abandon me; you will have enough reason to do so."
They continued on their journey again until they reached a town. They asked the people there for food, but no one accepted them as their guests. They found there a wall of a house which was on the verge of tumbling to the ground. The companion of Moses repaired that wall. Moses said, "You should have received some money for your labor."
He replied, "This is where we should depart from one another. I shall give an explanation to you for all that I have done for which you could not remain patient.
"The boat belonged to some destitute people who were using it as a means of their living in the sea. The king had imposed a certain amount of tax on every undamaged boat. I damaged it so that they would not have to pay the tax.
And as for the boy, his parents were believers, and we feared that he would overburden them by transgression and disbelief.
so We decided that their Lord should replace him by a better and more virtuous son.
"The tumbling wall belonged to two orphans in the town whose father was a righteous person. Underneath the wall there was a treasure that belonged to them. Your Lord wanted the orphans to find

the treasure through the mercy of your Lord when they mature. I did not repair the wall out of my own desire. These were the explanations of my deeds about which you could not remain patient."

19:51
And mention in the Book, Moses. Indeed, he was chosen, and he was a messenger and a prophet.

20:9-36
(Muhammad), have you heard the story of Moses?
When he saw the fire, he said to his family, "Wait here for I can see a fire. Perhaps I shall bring you a burning torch or find a way to some fire".
When he came to it, he was called, "O, Moses.
Indeed, I am your Lord, so remove your sandals. Indeed, you are in the sacred valley of Tuwa.
And I have chosen you, so listen to what is revealed [to you].
Indeed, I am God. There is no deity except Me, so worship Me and establish prayer so you always remember Me.
Although it is certain that the Day of Judgment will come, I prefer to keep it almost a secret so that every soul will receive the recompense for what it has done (on its own).
Let not the unbelievers who follow their vain desires make you forget the Day of Judgment, lest you will perish."
(God said) "What is this in your right hand, Moses?"
He said, "It is my staff; I lean upon it, and I bring down leaves for my sheep and I have therein other uses."

He said, "Throw it down, Moses."
So he threw it down, and thereupon it was a snake, moving swiftly.
The Lord said, "Hold the serpent and do not be afraid; We will bring it back to its original form."
"Now - as another Sign - place your hand under your arm and it will

come out sheer white without harm (or stain).
That We may show you [some] of Our greater miracles.
(God said) Go to Pharaoh. Indeed, he has transgressed."
Moses said, "Lord, grant me courage.
Make my task easy
And untie the knot from my tongue (Moses stuttered)
That they may understand my speech.
Appoint a deputy (for me) from my own people.
Aaron, my brother.
Increase through him my strength
And let him share my task
That we may glorify You much
And remember You much.
You are Well Aware of our situation."
(God) said, "Your request is granted, O Moses.

20:49
(Pharaoh) said, "Who is your Lord, O Moses."

20:57
He said, "Did you come here to take us out of our land with your magic, O Moses?

20:61
Moses said to them, "Woe to you. Do you fabricate lies to fight **GOD** *and thus incur His retribution? Such fabricators will surely fail."*

20:65
They said, "O Moses, either you throw, or we will be the first to throw."

20:67
Moses harbored some fear.

MOSES

20:70
The magicians fell prostrate, saying, "We believe in the Lord of Aaron and Moses."

20:77
We inspired Moses: "Lead My servants out, and strike for them a dry road across the sea. You shall not fear that you may get caught, nor shall you worry."

20:83
"Why did you rush away from your people, O Moses?"

20:86
Moses returned to his people, angry and disappointed, saying, "O my people, did your Lord not promise you a good promise? Could you not wait? Did you want to incur wrath from your Lord? Is this why you broke your agreement with me?"

20:88
He produced for them a sculpted calf, complete with a calf's sound.* They said, "This is your God, and the God of Moses." Thus, he forgot.

20:91
They said, "We will continue to worship it, until Moses comes back."

20:92
(Moses) said, "O Aaron, what is it that prevented you, when you saw them go astray,

21:48
We gave Moses and Aaron the principals (standards for discerning right from wrong), a beacon, and a reminder for the righteous.

23:45
Then we sent Moses and his brother Aaron with our revelations and a profound proof.

23:49
We gave Moses the scripture, that they may be guided.

25:35
We have given Moses the scripture, and appointed his brother Aaron to be his assistant.

26:10
Recall that your Lord called Moses: "Go to the transgressing people.

26:43
Moses said to them, "Throw what you are going to throw."

26:45
Moses threw his staff, whereupon it swallowed what they fabricated.

26:48
"The Lord of Moses and Aaron."

26:52
We inspired Moses: "Travel with My servants; you will be pursued."

26:61
When both parties saw each other, Moses' people said, "We will be caught."

26:63
We then inspired Moses: "Strike the sea with your staff," whereupon it parted. Each part was like a great hill.

MOSES

26:65
We thus saved Moses and all those who were with him.

27:7
Recall that Moses said to his family, "I see a fire; let me bring you news therefrom, or a torch to warm you."

27:9
"O Moses, this is Me, God, the Almighty, Most Wise.

27:10
"Throw down your staff." When he saw it moving like a demon, he turned around and fled. "O Moses, do not be afraid. My messengers shall not fear.

28:3
We recite to you herein some history of Moses and Pharaoh, truthfully, for the benefit of people who believe.

28:7
We inspired Moses' mother: "Nurse him, and when you fear for his life, throw him into the river without fear or grief. We will return him to you, and will make him one of the messengers."

28:10
The mind of Moses' mother was growing so anxious that she almost gave away his identity. But we strengthened her heart, to make her a believer.

28:15
Once he entered the city unexpectedly, without being recognized by the people. He found two men fighting; one was (a Hebrew) from his people, and the other was (an Egyptian) from his enemies. The one from his people called on him for help against his enemy.

Moses punched him, killing him. He said, "This is the work of the devil; he is a real enemy, and a profound misleader."

28:18
In the morning, he was in the city, afraid and watchful. The one who sought his help yesterday, asked for his help again. Moses said to him, "You are really a troublemaker."

28:19
Before he attempted to strike their common enemy, he said, "O Moses, do you want to kill me, as you killed the other man yesterday? Obviously, you wish to be a tyrant on earth; you do not wish to be righteous."

28:20
A man came running from the other side of the city, saying, "O Moses, the people are plotting to kill you. You better leave immediately. I am giving you good advice."

28:30
*When he reached it, he was called from the edge of the right side of the valley, in the blessed spot where the burning bush was located: "O Moses, this is Me. **GOD**; Lord of the universe.*

28:31
"Throw down your staff." When he saw it moving like a demon, he turned around and fled. "O Moses, come back; do not be afraid. You are perfectly safe.

28:36
When Moses went to them with our proofs, clear and profound, they said, "This is fabricated magic. We have never heard of this from our ancient ancestors."

MOSES

28:37
Moses said, "My Lord knows best who brought the guidance from Him, and who will be the ultimate victors. Surely, the transgressors never succeed."

28:38
Pharaoh said, "O you elders, I have not known of any God for you other than me. Therefore, fire the adobe, O Hāmān, in order to build a tower, that I may take a look at the God of Moses. I am sure that he is a liar."

28:43
We gave Moses the scripture—after having annihilated the previous generations, and after setting the examples through them—to provide enlightenment for the people, and guidance, and mercy, that they may take heed.

28:44
You were not present on the slope of the western mount, when we issued the command to Moses; you were not a witness.

28:46
Nor were you on the slope of Mount Sinai when we called (Moses). But it is mercy from your Lord, (towards the people,) in order to warn people who received no warner before you, that they may take heed.

28:48
Now that the truth has come to them from us, they said, "If only we could be given what was given to Moses!" Did they not disbelieve in what was given to Moses in the past? They said, "Both (scriptures) are works of magic that copied one another." They also said, "We are disbelievers in both of them."

28:76
Qăroon (the slave driver) was one of Moses' people who betrayed them and oppressed them. We gave him so many treasures that the keys thereof were almost too heavy for the strongest band. His people said to him, "Do not be so arrogant; God does not love those who are arrogant.

29:39
Also Qăroon, Pharaoh, and Hămăn; Moses went to them with clear signs. But they continued to commit tyranny on earth. Consequently, they could not evade (the retribution).

32:23
We have given Moses the scripture—do not harbor any doubt about meeting Him—and we made it a guide for the Children of Israel.

33:7

Recall that we took from the prophets their covenant, including you (O Muhammad), Noah, Abraham, Moses, and Jesus the son of Mary. We took from them a solemn pledge.

33:69
O you who believe, do not be like those who hurt Moses, then God absolved him of what they said. He was, in the sight of God, honorable.

37:114
We also blessed Moses and Aaron.

37:120
Peace be upon Moses and Aaron.

40:23
We sent Moses with our signs and a profound authority.

MOSES

40:26
Pharaoh said, "Let me kill Moses, and let him implore his Lord. I worry lest he corrupts your religion, or spreads evil throughout the land."

40:27
Moses said, "I seek refuge in my Lord and your Lord, from every arrogant one who does not believe in the Day of Reckoning."

40:37
"I want to reach the heaven, and take a look at the God of Moses. I believe he is a liar." Thus were the evil works of Pharaoh adorned in his eyes, and thus was he kept from following (the right) path. Pharaoh's scheming was truly evil.

40:53
We have given Moses the guidance, and made the Children of Israel inherit the scripture.

41:45
We have given Moses the scripture and it was also disputed. If it were not for your Lord's predetermined decision, they would have been judged immediately. Indeed, they harbor too many doubts.

42:13
He decreed for you the same religion decreed for Noah, and what we inspired to you, and what we decreed for Abraham, Moses, and Jesus: "You shall uphold this one religion, and do not divide it."

43:46
For example, we sent Moses with our proofs to Pharaoh and his elders, proclaiming: "I am a messenger from the Lord of the universe."

46:12
Before this, the book of Moses provided guidance and mercy. This too is a scripture that confirms, in Arabic, to warn those who transgressed, and to give good news to the righteous.

46:30
They said, "O our people, we have heard a book that was revealed after Moses, and confirms the previous scriptures. It guides to the truth; to the right path.

51:38
And in Moses [was a sign], when We sent him to Pharaoh with clear authority.

53:36
Was he not informed of the teachings in the scripture of Moses?

61:5
Recall that Moses said to his people, "O my people, why do you hurt me, even though you know that I am God's messenger to you?" When they deviated, God diverted their hearts. For God does not guide the wicked people.

Jesus & Mary

Mary has a whole chapter in the Quran by herself: Chapter 19 (Maryam). The chapter starts with Zachariah complaining to God for not having a son to carry his name, as he is getting old and his wife is barren. God gives him the good news of a baby boy named Yahyah (John), who is on his way. Then the chapter moves into how Mary is confronted by an angel. The angel gives Mary the good news of a pure boy. Mary responds asking how she can have a boy when no man has ever touched her. God blew from His own soul into Jesus. That is why Muslims call Jesus, "Ruhollah." In Arabic it means "God spirit." The virgin birth of Jesus, God equipping Jesus with the Holy Spirit, and giving Jesus miracles since childhood is all well-known and documented in the Quran. The Quran also mentions Jesus will return on Judgment Day (43:61).

43:61
(Muhammad), tell them, "Jesus is a sign of the Hour of Doom. Have no doubt about it and follow me; this is the straight path.

The Quran is very specific about who is God and who is not. God does not share his power with anyone. He sits alone on the throne. The Quran condemns giving a partner to God or giving any relation to God, as it is specific that God does not give birth to anyone and was not born from anyone (112:3). It also opposes the idea of the Trinity. According to Islam, Jesus was a man and a prophet of God. Jesus never told anyone to worship him.

5:110
GOD will say, "O Jesus, son of Mary, remember My blessings upon you and your mother. I supported you with the Holy Spirit, to enable you to speak to the people from the crib, as well as an adult. I taught you the scripture, wisdom, the Torah, and the Gospel. Recall that you created from clay the shape of a bird by My leave, then blew into it, and it became a live bird by My leave. You healed the blind and the leprous by My leave, and revived the dead by My leave. Recall that I protected you from the Children of Israel who wanted to hurt you, despite the profound miracles you had shown them. The disbelievers among them said, 'This is obviously magic.'

4:171
People of the Book, do not exceed the limits of devotion in your religion or say anything about God which is not the Truth. Jesus, son of Mary, is only a Messenger of God, His Word, and a spirit from Him whom He conveyed to Mary. So have faith in God and His Messengers. Do not say that there are three Gods. It is better for you to stop believing in the Trinity. There is only One God. He is too glorious to give birth to a son. To God belongs all that is in the heavens and the earth. God alone is a Sufficient Guardian for all.

5:15
Oh people of the book, our messenger has come to you making clear of what you have concealed from the Scriptures and overlooking many. Surely there has come to you a light from God and a clear Book.

5:110
When God said, "Jesus, son of Mary, recall My favors to you and your mother. (Recall) how I supported you by the holy spirit, made you speak to people from your cradle and when you grew up, taught you the Book, gave you wisdom, the Torah, and the Gospel.

(Recall) when, by My will, you made a sculpture of a bird out of clay, blew into it, and it turned into a real bird by My Will. (Recall) how, by My will, you healed the deaf, the lepers, and raised the dead. (Recall) when you came to the Israelites in the house with clear miracles and I saved you from their mischief, even though the disbelievers among them said, "This is obviously magic".

3:183
(Muhammad), say to those who say, 'God has commanded us not to believe any Messenger unless he offers a burnt offering,' (Muhammad) say, "Messengers came to you before me with certain miracles and with that which you had asked for (burnt offering). Why, then, did you slay them if you were true in your claim?"

In Islam, Jesus is not considered God or the son of God. He is loved and respected the same as Noah, Moses, and Muhammad, and his creation is considered similar to Adam's.

The following verses from the Quran describe Jesus, son of Mary, and Mary.

2:136
(Muslims), say, "We believe in God and what He has revealed to us and to Abraham, Ishmael, Isaac, and their descendants, and what was revealed to Moses, Jesus, and the Prophets from their Lord. We make no distinction among them and to God we have submitted ourselves." 3:52
When Jesus found them denying the truth, he said, "Who will help me in the cause of God?" The disciples replied, "We are the helpers of God. We believe in Him. Jesus, bear witness that we have submitted ourselves to His will."

3:55
He told Jesus, "I will save you from your enemies, raise you to Myself, keep you clean from the association with the disbelievers,

and give superiority to your followers over the unbelievers until the Day of Judgment. On that day you will all return to Me and I shall resolve your dispute

3:52
When Jesus sensed their disbelief, he said, "Who are my supporters towards GOD?" The disciples said, "We are GOD's supporters; we believe in GOD, and bear witness that we are submitters.

3:53
"Our Lord, we have believed in what You have sent down, and we have followed the messenger; count us among the witnesses."

3:55
Thus, GOD said, "O Jesus, I am terminating your life, raising you to Me, and ridding you of the disbelievers. I will exalt those who follow you above those who disbelieve, till the Day of Resurrection. Then to Me is the ultimate destiny of all of you, then I will judge among you regarding your disputes.

3:56
"As for those who disbelieve, I will commit them to painful retribution in this world, and in the Hereafter. They will have no helpers."

3:57
As for those who believe and lead a righteous life, He will fully recompense them. GOD does not love the unjust.

3:59
The example of Jesus, as far as God is concerned, is the same as that of Adam; He created him from dust, then said to him, "Be," and he was.

JESUS & MARY

3:84
Say, "We believe in God and in what was sent down to us, and in what was sent down to Abraham, Ismail, Isaac, Jacob, and the Patriarchs, and in what was given to Moses, Jesus, and the prophets from their Lord. We make no distinction among any of them. To Him alone we are submitters."

4:163
(Muhammad), We have sent revelations to you just as were sent to Noah and the Prophets who lived after him and to Abraham, Ishmael, Isaac, Jacob, his descendants, Jesus, Job, Jonah, Aaron, and Solomon. We gave the Psalms to David.

6:85
Also, Zachariah, John, Jesus, and Elias; all were righteous.

43:61
Muhammad), tell them, "Jesus is a sign of the Hour of Doom. Have no doubt about it and follow me; this is the straight path.

43:63
When Jesus came with clear proof (in support of his truthfulness), he said, "I have come to you with wisdom to clarify for you some of the matters in which you have disputes. Have fear of God and obey me.

2:87
And We did certainly give Moses the Torah and followed up after him with messengers. And We gave Jesus, the son of Mary, clear proofs and supported him with the Pure Spirit. But is it [not] that every time a messenger came to you, [O Children of Israel], with what your souls did not desire, you were arrogant? And a party [of messengers] you denied and another party you killed

2:253

We gave some of Our Messengers preference over others. To some of them God spoke and He raised the rank of some others. We gave authoritative proofs to Jesus, son of Mary, and supported him by the Holy Spirit. Had God wanted, the generations who lived after those Messengers would not have fought each other after the authority had come to them. But they differed among themselves, some of them believed in the authority and others denied it. They would not have fought each other had God wanted, but God does as He wills.

3:33

God chose (and gave distinction to) Adam, Noah, the family of Abraham, and Imran over all the people of the world

3:37

Her Lord graciously accepted the offer and made Mary grow up, pure, and beautiful. Zachariah took custody of her. Whenever he went to visit her in her place of worship, he would find with her some food. He would ask her, "Where did this food come from?" She would reply, "God has sent it." God gives sustenance to whomever He wants without keeping an account.

3:42

The angels said, "O Mary, God has chosen you and purified you. He has chosen you from all the women.

3:43

"O Mary, you shall submit to your Lord, and prostrate and bow down with those who bow down."

3:45

The angels said, "O Mary, God gives you good news: a Word from Him whose name is 'The Messiah, Jesus the son of Mary.' He will be prominent in this life and in the Hereafter, and one of those closest to Me.

4:156
Their hearts were also sealed because of their lack of faith, their gravely slanderous accusation against Mary,

4:157
And [for] their saying, "Indeed, we have killed the Messiah, Jesus, the son of Mary, the messenger of God." And they did not kill him, nor did they crucify him; but [another] was made to resemble him to them. And indeed, those who differ over it are in doubt about it. They have no knowledge of it except the following of assumption. And they did not kill him, for certain

4:171
People of the Book, do not exceed the limits of devotion in your religion or say anything about God which is not the Truth. Jesus, son of Mary, is only a Messenger of God, His Word, and a spirit from Him whom He conveyed to Mary. So have faith in God and His Messengers. Do not say that there are three Gods. It is better for you to stop believing in the Trinity. There is only One God. He is too glorious to give birth to a son. To God belongs all that is in the heavens and the earth. God alone is a Sufficient Guardian for all.

43:61
(Muhammad), tell them, "Jesus is a sign of the Hour of Doom. Have no doubt about it and follow me; this is the straight path.

5:17
Those who have said that the Messiah, son of Mary, is God, have, in fact, committed themselves to disbelief. (Muhammad), ask them, "Who can prevent God from destroying the Messiah, his mother

and all that is in the earth?" To God belongs all that is in the heavens, the earth, and all that is between them. God creates whatever He wants and He has power over all things.

5:46
And We sent, following in their footsteps, Jesus, the son of Mary, confirming that which came before him in the Torah; and We gave him the Gospel, in which was guidance and light and confirming that which preceded it of the Torah as guidance and instruction for the righteous

5:72
Those who say that Jesus, the son of Mary, is God, have, in fact, turned to disbelief. Jesus said to the Israelites, "Worship God, my Lord and yours. God will deprive anyone who considers anything equal to God of Paradise and his dwelling will be fire. The unjust people have no helpers."

5:75
Jesus, the son of Mary, was no more than a Messenger before whom there lived many other Messengers. His mother was a truthful woman and both of them ate earthly food. Consider how We explain the evidence (of the Truth) to them and see where they then turn.

5:78
The unbelievers among the Israelites, because of their disobedience and transgression, were condemned by David and Jesus, the son of Mary for their disobedience; they were transgressors.

5:110
When God said, "Jesus, son of Mary, recall My favors to you and your mother. (Recall) how I supported you by the holy spirit, made

you speak to people from your cradle and when you grew up, taught you the Book, gave you wisdom, the Torah, and the Gospel. (Recall) when, by My will, you made a sculpture of a bird out of clay, blew into it, and it turned into a real bird by My Will. (Recall) how, by My will, you healed the deaf, the lepers, and raised the dead. (Recall) when you came to the Israelites in the house with clear miracles and I saved you from their mischief, even though the disbelievers among them said, "This is obviously magic"

5:112
Recall that the disciples said, "O Jesus, son of Mary, can your Lord send down to us a feast from the sky?" He said, "You should reverence God, if you are believers."

5:114
Said Jesus, the son of Mary, "Our God, our Lord, send down to us a feast from the sky. Let it bring plenty for each and every one of us, and a sign from You. Provide for us; You are the best Provider."

5:116
And [beware the Day] when God will say, "O Jesus, Son of Mary, did you say to the people, 'Take me and my mother as deities besides God?'" He will say, "Exalted are You! It was not for me to say that to which I have no right. If I had said it, You would have known it. You know what is within myself, and I do not know what is within Yourself. Indeed, it is You who is Knower of the unseen.

9:31
They have taken their scholars and monks as lords besides God, and [also] the Messiah, the son of Mary. And they were not commanded except to worship one God; there is no deity except Him. Exalted is He above whatever they associate with Him.

19:16
And mention, [O Muhammad], in the Book [the story of] Mary, when she withdrew from her family to a place toward the east.

19:27
Then she brought him to her people, carrying him. They said, "O Mary, you have certainly done a thing unprecedented.

19:34
Such was the true story of Jesus, the son of Mary, about which they dispute bitterly.

21:91
As for the one who maintained her virginity, we blew into her from our spirit, and thus, we made her and her son a portent for the whole world.

23:50
And We made the son of Mary and his mother a sign and sheltered them within a high ground having level [areas] and flowing water.

27:61
Is He [not best] who made the earth a stable ground and placed within it rivers and made for it firmly set mountains and placed between the two seas a barrier? Is there a deity with God? [No], but most of them do not know

33:7
And [mention, O Muhammad], when We took from the prophets their covenant and from you and from Noah and Abraham and Moses and Jesus, the son of Mary; and We took from them a solemn covenant.

61:6

And [mention] when Jesus, the son of Mary, said, "O children of Israel, indeed I am the messenger of God to you confirming what came before me of the Torah and bringing good tidings of a messenger to come after me, whose name is Ahmad." But when he came to them with clear evidences, they said, "This is obvious magic."

61:14

Believers, be the helpers of God just as when Jesus, the son of Mary, asked the disciples, "Who will be my helpers for the cause of God?" and the disciples replied, "We are the helpers of God." A group of the Israelites believed in him and others rejected him. We helped the believers against their enemies and they became victorious

66:12

And [the example of] Mary, the daughter of 'Imran, who guarded her chastity, so We blew into [her garment] through Our angel, and she believed in the words of her Lord and His scriptures and was of the devoutly obedient.

Dealing with Our Enemies

I had promised myself not to bring politics into this book, and to leave it for the next book. But these days, with the Trump administration and their views and comments on Muslims and Islam, politics is the eight-hundred-pound gorilla in the room and cannot be ignored, despite the fact that I am advised to disregard it!

33:48
Do not yield to the disbelievers or the hypocrites. Disregard their insult and put your trust in God. God is your all Sufficient Protector.

Islam and Muslims have two sets of enemies, enemies from the inside and enemies from the outside. Our enemies from the inside are ignorant and backward religious leaders, *Ayatollahs*, *Muftis*, and *Mullahs* that have constantly pushed Islam and Muslims backward with their wrong way of thinking, lack of vision, and ignorance. We also have fanatics like any other religion, who harm from within. Currently some of our fanatics are supported and controlled by outside forces such as ISIS, Al-Qaida, and other similar groups who have become a menace to our societies and to the world.

Enemies from the outside are Israel, the US, England, Zionist groups, neocons, and far right political groups and organizations that constantly try to undermine Islam and Muslims.

The following is an excerpt from a Global Research website article in 2006:
http://www.globalresearch.ca/plans-for-redrawing-the-middle-east-the-project-for-a-new-middle-east/3882

"Hegemony is as old as mankind" (Zbigniew Brzezinski, former US National Security Advisor). The term "New Middle East" was introduced to the world in June 2006 in Tel Aviv by US Secretary of State Condoleezza Rice (who was credited by the Western media for coining the term) in replacement of the older and more imposing term, the "Greater Middle East."

The "New Middle East" project was introduced publicly by Washington and Tel Aviv with the expectation that Lebanon would be the pressure point for realigning the whole Middle East and thereby unleashing the forces of "constructive chaos." This "constructive chaos"—which generates conditions of violence and warfare throughout the region— would in turn be used so that the United States, Britain, and Israel could redraw the map of the Middle East in accordance with their geo-strategic needs and objectives.

All the recent wars in the Middle East were planned in advance and are the handiwork of these three countries. They will not stop until they destroy all the Middle East.

Which other countries in the world would do such a thing, besides these three! Presently the only people who do not know that the US and their allies directly and indirectly support the terrorist groups such as ISIS, Al-Qaida, al-Sham, and al-Nusra, are the Americans.

According to Hillary Clinton's leaked email in WikiLeaks, Saudi Arabia and Qatar are responsible for financing ISIS.

http://dailycaller.com/2016/10/10/hillary-in-leaked-email-saudi-arabia-and-qatar-are-funding-isis/

http://www.independent.co.uk/voices/hillary-clinton-wikileaks-email-isis-saudi-arabia-qatar-us-allies-funding-barack-obama-knew-all-a7362071.html

DEALING WITH OUR ENEMIES

Retired four-star general Wesley Clark in his interview with Amy Goodman on March 2, 2007, on the *Democracy Now* TV program said he was told by the Pentagon that, "We are going to take out seven countries in five years: Iraq, Syria, Lebanon, Libya, Sudan, Somalia, Iran."

Israel has become the mahout of this big war elephant called the US. The constant acts of sabotage and wars orchestrated by Israel and enforced by the US and their allies do not allow the countries in that region to have a moderate Islam. They constantly have to stay on guard, as the above three countries have already shown their true intentions and hatred in action for the past forty plus years. They have constantly tried and are still trying to create a big Sunni-Shia war, so the Muslims kill each other off to appease Israel. Unfortunately some Muslim countries think if they ally themselves with these three, they have elevated themselves. They should take heed from the following verses.

4:139
They are the ones who ally themselves with disbelievers instead of believers. Are they seeking dignity with them? All dignity belongs with GOD alone.

5:51
O you who believe, do not take certain Jews and Christians as allies; these are allies of one another. Those among you who ally themselves with these belong with them. GOD does not guide the transgressors.

4:94
O you who believe, if you strike in the cause of GOD, you shall be absolutely sure. Do not say to one who offers you peace, "You are not a believer," seeking the spoils of this world. For GOD possesses infinite spoils. Remember that you used to be like them, and

GOD blessed you. Therefore, you shall be absolutely sure (before you strike). GOD is fully Cognizant of everything you do.

4:93
Anyone who kills a believer on purpose, his retribution is Hell, wherein he abides forever, GOD is angry with him, and condemns him, and has prepared for him a terrible retribution.

So if you are a Muslim and you think all of these are going to blow away after ISIS is defeated and the situation will be normal again like before, I would have to say with disappointment you are mistaken. I will explain in the next book the reason why this will continue, as it is a lengthy subject.

As I am finishing this book, Donald Trump declared a Muslim ban against seven Muslim countries under the pretense of a terrorist attack, which provoked me to add this section, "Dealing with Our Enemies," and make a few other political comments in other chapters. The countries that are listed in the ban are Syria, Iran, Sudan, Libya, Somalia, Yemen, and Iraq. No one can figure out why he has declared a ban on these countries, despite the fact that there have been zero terrorist attacks from these countries on the US for the past forty years! Trump keeps saying the list of the countries is based on their intelligence report, an agency that he himself mocked because of their incompetence in their weapons of mass destruction report prior to the Iraq War.

The 9/11 attack was carried out by nineteen men, fifteen from Saudi Arabia, two from the United Arab Emirates, one from Egypt, and one from Libya. All were Wahhabi Sunni Muslims.

The Trump administration has declared Iran, a Shia Muslim country, the center of the Islamic terrorism around the world and in the United States. But all the terrorist attacks around the world have been done by Wahhabi Muslim groups such as Al-Qaida and ISIS that are supported by the US, Saudi Arabia, and Qatar.

DEALING WITH OUR ENEMIES

Recently a very brave US representative, Ms. Tulsi Gabbard, submitted a bill to Congress called the "Stop Arming Terrorists Act," or HR 608 according to:

https://www.congress.gov/bill/115th-congress/house-bill/608

https://gabbard.house.gov/news/StopArmingTerrorists

"We have spent trillions of dollars on regime change wars in the Middle East while communities like Hawai'i face a severe lack of affordable housing, aging infrastructure, the need to invest in education, health care, and so much more." -Rep. Tulsi Gabbard

It appears the Trump administration is trying to mislead Americans as to where the real terrorists to America, Syria, and around the world come from. It also appears that the Trump administration is trying to start another false flag war, this time with Iran. The Trump administration bases their opinions and actions on what they like to call "alternative facts," or said another way, "pure lies."

Wesley Clark has devoted a whole website against the war with Iran: www.stopiranwar.com.

They will try to come up with another "weapons of mass destruction fake news" against Iran and have the media jump on the bandwagon to start another war, similar to what they and the media did in Iraq, and are currently doing with Syria. According to Wikipedia the US killed approximately 180,000 civilians in the Iraq War. And now all of a sudden they say the Assad regime in Syria has used chemical weapons that have killed seventy some people. The United States aided Saddam Hussein with chemical weapons to be used against Iranians and Kurdish villages in the Iran-Iraq War. Mr. Trump told the media how bad he felt when he saw the picture of those children under chemical attack and that he has decided to change the regime in Syria, yet he does not allow any Syrian refugees into the US. CNN and Fox News are literally drilling the American audience with this alleged chemical attack news almost 24/7 to push for another regime change on the list, according to the 2006 "New Middle East" project in Tel Aviv, Israel.

It appears the Trump administration is trying to create a Christian-Muslim war! According to the press and media, his mentor and advisor, Mr. Bannon, thinks the Muslims are going to take over America! A population of three million, which are mostly middle-class and blue-collar workers are going to take over a country of over three hundred million! Really!? How? Financially or politically? Because we have neither one! Most Muslims in this country, like everybody else, try very hard to keep their heads above the water. Racism does not come with a head or tail. Mr. Bannon, his mentor and advisor, in his interview with *Vanity Fair* stated: Trump is a "blunt instrument for us... I don't know whether he really gets it or not"

http://www.vanityfair.com/news/2017/01/is-donald-trump-a-pawn-in-steve-bannons-game.

A blunt instrument for who? For what purpose? What was that saying, that they relate to Sinclair Lewis? "When fascism comes to America it will be wrapped in the flag and carrying a cross."

The tree they planted in Washington will bear the same fruit it gave in New York!

To uphold and praise unworthy leaders
And expecting to see a rosy future

Is only losing your reins and direction
Is growing a snake, in your own cradle

DEALING WITH OUR ENEMIES

A tree that only gives bitter fruit
Even if planted, in the gardens of Heaven

Cared and watered by the streams of heaven
Honeyed and syruped down to the root

Finally it will bring you its fruit
The same bitter fruit, that it always gave to you

> Ferdowsi, Persian poet 10th centruy
> Shahnameh (Book of Kings)
> Transalted and ryhm
> Faramarz Franco Davati

We saw their "fake news" during the Bush administration, in which under the false pretenses of "weapons of mass destruction," the US and their allies killed hundreds of thousands of civilians in Iraq, with no remorse, to steal their oil. As a matter of fact, the politicians and neocons are so belligerent they say they would do it all over again!

Just because you have a blade, it's not for killing
God doesn't forget the ones, who do the killing

Steel is not forged, just for making blades
And grapes aren't crushed, just for making wine

Jesus saw a dead man who was lying on the ground
Jesus was dismayed and asked in puzzle

Who have you ever slain? Get slain this bizarre?
And who will slay the one, who slewed you now?

ALCHEMY OF THE QURAN

Don't you lay finger, in hurting a soul
So you don't hurt too, when God throws a punch

Nasir Khusraw, Persian poet, 11th century
Translation and Rhyme
Faramarz F. Davati

Now they are trying to create another false flag war under the pretense of "weapons of mass destruction" or any other excuse they can find to start a war with Iran. Donald Trump appears to be putting together a war cabinet. Years ago Dick Cheney commented in an interview on some kind of nuclear attack or accident on a nuclear facility in the US which would result in far graver American casualties than 9/11. They have been showing the US cyber-attack on Natanz nuclear facility in Iran on HBO and other channels lately to get the public ready. I would not be surprised if they create some kind of false flag accident here in US. Then blame Iran for it to start a war, the same way they did with Iraq.

You fooled the American people, troops, and their family once, shame on you. You fool them again, shame on you again! Since you control the media and their mind.

God help the people and Muslims in Iran, around the world, and in this country. If any Muslim wants to send money or medicine back home to their family, they should do it now, before the Trump administration stops it.

3:139
So do not weaken and do not grieve, and you will be superior if you are [true] believers.

In the coming years, the Trump administration will try to put many obstacles and stumbling blocks in front of the Muslims who live here in America. As long as we Muslims keep God in the first place, trust in Him, pray to Him to vindicate us against

DEALING WITH OUR ENEMIES

our enemies, confront our enemies politically here in the US, and move forward with our lives, we will be fine. We have seen pharaohs come and go. Trump and his administration will be gone too. When your president and his advisers are racist, we Muslims have to take the high road. The best way to combat and protect yourself against Trump, Bannon, and the rest of the black crows and dark forces in his administration, is to fill yourself with the light of God. That is your best shield against these dark forces. When you are stressed, at night after your prayer, logon to the www.recitequran.com or any other similar site, CD, or anything that works for you. Play the Quran in English or any other translation that you like, and meditate.

In your meditation fill your inside with the light and love of God. When you fill your inside with the light of God, those light forces inside you protect you like a shield. Love is the strongest force in the universe. By constantly filling yourself with the light and love of God, you bring more and more of a smile to your face, you become more and more stress free, and it's your love of God, love of your life, loving yourself for whatever shape, look, weight and race you are and thanking God for everything he has given you that reflects in that "mirror" of life and gives you back exactly in life the picture you see in that mirror.

The power of Love is limitless. The power of God is limitless and can have no boundary, no limitations, no obstacles, and no conditions. You simply love God and give Him your love no matter what the condition is, and you remain patient. He will reflect back in your life what you are radiating. This is the secret of staying happy. Fill yourself with the love and light of God and be happy. You automatically defeat the enemy. Trump, Bannon, and the rest of their dark forces and supporting media will self-destruct and crumble in their own hatred for others. Moses, with only a staff in hand, and his trust-in- Lord brought down the pharaohs. We have God. They have nothing!

10:88
Moses said, "Lord, You have given the Pharaoh and his people great riches and splendor in this life and this makes them stray from Your path. Lord, destroy their wealth and harden their hearts in disbelief so that they will suffer the most painful torment."

10:89
God said, "Your prayer has been answered, so be steadfast on the right course, and do not follow the ways of those who do not know."

And if they close on you roads and byways
He will show a hidden road they do not know.

Rumi, Persian poet 13th century
Translation and Rhyme
Faramarz F. Davati

Our Relationship with Other Abrahamic Faiths

❖

(2:62, 5:69)
Surely, those who believe, those who are Jewish, Sabeans (people of the land of Sheba, today's Yemen) the Christians, and anyone who believes in GOD, and believes in the Last Day, and leads a righteous life, will receive their recompense from their Lord. They have nothing to fear, nor will they grieve.

5:48
We revealed to you [O Muhammad], the Book (Quran) in truth confirming what was before it and a protector over it. So judge among them based on what has been revealed to you and avoid their vain desires, and do not distance yourself from the truth that has come to you and do not follow them. For each of you WE have made a law and a clear way. And if God willed he would have made you one community. But he wants to test you in what he has given you. So try to compete with each other (Jews, Christians, Muslims) in doing good things. The return of all of you is to the God. Then he will reveal to you on what you were differing about.

We believe in God, the creator of the universe. For us Muslims, He is the One and Only One, the everlasting refuge and shelter. He was not born from anyone and does not give birth to anyone, and no one is equivalent to Him. Judaism also believes in our God. Christians refer to Him as Father and refer to Jesus as Son. In Hebrew, God has reportedly seven names, and one is called Eloah (God). In Islam he is Allah. In this book I have simply referred to him as God or Lord.

We pray to the same God as the Jews pray. When Muhammad and some of his followers were escaping from his enemies from Mecca, they all sought refuge in a Christian church for safety. The priest and his monks gave Muhammad and his followers refuge, safety, and food and protected them inside the church against Muhammad's enemies.

In 5:48 in the Quran, God encourages the believers of the three religions to race toward good and help mankind together.

5:48
We revealed to you [O Muhammad], the Book (Quran) in truth confirming what was before it and a protector over it. So judge among them based on what has been revealed to you and avoid their vain desires, and do not distance yourself from the truth that has come to you and do not follow them. For each of you WE have made a law and a clear way. And if God willed he would have made you one community. But he wants to test you in what he has given you. So try to compete with each other (Jews, Christians, Muslims) in doing good things. The return of all of you is to the God. Then he will reveal to you on what you were differing about.

The following are some of the verses regarding the relationships between the three religions.

(2:62, 5:69)
Surely, those who believe, those who are Jewish, Sabeans (people of the land of Sheba, today's Yemen) the Christians, and anyone who believes in GOD, and believes in the Last Day, and leads a righteous life, will receive their recompense from their Lord. They have nothing to fear, nor will they grieve.

OUR RELATIONSHIP WITH OTHER ABRAHAMIC FAITHS

[42:15] This is what you shall preach, and steadfastly maintain what you are commanded to do, and do not follow their wishes. And proclaim: "I believe in all the scriptures sent down by GOD. I was commanded to judge among you equitably. GOD is our Lord and your Lord. We have our deeds and you have your deeds. There is no argument between us and you. GOD will gather us all together; to Him is the ultimate destiny."

2:87
And indeed we gave Moses the Book and we followed him up (with a succession of) messengers. And we gave Jesus, the son of Maryam, clear signs and supported him with the Holy Spirit. Is it not so, that whenever there came to you a messenger with what you yourselves did not desire, you acted arrogantly? So a party (of Messengers) you denied and another party you killed.

2:105
Neither those who are non-believers among the people of the book, nor those who choose a partner with God, do not like anything good to come to you. But God choses whom to send his blessings, And God has endless resources and wealth.

2:109
Many of the people of the book wish they could turn you to disbelief after you have believed, out of jealousy within them, even after the truth has become clear to them. So forgive them and overlook until God brings His command. Indeed, God has power over everything.

2:113
The Jews say, "The Christians have nothing (true to stand) upon". And the Christians say, "The Jews have nothing (true to stand) upon, Although they both recite the Book. Thus say those who do not know (the Book, making) similar statements. God will judge

between them on the Day of Resurrection in (all those matters over) which they were differing (between themselves).

2:145
And even if you bring to those who were given the Book all the signs (miracles), they would not follow your direction of prayer, nor will you follow their direction of prayer. And nor would they be followers of each other's direction of prayer. And if you follow their desires after knowledge has come to you, then surely you will be among the wrong doers.

2:146
Those to whom we gave the Book, recognize it like they recognize their sons. But indeed a group of them knowingly conceal the truth.

2:177
It is not righteousness that you turn your faces towards the east or the west but righteous is he who believes in God, the Last Day, the Angels, the Book, and the Prophets and gives wealth in spite of love for it to the near relative the orphans, the needy, the drifter, and those who ask, and in freeing the slaves; and who establishes prayer and gives charity (zakat) and he who fulfills the covenant when makes it; and he who is patient in suffering, hardship, and periods of stress. Those are the ones who are true and it is those who are the righteous.

2: 285
The Messenger has believed in what was revealed to him from his Lord, and (so have) the believers. All of them have believed in God and his Angels and His book and His Messengers, (saying) " We do not make distinction between any of his messengers". And they said, " We hear and obey. Grant us Your forgiveness, our Lord, and to You is the return".

OUR RELATIONSHIP WITH OTHER ABRAHAMIC FAITHS

3:7
He is the one who revealed to you the Book, in it are verses which are absolutely clear – they are the foundation of the Book and others are symbolic, (representation, similar). Then as for those in whose hearts is perversity- they follow what is symbolic from the book, seeking discord and seeking its interpretation. And none except God knows it's true interpretation. And those who are firm in knowledge say, we believe in it. All (of it) is from our Lord." And no one will notice except men of understanding.

3:65
O People of the Book! Why do you argue about Abraham while the Tauraut and injeel were not revealed until after him? Then why don't you use your intellect?

3:113
They are not (all) the same among the people of the book (amongst) them is a group that stands (stands for) and recite the verses of God in the hours of night and they face down to the ground and pray to God.

3:199
Surely, some followers of the previous scriptures do believe in GOD, and in what was revealed to you, and in what was revealed to them. They reverence GOD, and they never trade away GOD's revelations for cheap. These will receive their recompense from their Lord. GOD is the most efficient in reckoning.

4:136
Oh you who believe! Believe in God and His Messenger, and the Book which He revealed before. And whoever disbelieves in God, His Angels, His books, His Messengers and the Last day, then surely he has gone stray too far.

4:140
And surely He has revealed to you in the Book that when you hear the Verses of God being rejected and ridiculed, then do not sit with them until they engage in some other conversation. Indeed, you would then be them. Indeed, God will gather the hypocrites and disbelievers in Hell all together.

4:171
Oh people of the Book do not exaggerate in your religion and do not say about God but the truth about the savior Isa son of Maryam, a messenger of God and His word which he conveyed to Maryam and a spirit from Him. So believe in God and his messengers and do not say three desist. It is better for you only one God. Glorious and dignified he is from having a son. Whatever it is in the heaven and on earth belong to him. And is enough to take care of the affairs.

5:15
Oh people of the book, our messenger has come to you making clear of what you have concealed from the Scriptures and overlooking many. Surely there has come to you a light from God and a clear Book.

5:19
O people of the Book! Surely has come to you Our Messenger to make clear to you (the religion) after an interval (of interruption) of prophets to clear His message to you, so you do not say we did not had (prophet) who bring a good news and a warner. God is All-powerful over everything.

5:48
We revealed to you the Book (Quran) in truth confirming what was before it and a protector over it. So judge among them based on

OUR RELATIONSHIP WITH OTHER ABRAHAMIC FAITHS

what has been revealed to you and avoid their vain desires, and do not distance yourself from the truth that has come to you and do not follow them. For each of you WE have made a law and a clear way. And if God willed he would have made you one community. But he wants to test you in what he has given you. So try to compete with each other (Jews, Christians, Muslims) in doing good things. The return of all of you is to the God. Then he will reveal to you on what you were differing about.

5:57
Oh you who believe do not take those who ridicule and make fun of your religion as friend, regardless if they are from the people of the Book or disbelievers. And fear God if you are a believer.

5:59
Say O' People of Book isn't it that you resent us because we believe in God and what has been revealed to us and what was revealed before and most of you are defiantly disobedient.

5:65
And if the people of the Book had believed and feared God, we would have removed from them their sins and surely we would have admitted them to gardens of pleasure.

5:68
Say O' people of the Book, you are not (standing) on anything until you uphold the (laws) of Taurat and the Gospel and what has been revealed to you from your Lord. And surely many of them will rebel against you for what has been revealed to you from your Lord with disbelief, so do not grieve over the disbelieving people.

5:77
Say O' people of the book do not exaggerate in your religion other than the truth and do not follow (vain) desires of people who went

astray in the past and misled many and went astray from the right path.

5:110
Then God said O, Isa (Jesus) son of Maryam, remember my favors upon you and your mother when I strengthened you with Holy spirit. You spoke to the people in the cradle and in maturity I taught you the Book, the wisdom, the Taurat, Injeel, and when you make a bird with clay and by my permission when you breath into it, it became a bird, by my permission you heal the born blind and the leper, by my permission your brought back the dead, by my permission I restrained the children of Israel from you. When you came to them with proof then said those who disbelieved this is nothing but clear magic.

6:89
Those are the one that we gave them prophet hood, judgment and the Book. But if they (people who place an associate with God) disbelieve in it, we will entrust it to a group of people who are not disbelievers.

6:91
And they did not praise the Lord the way they should have and they said God did not reveal anything to human beings, say who revealed the book to Moses, as a light and guidance to people? You made it into rolled up papers and disclosed some of it and concealed much of it. And you were taught things that you and your forefathers did not know. Say God revealed it, then leave them playing in their debates.

6:114
Then is it other than God I should seek as judge while it is HE Who has revealed to you the Book explained in detail? And those to

whom We gave the Book know that it is sent down from your Lord in truth, so do not be among the doubters.

6:155
And this is a blessed book which we have revealed, so follow it and fear God so that you may receive mercy.

6: 156
We revealed it, so you do not say, the Book was only revealed to the two groups before us, and indeed was unaware about their study.

7:170
And those who cling (refuge) to the Book and establish the prayer, We indeed will not let the reward of the reformers go to waste. (We will not disappoint them)

10:37
And isn't this that the Quarn, could not have been produced by other than God, and it is a confirmation of what it came before it and a detailed explanation of the Book, there is no doubt in it, (it is) from the Lord of the world.

10:61
And not you are in any situation and not you recite from Quran and you do not do any deed except We are witness over you when you are engaged in it. And even the smallest weight cannot escape from your Lord neither on earth or heaven. And there is nothing smaller or bigger that will not be recorded in the clear book (book of deeds).

10:94
So if you (Muhammad) are in doubt of what we have revealed to you, then ask those who have been reading the Book before you.

Certainly, the truth has come to you from you're your Lord, so do not be among the doubters.

11:1

Alif Lam Ra (A L R, alphabets), (This is) a Book that is verses are perfected and then its presented in detail from the one who explained in detail by the one who is wise and aware.

11:17
Then is he, who is on a clear proof from his Lord and recites it, a witness from Him. And before it (was) a book of Moses (as) a guide and (as) mercy for those who believe in it. But whoever disbelieves in it among the sects, then the Fire (will be) his promised (meeting) place. So (do) not be in doubt about it. Indeed it is the truth from Your Lord, but most of the people do not believe.

14:01
Alif, Lam, Ra. [This is] a book which We have revealed to you, [O Muhammad], that you might bring mankind out of darkness into the light by permission of their lord to the path of Almighty, the praiseworthy.

16:64
We have sent you the book for no other reason than to settle their differences and to be a guide and mercy for those who believe.

17:55
And your Lord is most knowing whoever is in the heavens and the earth. And indeed we have preferred some of the prophets above others. And we gave David the book of Psalm.

19:56
And mention in the Book, Enoch (Idrees). Indeed, he was a man of truth and a prophet.

OUR RELATIONSHIP WITH OTHER ABRAHAMIC FAITHS

21:105
And we have already written in the book of Psalm, after the previous mention, that my righteous slaves will inherit the earth

23:49
We gave the Book to Moses so that perhaps they may have guidance.

29:45
(Muhammad), recite to them what has been revealed to you in the Book and be steadfast in prayer; prayer keeps one away from indecency and evil. It is the greatest act of worshipping God. God knows what you do.

32:02
There is no doubt that this Book is revealed by the Lord of the Universe.

35:29
Those who recite the Book of God, who are steadfast in prayer and, who spend out of what We have given them for the cause of God, both in public and in private, hope for a gain which will not perish.

39:41
(Muhammad), We have revealed the Book to you for mankind in all truth. Whoever seeks guidance does so for his own good. Whosoever goes astray goes against his own soul. You are not their representative

[42:15] This is what you shall preach, and steadfastly maintain what you are commanded to do, and do not follow their wishes. And proclaim: "I believe in all the scriptures sent down by GOD. I was commanded to judge among you equitably. GOD is our Lord and your Lord. We have our deeds and you have your deeds. There is

no argument between us and you. GOD will gather us all together; to Him is the ultimate destiny."

42:52
Thus, We have revealed to you an inspiration of Our command, (Muhammad). Before, you did not even know what a Book or Faith was, but We have made the Quran as a light by which We guide whichever of Our servants We want. You certainly guide (people) to the right path.

Loving God and Why Are We Here?

❖

The following is the author's own point of view. It is not from the Quran:

Many of my friends raised their eyebrows when I wrote this book, as they know me through my lighthearted conversations and jokes. I have mostly kept my religious and spiritual side to myself, as it has been a personal passion. I hope the following line from one of Hafez's poems will be sufficient to all my friends or my critics.

The universe couldn't wait for destiny
Of all people, it picked crazy me!

> Hafez, Persian poet 14th century
> Translation and Rhyme
> Faramarz F, Davati

It has taken me over ten years to write this book, which has been ten years of pure joy, wandering through this heavenly treasure and the old scholars' notes and poems. I only did one to two hours almost every morning. The saddest day was the last day when I finished this book.

What is interesting for me is that I learned something new about myself by writing this book! I have never, ever said a poem or translated a poem in my life in any language. It was only through the last year of this book when I attempted to rhyme the story of "Moses and Shepherd" by Rumi, that I realized how much I enjoyed translating and literally saying those poems in English within the same content. I know I have to work on it, but I think I may have an inclination in this field! I consider it a gift from God for my retirement days! I came across over 1,200 lines of Rumi's poetry that are directly related to different verses in the Quran, and most poems carry verbatim parts of the Quran's verses. Rumi has even more poems that he has taken from different verses of the Quran. Perhaps if time allows, I will write a separate book for all of those. Deciphering, analyzing, and arguing his poetry is hard and heavy enough for those who are familiar with his work, let alone trying to translate and rhyme it, as I tried to do some in this book.

During my research and going through some of the work of Old Persian scholars in Islam, I realized how advanced they were in their thinking and analysis of the Quran, compared to today's Islam and its interpretation of not only the Quran but the religion itself. Unfortunately we have lost what was gained before and have gone backward. Hopefully in the coming years logic and common sense will take priority in the interpretation of our holy book, the Quran, without compromising the fundamentals of Islam. (Chapter 3, General Fundamentals of Islam).

The questions of why we are here and what the purpose of this life is, have been asked since the dawn of man. From what we learn from the Quran and other religions, God is eternal. Among His many characteristics He is also loving; therefore His love is eternal.

In my opinion, despite the fact that God is perfect, He is lonely! He has built this vast universe with billions of planets of rocks, dirt, gases, and minerals, all empty as far as we can see! And now what? Imagine someone very capable who is also very loving, living in the biggest, most luxurious castle all by Himself. Lonely. No one around, except some servants called angels. Now what?

How many millions of years can God watch these planets turn around themselves? And for what purpose? Do any of them give God love? No.

76:1
There was certainly a time when there was no mention of the human being.

God does not need anyone, but He is certainly appreciative those who love Him back.

39:7
If you disbelieve, GOD does not need anyone. But He dislikes to see His servants make the wrong decision. If you decide to be appreciative, He is pleased for you. No soul bears the sins of any other soul. Ultimately, to your Lord is your return, then He will inform you of everything you had done. He is fully aware of the innermost thoughts.

For a loving God, He is pleased with someone who appreciates Him. Not that He needs it, but He appreciates it. And I believe He definitely notices the ones that appreciate Him. How can He not!

He created Adam in His own image, with some of His own capabilities and characteristics, including love. He loved Adam and taught him the name of things. God showed him off in front of the angels, as they did not know the names, but Adam knew. His love for Adam was so great that it created jealousy among the angels. Adam did not need anything, as everything was ready and available for him in Paradise.

Adam roaming around lonely in Paradise is a reflection of the Almighty Himself in His vast universe. It is somewhat of a giveaway of His loneliness. At the beginning God created just Adam, as lonely as Himself. There was no plan of Eve. When God saw how lonely Adam was, that's when He created Eve.

They were cast out from heaven to earth and were instructed to populate the earth. The rules were simple and have been taught by many prophets of God: Love God, pray to God, praise and thank Him, and do good, and in return you will be blessed and God will love you back. He will love you back in the form of blessings in your life, answering your prayers and needs.

Now, how do we love God, besides praying and worshiping Him? We try to become His friend.

How do we become a friend of God? By helping others who are in need. Some say by becoming an angel of God on earth.

To become God's friend means we do good deeds and help others not because we are worried about Hell and the Judgment Day, or expect blessings, or want to score points and credit with God to go to heaven!

We help others because we consider ourselves a friend of God, we like Him and we consider ourselves an extension of his hands to do his work to help others.

4:125
Who is better guided in his religion than one who submits totally to GOD, leads a righteous life, according to the creed of Abraham: monotheism? **GOD has chosen Abraham as a beloved friend.**

9:76
*And they feed, for **love of Him,** the poor, the orphan, and the prisoner*

2:177
Righteousness is not determined by facing East or West during prayer. Righteousness consists of the belief in God, the Day of Judgment, the angels, the Books of God, His Prophets; to give

*money **for the love of Him** to relatives, orphans, the destitute, and those who are on a journey and in urgent need of money, beggars; to set free slaves and to be steadfast in prayer, to pay the religious tax (zakah) to fulfill one's promises, and to exercise patience in poverty, in distress, and in times of war. Such people who do these are truly righteous and pious.*

As mentioned, the rules are simple. You love God and He will love you back. We are not forced to love God, as He has given us a choice. If you love Him, you will receive His blessings.

[5:54]
*O you who believe, if you revert from your religion, then GOD <u>will substitute in your place people</u> whom **He loves** and **who love Him.** They will be kind with the believers, stern with the disbelievers, and will strive in the cause of GOD without fear of any blame. Such is GOD's blessing; He bestows it upon whomever He wills. GOD is giving and, All knowing.*

19:96
*To the righteously striving believers **God will grant love.***

He loves to love those who love Him, and their love for Him is as genuine as His is for them. That is why He tests us (29:2, 3:186, 21:35, 21:111).

21:35
Every soul will taste death, after we put you to the test through adversity and prosperity, then to us you ultimately return.

21:111
"For all that I know, this world is a test for you, and a temporary enjoyment."

You cannot fool God! It's a two-way street in this exchange. The more you love God, the more love you get back from Him. That is why all the scholars have agreed that love is the strongest force in the universe.

This exchange and cycle of love, prayer, and worship between God and *his own image* have been going on for thousands of years.

6:162
Say, "Indeed, my prayer, my rites of sacrifice, <u>my living and my dying are for God</u>, Lord of the worlds

48:9
That you people may believe in GOD and His messenger, and reverence Him, and observe Him, and glorify Him, day and night.

This cycle will continue until the day life comes to an end on this planet, when He decides it. The Quran gives a hint that it all will be ended by a meteor (44:10-11 *"Then wait for the day when the sky will bring a visible smoke that shall overtake people; this is a painful torment"*). There will be a Judgment Day after it, but where and when only God knows.

Even then, I would not be surprised if He starts again brand new on other planets, if He hasn't already done so. As this cycle of love exchange between God and His subjects will go on and last forever, because God and His love are eternal and last forever.

29:19
Have they not seen how GOD initiates the creation, then repeats it? This is easy for GOD to do.

Some may argue or criticize that God only brings us to this world for His own amusement and love. And some may argue back that for the same reason, we decide to have children and have the love of the children!

You love your children, take care of them, and like to see how far they go!

It's perhaps something like that—God would like to see how far His own image can go with the capabilities that He has given them! And He does not want to see us go down the wrong path or make the wrong decision (39:7).

The key here is understanding the enormous power of "love" and how it can create a response back from the Almighty, Who moves the universe.

Granted, when we are faced with Evil and our enemies, we have to stand up to them and fight them as God has instructed us to do so, and not befriend them. But in our personal relationships with others, "love" is the answer.

Now that it seems the secret behind our creation might have been "love," and this "love" in everything is the strongest force in the universe, it is up to us to decide how we will use this enormous power God has given us.

Drunk and stuck up we are, we don't care what others do
If the world implodes one day, forever Your love remains

Your love if starts boiling, will put up hundreds of earths
In the hollows of the cosmos, will be born thousands of years

*Drunk here means "Drunk" with the Love of God

Rumi, Persian poet 13th century
Translation and Rhyme
Faramarz F, Davati

Now you have at least a basic introduction to the Quran, the message it contains, and how to apply it in your life. I have also included additional information in the appendices. For those who are interested, there is a collection of some verses from the Quran in Appendix 1, as well as instruction on how to pray in Appendix 2.

Appendix – I

Miscellaneous Verses from the Quran

[9:51] Say, "Nothing happens to us, except what GOD has decreed for us. He is our Lord and Master. In GOD the believers shall trust."

[10:63] They are those who believe and lead a righteous life.

[2:161] Those who disbelieve and die as disbelievers, have incurred the condemnation of GOD, the angels, and all the people (on the Day of Judgment).

[2:172] O you who believe, eat from the good things we provided for you, and be thankful to GOD, if you do worship Him alone.

[2:256]
There is no persuasion in religion. Certainly, right has become clearly distinct from wrong. Whoever rejects the devil and believes in God has firmly taken hold of a strong handle that never breaks. God is All-hearing and knowing.

[9:38] O you who believe, when you are told, "Mobilize in the cause of GOD," why do you become heavily attached to the ground? Have you chosen this worldly life in place of the Hereafter? The materials of this world, compared to the Hereafter, are nil.

[9:111] GOD has bought from the believers their lives and their money in exchange for Paradise. Thus, they fight in the cause of GOD, willing to kill and get killed. Such is His truthful pledge in the

Torah, the Gospel, and the Quran-and who fulfills His pledge better than GOD? You shall rejoice in making such an exchange. This is the greatest triumph.

[10:45] On the day when He summons all of them, they will feel as if they lasted in this world one hour of the day, during which they met. Losers indeed are those who disbelieved in meeting GOD; and chose to be misguided.

[13:33] Is there any equal to the One who controls every single soul? Yet, they set up idols to rival God. Say, "Name them. Are you informing Him of something on earth that He does not know? Or, are you fabricating empty statements?" Indeed, the schemes of those who disbelieve have been adorned in their eyes. They are thus diverted from the right path. Whomever GOD sends astray can never find a guiding teacher.

[57:28] O you who believe, you shall reverence God and believe in His messenger. He will then grant you double the reward from His mercy, endow you with light to guide you, and forgive you. God is Forgiver, Most Merciful.

[2: 285] The Messenger has believed in what was revealed to him from his Lord, and (so have) the believers. All of them have believed in God and his Angels and His book and His Messengers, (saying) " We do not make distinction between any of his messengers". And they said, " We hear and obey. Grant us Your forgiveness, our Lord, and to You is the return".

[3:67] Abraham was neither a Jew or a Christian, but he was a true believer and he was not of those who associated partners with God. (believed God has a partner)

APPENDIX – I

[2:25] And give good news to those who believe and do righteous deeds that they will have gardens [in Paradise] beneath which rivers flow. Whenever they are provided with a provision of fruit therefrom, they will say, "This is what we were provided with before." And it is given to them in likeness. And they will have therein purified spouses, and they will abide therein eternally.

[2:62] Surely, those who believe those who are Jewish, the Christians, and the converts; anyone who (1) believes in GOD, and (2) believes in the Last Day, and (3) leads a righteous life, will receive their recompense from their Lord. They have nothing to fear, nor will they grieve.

Indeed, those who believed and those who were Jews or Christians or Sabeans [before Prophet Muhammad] - those [among them] who believed in God and the Last Day and did righteousness - will have their reward with their Lord, and no fear will there be concerning them, nor will they grieve.

[2:109] Many of the people of the book wish they could turn you to disbelief after you have believed, out of jealousy within them, even after the truth has become clear to them. So forgive them and overlook until God brings His command. Indeed, God has power over everything.

[2:257] God is the Guardian of the believers and it is He who takes them out of darkness into light. The Devil is the guardian of those who deny the Truth and he leads them from light to darkness. These are the dwellers of hell wherein they will live forever.

[2:258] (Muhammad), have you heard about the one who argued with Abraham about his Lord for His granting him authority? Abraham said, "It is only my Lord who gives life and causes things to

die." His opponent said, "I also can give life and make things die." Abraham said, "God causes the sun to come up from the East. You make it come from the West." Thus the unbeliever was confounded. God does not guide the unjust people

[2:260] When Abraham prayed, "Lord, show me how you bring the dead back to life," the Lord said, "Do you not yet believe?" Abraham replied, "I believe but want more confidence for my heart." God told him, "Take four birds, induce them to come to you, cut and scatter their bodies leaving parts on every mountain top, then call them and they will swiftly come to you." Know that God is Majestic and Wise

[2:285] The messenger has believe in what was sent down to him from his Lord, and so did the believers. They believe in GOD, His angels, His scripture, and His messengers: "We make no distinction among any of His messengers." They say, "We hear, and we obey.* Forgive us, our Lord. To You is the ultimate destiny."

[3:39] The angels called him when he was praying in the sanctuary: "GOD gives you good news of John; a believer in the word of GOD, honorable, moral, and a righteous prophet."

[3:49] As a messenger to the Children of Israel: "I come to you with a sign from your Lord-I create for you from clay the shape of a bird, then I blow into it, and it becomes a live bird by GOD's leave. I restore vision to the blind, heal the leprous, and I revive the dead by GOD's leave. I can tell you what you eat, and what you store in your homes. This should be a proof for you, if you are believers.

[3:52] When Jesus sensed their disbelief, he said, "Who are my supporters towards GOD?" The disciples said, "We are GOD's supporters; we believe in GOD, and bear witness that we are submitters.

APPENDIX – I

[3:53] "Our Lord, we have believed in what You have sent down, and we have followed the messenger; count us among the witnesses."

[3:55] Thus, GOD said, "O Jesus, I am terminating your life, raising you to Me, and ridding you of the disbelievers. I will exalt those who follow you above those who disbelieve, till the Day of Resurrection. Then to Me is the ultimate destiny of all of you, then I will judge among you regarding your disputes.

[3:56] "As for those who disbelieve, I will commit them to painful retribution in this world, and in the Hereafter. They will have no helpers."

[3:57] As for those who believe and lead a righteous life, He will fully recompense them. GOD does not love the unjust.

[3:68] The people most worthy of Abraham are those who followed him, and this prophet, and those who believe. GOD is the Lord and Master of the believers.

[3:84] Say, "We believe in GOD, and in what was sent down to us, and in what was sent down to Abraham, Ismail, Isaac, Jacob, and the Patriarchs, and in what was given to Moses, Jesus, and the prophets from their Lord. We make no distinction among any of them. To Him alone we are submitters."

[3:114] They believe in GOD and the Last Day, they advocate righteousness and forbid evil, and they hasten to do righteous works. These are the righteous.

[3:118] O you who believe, do not befriend outsiders who never cease to wish you harm; they even wish to see you suffer. Hatred flows out of their mouths and what they hide in their chests is far worse. We thus clarify the revelations for you, if you understand.

[3:119] Here you are loving them, while they do not love you, and you believe in all the scripture. When they meet you they say, "We believe," but as soon as they leave they bite their fingers out of rage towards you. Say, "Die in your rage." GOD is fully aware of the innermost thoughts.

[3:139] So do not weaken and do not grieve, and you will be superior if you are [true]believers.

[3:140] If you suffer hardship, the enemy also suffers the same hardship. We alternate the days of victory and defeat among the people. GOD thus distinguishes the true believers, and blesses some of you with martyrdom. GOD dislikes injustice.

[3:141] GOD thus toughens those who believe and humiliates the disbelievers. disbelievers.

[3:149] O you who believe, if you obey those who disbelieve, they will turn you back on your heels, then you end up losers.

[3:164] GOD has blessed the believers by raising in their midst a messenger from among them, to recite for them His revelations, and to purify them, and to teach them the scripture and wisdom. Before this, they had gone totally astray.

[3:175] It is the devil's system to instill fear into his subjects. Do not fear them and fear Me instead, if you are believers.

[3:176]. Do not be saddened by those who hasten to disbelieves. They never hurt GOD in the least. Instead, GOD has willed that they will have no share in the Hereafter. They have incurred a terrible retribution.

APPENDIX – I

[3:179] GOD is not to leave the believers as you are, without distinguishing the bad from the good. Nor does GOD inform you of the future, but GOD bestows such knowledge upon whomever He chooses from among His messengers.* Therefore, you shall believe in GOD and His messengers. If you believe and lead a righteous life, you receive a great recompense.

[3:196] Do not be impressed by the apparent success of disbelievers.

[3:200] O you who believe, you shall be steadfast, you shall persevere, you shall be united, you shall observe GOD, that you may succeed.

[4:19] O you who believe, it is not lawful for you to inherit what the women leave behind, against their will. You shall not force them to give up anything you had given them, unless they commit a proven adultery. You shall treat them nicely. If you dislike them, you may dislike something wherein GOD has placed a lot of good.

[4:29] O you who believe, do not consume each other's' properties illicitly- only mutually acceptable transactions are permitted. You shall not kill yourselves. GOD is Merciful towards you.

[4:57] As for those who believe and lead a righteous life, we will admit them into gardens with flowing streams; they abide therein forever. They will have pure spouses therein. We will admit them into a blissful shade.

[4:59] O you who believe, you shall obey GOD, and you shall obey the messenger, and those in charge among you. If you dispute in any matter, you shall refer it to GOD and the messenger, if you do believe in GOD and the Last Day. This is better for you, and provides you with the best solution.

[4:60] Have you noted those who claim that they believe in what was revealed to you, and in what was revealed before you, then uphold the unjust laws of their idols? They were commanded to reject such laws. Indeed, it is the devil's wish to lead them far astray.

[4:76] Those who believe are fighting for the cause of GOD, while those who disbelieve are fighting for the cause of tyranny. Therefore, you shall fight the devil's allies; the devil's power is nil.

[4:84] You shall fight for the cause of GOD; you are responsible only for your own soul, and exhort the believers to do the same. GOD will neutralize the power of those who disbelieve. GOD is much more powerful, and much more effective.

[4:89] They wish that you disbelieve as they have disbelieve, then you become equal. Do not consider them friends, unless they mobilize along with you in the cause of GOD. If they turn against you, you shall fight them, and you may kill them when you encounter them in war. You shall not accept them as friends, or allies.*

[4:93] Anyone who kills a believer on purpose, his retribution is Hell, wherein he abides forever, GOD is angry with him, and condemns him, and has prepared for him a terrible retribution.

[4:94] O you who believe, if you strike in the cause of GOD, you shall be absolutely sure. Do not say to one who offers you peace, "You are not a believer," seeking the spoils of this world. For GOD possesses infinite spoils. Remember that you used to be like them, and GOD blessed you. Therefore, you shall be absolutely sure (before you strike). GOD is fully Cognizant of everything you do.

[4:95] Not equal are the sedentary among the believers who are not handicapped, and those who strive in the cause of GOD with their money and their lives. GOD exalts the strivers with their money

APPENDIX – I

and their lives above the sedentary. For both, GOD promises salvation, but GOD exalts the strivers over the sedentary with a great recompense.

[4:101] When you travel, during war, you commit no error by shortening your Contact Prayers (Salat), if you fear that the disbelievers may attack you. Surely, the disbelievers are your ardent enemies.

[4:103] Once you complete your Contact Prayer (Salat), you shall remember GOD while standing, sitting, or lying down.* Once the war is over, you shall observe the Contact Prayers (Salat); the Contact Prayers (Salat) are decreed for the believers at specific times.

[4:122] As for those who believe and lead a righteous life, we will admit them into gardens with flowing streams, wherein they live forever. Such is the truthful promise of GOD. Whose utterances are more truthful than GOD's?

[4:135] O you who believe, you shall be absolutely equitable, and observe GOD, when you serve as witnesses, even against yourselves, or your parents, or your relatives. Whether the accused is rich or poor, GOD takes care of both. Therefore, do not be biased by your personal wishes. If you deviate or disregard (this commandment), then GOD is fully Cognizant of everything you do.

[4:136] O you who believe, you shall believe in GOD and His messenger, and the scripture He has revealed through His messenger, and the scripture He has revealed before that. Anyone who refuses to believe in GOD, and His angels, and His scriptures, and His messengers, and the Last Day, has indeed strayed far astray.

[4:139] They are the ones who ally themselves with disbelievers instead of believers. Are they seeking dignity with them? All dignity belongs with GOD alone

ALCHEMY OF THE QURAN

[4:140] He has instructed you in the scripture that: if you hear GOD's revelations being mocked and ridiculed, you shall not sit with them, unless they delve into another subject. Otherwise, you will be as guilty as they are. GOD will gather the hypocrites and the disbelievers together in Hell.

[4:144] O you who believe, you shall not ally yourselves with the disbelievers, instead of the believers. Do you wish to provide GOD with a clear proof against you?

[4:146] Only those who repent, reform, hold fast to GOD, and devote their religion absolutely to GOD alone, will be counted with the believers. GOD will bless the believers with a great recompense.

[4:147] What will GOD gain from punishing you, if you became appreciative and believe d? GOD is Appreciative, Omniscient.

[4:152] As for those who believe in GOD and His messengers, and make no distinction among them, He will grant them their recompense. GOD is Forgiver, Most Merciful.

[4:155] (They incurred condemnation) for violating their covenant, rejecting GOD's revelations, killing the prophets unjustly, and for saying, "Our minds are made up!" In fact, GOD is the One who sealed their minds, due to their disbelief, and this is why they fail to believe, except rarely.

[4:159] Everyone among the people of the scripture was required to believe in him before his death. On the Day of Resurrection, he will be a witness against them.

[4:170] O people, the messenger has come to you with the truth from your Lord. Therefore, you shall believe for your own good. If you disbelieve, then to GOD belongs everything in the heavens and the earth. GOD is Omniscient, Most Wise.

APPENDIX – I

[4:173] As for those who believe and lead a righteous life, He will fully recompense them, and shower them with His grace. As for those who disdain and turn arrogant, He will commit them to painful retribution. They will find no lord beside GOD, nor a savior.

[4:175] Those who believe in GOD, and hold fast to Him, He will admit them into mercy from Him, and grace, and will guide them to Him in a straight path.

[5:1] O you who believe, you shall fulfill your covenants. Permitted for you to eat are the livestock, except those specifically prohibited herein. You shall not permit hunting throughout Hajj pilgrimage. GOD decrees whatever He wills.

[5:8] O you who believe, you shall be absolutely equitable, and observe GOD, when you serve as witnesses. Do not be provoked by your conflicts with some people into committing injustice. You shall be absolutely equitable, for it is more righteous. You shall observe GOD. GOD is fully Cognizant of everything you do.

[5:9] GOD promises those who believe and lead a righteous life forgiveness and a great recompense.

[5:11] O you who believe, remember GOD's blessings upon you; when some people extended their hands to aggress against you, He protected you and withheld their hands. You shall observe GOD; in GOD the believers shall trust.

[5:12] GOD had taken a covenant from the Children of Israel, and we raised among them twelve patriarchs. And GOD said, "I am with you, so long as you observe the Contact Prayers (Salat), give the obligatory charity (Zakat), and believe in My messengers and respect them, and continue to lend GOD a loan of righteousness. I will then remit your sins, and admit you into gardens with flowing

streams. Anyone who disbelievers after this, has indeed strayed off the right path."

[5:35] O you who believe you shall reverence GOD and seek the ways and means to Him, and strive in His cause, that you may succeed.

[5:44] We have sent down the Torah,* containing guidance and light. Ruling in accordance with it were the Jewish prophets, as well as the rabbis and the priests, as dictated to them in GOD's scripture, and as witnessed by them. Therefore, do not reverence human beings; you shall reverence Me instead. And do not trade away My revelations for a cheap price. Those who do not rule in accordance with GOD's revelations, are the disbelievers.

[5:51] O you who believe, do not take certain Jews and Christians as allies; these are allies of one another. Those among you who ally themselves with these belong with them. GOD does not guide the transgressors.

[5:55] Your real allies are GOD and His messenger, and the believers who observe the Contact Prayers (Salat), and give the obligatory charity (Zakat), and they bow down.

[5:56] Those who ally themselves with GOD and His messenger, and those who believed, belong in the party of GOD; absolutely, they are the victors.

[5:57] O you who believe, do not befriend those among the recipients of previous scripture who mock and ridicule your religion, nor shall you befriend the disbelievers. You shall reverence GOD, if you are really believers.

APPENDIX – I

[5:69] Surely, those who believe, those who are Jewish, the converts, and the Christians; any of them who (1) believe in GOD and (2) believe in the Last Day, and (3) lead a righteous life, have nothing to fear, nor will they grieve.

[5:83] When they hear what was revealed to the messenger, you see their eyes flooding with tears as they recognize the truth therein, and they say, "Our Lord, we have believed, so count us among the witnesses.

[5:84] "Why should we not believe in GOD, and in the truth that has come to us, and hope that our Lord may admit us with the righteous people?"

[5:87] O you who believe, do not prohibit good things that are made lawful by GOD, and do not aggress; GOD dislikes the aggressors.

[5:88] And eat from the good and lawful things that GOD has provided for you. You shall reverence GOD, in whom you are believers.

[5:90] O you who believe, intoxicants, and gambling, and the altars of idols, and the games of chance are abominations of the devil; you shall avoid them, that you may succeed.

[5:93] Those who believe and lead a righteous life bear no guilt by eating any food, so long as they observe the commandments, believe and lead a righteous life, then maintain their piety and faith, and continue to observe piety and righteousness. GOD loves the righteous.

[5:111] "Recall that I inspired the disciples: 'You shall believe in Me and My messenger.' They said, 'We have believed, and bear witness that we are submitters.' "

[5:112] Recall that the disciples said, "O Jesus, son of Mary, can your Lord send down to us a feast from the sky?" He said, "You should veneration GOD, if you are believers."

[5:115] GOD said, "I am sending it down. Anyone among you who disbelieve after this, I will punish him as I never punished anyone else."*

[6:1] Praise be to GOD, who created the heavens and the earth, and made the darkness and the light. Yet, those who disbelieve in their Lord continue to deviate.

[6:20] Those to whom we have given the scripture recognize this as they recognize their own children. The ones who lose their souls are those who do not believe.

[6:31] Losers indeed are those who disbelieve in meeting GOD, until the Hour comes to them suddenly then say, "We deeply regret wasting our lives in this world." They will carry loads of their sins on their backs; what a miserable load!

[6:35] If their rejection gets to be too much for you, you should know that even if you dug a tunnel through the earth, or climbed a ladder into the sky, and produced a miracle for them (they still would not believe). Had GOD willed, He could have guided them, unanimously. Therefore, do not behave like the ignorant ones.

[6:48] We do not send the messengers except as deliverers of good news, as well as warners. Those who believe and reform have nothing to fear, nor will they grieve.

[6:82] Those who believe, and do not pollute their belief with idol worship, have deserved the perfect security, and they are truly guided.

APPENDIX – I

[6:92] This too is a blessed scripture that we have revealed, confirming the previous scriptures, that you may warn the most important community* and all those around it. Those who believe in the Hereafter will believe in this (scripture), and will observe the Contact Prayers (Salat).

[6:99] He is the One who sends down from the sky water, whereby we produce all kinds of plants. We produce from the green material multitudes of complex grains, palm trees with hanging clusters, and gardens of grapes, olives and pomegranate; fruits that are similar, yet dissimilar. Note their fruits as they grow and ripen. These are signs for people who believe.

[6:109] They swore by GOD, solemnly, that if a miracle came to them, they would surely believe. Say, "Miracles come only from GOD." For all you know, if a miracle did come to them, they would continue to disbelieve.

[6:113] This is to let the minds of those who do not believe in the Hereafter listen to such fabrications, and accept them, and thus expose their real convictions.*

[6:154] And we gave Moses the scripture, complete with the best commandments, and detailing everything, and a beacon and mercy, that they may believe in meeting their Lord.

[6:158] Are they waiting for the angels to come to them, or your Lord, or some physical manifestations of your Lord? The day this happens, no soul will benefit from believing if it did not believe before that, and did not reap the benefits of belief by leading a righteous life.* Say, "Keep on waiting; we too are waiting."

[6:163] "He has no partner. This is what I am commanded to believe, and I am the first to submit."

[7:2] This scripture has been revealed to you-you shall not harbor doubt about it in your heart-that you may warn with it, and to provide a reminder for the believers.

[7:27] O children of Adam, do not let the devil dupe you as he did when he caused the eviction of your parents from Paradise, and the removal of their garments to expose their bodies. He and his tribe see you, while you do not see them. We appoint the devils as companions of those who do not believe.

[7:30] Some He guided, while others are committed to straying. They have taken the devils as their masters, instead of GOD, yet they believe that they are guided.

[7:37] Who is more evil than those who invent lies about GOD, or reject His revelations? These will get their share, in accordance with the scripture, then, when our messengers come to terminate their lives, they will say, "Where are the idols you used to implore beside GOD?" They will say, "They have abandoned us." They will bear witness against themselves that they were disbelievers.

[7:42] As for those who believe and lead a righteous life-we never burden any soul beyond its means-these will be the dwellers of Paradise. They abide in it forever.

[7:52] We have given them a scripture that is fully detailed, with knowledge, guidance, and mercy for the people who believe.

[7:85] To Midyan we sent their brother Shu'aib. He said, "O my people, worship GOD; you have no other God beside Him. Proof has come to you from your Lord. You shall give full weight and full measure when you trade. Do not cheat the people out of their rights. Do not corrupt the earth after it has been set straight. This is better for you, if you are believers.

APPENDIX – I

[7:86] "Refrain from blocking every path, seeking to repel those who believe from the path of GOD, and do not make it crooked. Remember that you used to be few and He multiplied your number. Recall the consequences for the wicked.

[7:96] Had the people of those communities believed and turned righteous, we would have showered them with blessings from the heaven and the earth. Since they decided to disbelieve, we punished them for what they earned.

[7:101] We narrate to you the history of those communities: their messengers went to them with clear proofs, but they were not to believe in what they had rejected before. GOD thus seals the hearts of the disbelievers.

[7:126] "You persecute us simply because we believed in the proofs of our Lord when they came to us." "Our Lord, grant us steadfastness, and let us die as submitters."

[7:153] As for those who committed sins, then repented thereafter and believed, your Lord-after this-is Forgiver, Most Merciful.

[7:158] Say, "O people, I am GOD's messenger to all of you. To Him belongs the sovereignty of the heavens and the earth. There is no God except He. He controls life and death." Therefore, you shall believe in GOD and His messenger, the gentile prophet, who believes in GOD and His words. Follow him, that you may be guided.

[7:188] Say, "I have no power to benefit myself, or harm myself. Only what GOD wills happens to me. If I knew the future, I would have increased my wealth, and no harm would have afflicted me. I am no more than a warner, and a bearer of good news for those who believe."

[8:2] The true believers are those whose hearts tremble when GOD is mentioned, and when His revelations are recited to them, their faith is strengthened, and they trust in their Lord.

[8:4] Such are the true believers. They attain high ranks at their Lord, as well as forgiveness and a generous provision.

[8:15] O you who believe, if you encounter the disbelievers who have mobilized against you, do not turn back and flee.

[8:27] O you who believe, do not betray GOD and the messenger, and do not betray those who trust you, now that you know.

[8:29] O you who believe, if you reverence GOD, He will enlighten you, remit your sins, and forgive you. GOD possesses infinite grace.

[8:45] O you who believe, when you encounter an army, you shall hold fast and commemorate GOD frequently, that you may succeed.

[8:55] The worst creatures in the sight of GOD are those who disbelieved; they cannot believe.

[8:62] If they want to deceive you, then GOD will suffice you. He will help you with His support, and with the believers.

[8:65] O you prophet, you shall exhort the believers to fight. If there are twenty of you who are steadfast, they can defeat two hundred, and a hundred of you can defeat a thousand of those who disbelieved. That is because they are people who do not understand.

[8:66] Now (that many new people have joined you) GOD has made it easier for you, for He knows that you are not as strong as you

APPENDIX – I

used to be. Henceforth, a hundred steadfast believers can defeat two hundred, and a thousand of you can defeat two thousand by GOD's leave. GOD is with those who steadfastly persevere.

[8:73] Those who disbelieved are allies of one another. Unless you keep these commandments, there will be chaos on earth, and terrible corruption.

[9:13] Would you not fight people who violated their treaties, tried to banish the messenger, and they are the ones who started the war in the first place? Are you afraid of them? GOD is the One you are supposed to fear, if you are believers.

[9:14] You shall fight them, for GOD will punish them at your hands, humiliate them, grant you victory over them, and cool the chests of the believers.

[9:15] He will also remove the rage from the believers' hearts. GOD redeems whomever He wills. GOD is Omniscient, Most Wise.

[9:16] Did you think that you will be left alone without GOD distinguishing those among you who strive, and never ally themselves with GOD's enemies, or the enemies of His messenger, or the enemies of the believers? GOD is fully Cognizant of everything you do.

[9:18] The only people to frequent GOD's masjids are those who believe in GOD and the Last Day, and observe the Contact Prayers (Salat), and give the obligatory charity (Zakat), and do not fear except GOD. These will surely be among the guided ones.

[9:23] O you who believe, do not ally yourselves even with your parents and your siblings, if they prefer disbelieving over believing. Those among you who ally themselves with them are transgressing.

[9:28] O you who believe, the idol worshipers are polluted; they shall not be permitted to approach the Sacred Masjid after this year. If you fear loss of income, GOD will shower you with His provisions, in accordance with His will. GOD is Omniscient, Most Wise.

[9:34] O you who believe, many religious leaders and preachers take the people's money illicitly, and repel from the path of GOD. Those who hoard the gold and silver, and do not spend them in the cause of GOD, promise them a painful retribution.

[9:54] What prevented the acceptance of their spending is that they disbelieve in GOD and His messenger, and when they observed the Contact Prayers (Salat),* they observed them lazily, and when they gave to charity, they did so grudgingly.

[9:85] Do not be impressed by their money or their children; GOD causes these to be sources of misery for them in this world, and their souls depart as disbelievers.

[9:86] When a sura is revealed, stating: Believe in GOD, and strive with His messenger," even the strong among them say, "Let us stay behind!"

[9:88] As for the messenger and those who believed with him, they eagerly strive with their money and their lives. These have deserved all the good things; they are the winners.

[9:107] There are those who abuse the masjid by practicing idol worship, dividing the believers, and providing comfort to those who oppose GOD and His messenger. They solemnly swear: "Our intentions are honorable!" GOD bears witness that they are liars.

[9:113] Neither the prophet, nor those who believe shall ask forgiveness for the idol worshipers, even if they were their nearest of kin, once they realize that they are destined for Hell.

APPENDIX – I

[9:125] As for those who harbored doubts in their hearts, it actually added unholiness to their unholiness, and they died as disbelievers.

[10:13] Many a generation we have annihilated before you when they transgressed. Their messengers went to them with clear proofs, but they refused to believe. We thus requite the guilty people.

[10:40] Some of them believe (in this scripture), while others disbelieve in it. Your Lord is fully aware of the evildoers.

[10:78] They said, "Did you come to divert us from what we found our parents doing, and to attain positions of prominence for yourselves? We will never join you as believers."

[10:83] None believed with Moses except a few of his people, while fearing the tyranny of Pharaoh and his elders. Surely, Pharaoh was much too arrogant on earth, and a real tyrant.

[10:84] Moses said, "O my people, if you have really believed in GOD, then put your trust in Him, if you are really submitters."

[10:87] We inspired Moses and his brother. "Maintain your homes in Egypt for the time being, turn your homes into synagogues, and maintain the Contact Prayers (Salat). Give good news to the believers."

[10:90] We delivered the Children of Israel across the sea. Pharaoh and his troops pursued them, aggressively and sinfully. When drowning became a reality for him, he said, "I believe that there is no God except the One in whom the Children of Israel have believed; I am a submitter."

[10:98] Any community that believes will surely be rewarded for believing. For example, the people of Jonah: when they believed, we relieved the humiliating retribution they had been suffering in this world, and we made them prosperous.

[10:103] We ultimately save our messengers and those who believe. It is our immutable law that we save the believers.

[11:7] He is the One who created the heavens and the earth in six days-*and His (earthly) domain was completely covered with water-**in order to test you, to distinguish those among you who work righteousness. Yet, when you say, "You will be resurrected after death," those who disbelieve would say, "This is clearly witchcraft."

[11:19] They repel from the way of GOD and seek to make it crooked, and they are disbelievers in the Hereafter.

[11:23] As for those who believe and lead a righteous life, and devote themselves to their Lord, they are the dwellers of Paradise; they abide therein forever.

[11:86]
If you are true believers then know that the profit which God has left for you is better for you (than what you may gain through deceitful ways). I am not responsible for your deeds."

[12:57] Additionally, the reward in the Hereafter is even better for those who believe and lead a righteous life.

[12:103] Most people, no matter what you do, will not believe.

[12:111] In their history, there is a lesson for those who possess intelligence. This is not fabricated Hadith; this (Quran) confirms all previous scriptures, provides the details of everything, and is a beacon and mercy for those who believe.

APPENDIX – I

[13:32] Messengers before you have been ridiculed; I permitted the disbelievers to carry on, then I punished them. How terrible was My retribution!

[13:35] The allegory of Heaven, which is promised for the righteous, is flowing streams, inexhaustible provisions, and cool shade. Such is the destiny for those who observe righteousness, while the destiny for the disbelievers is Hell.

[13:42] Others before them have schemed, but to GOD belongs the ultimate scheming. He knows what everyone is doing. The disbelievers will find out who the ultimate winners are.

[13:43] Those who disbelieved will say, "You are not a messenger!" Say, "GOD suffices as a witness between me and you, and those who possess knowledge of the scripture."

[14:2] (The path of) GOD; the One who possesses everything in the heavens and everything on earth. Woe to the disbelievers; they have incurred a terrible retribution.

[14:8] Moses said, "If you disbelieve, along with all the people on earth, GOD is in no need, Praiseworthy."

[14:18] The allegory of those who disbelieve in their Lord: their works are like ashes in a violent wind, on a stormy day. They gain nothing from whatever they earn; such is the farthest straying.

[14:23] As for those who believe and lead a righteous life, they will be admitted into gardens with flowing streams. They abide therein forever, in accordance with the will of their Lord. Their greeting therein is: "Peace."

[14:27] GOD strengthens those who believe with the proven word, in this life and in the Hereafter. And GOD sends the transgressors astray. Everything is in accordance with GOD's will.

[14:31] Exhort My servants who believed to observe the Contact Prayers (Salat), and to give (to charity) from our provisions to them, secretly and publicly, before a day comes where there is neither trade, nor nepotism.

[16:22] Your God is one God. As for those who do not believe in the Hereafter, their hearts are denying, and they are arrogant.

[16:60] Those who do not believe in the Hereafter set the worst examples, while to GOD belongs the most sublime examples. He is the Almighty, the Most Wise.

[16:64] We have revealed this scripture to you, to point out for them what they dispute, and to provide guidance and mercy for people who believe.

[16:99] He (Satan) has no power over those who believe and trust in their Lord.

[16:104] Surely, those who do not believe in GOD's revelations, GOD does not guide them. They have incurred a painful retribution.

[16:106] Those who disbelieve in GOD, after having acquired faith, and become fully content with disbelief, have incurred wrath from GOD. The only ones to be excused are those who are forced to profess disbelief, while their hearts are full of faith.*

[17:9] This Quran guides to the best path, and brings good news to the believers who lead a righteous life, that they have deserved a great recompense.

APPENDIX – I

[17:45] When you read the Quran, we place between you and those who do not believe in the Hereafter an invisible barrier.

[17:82] We send down in the Quran healing and mercy for the believers. At the same time, it only increases the wickedness of the transgressors.

[17:99] Could they not see that the GOD who created the heavens and the earth, is able to create the same creations? He has predetermined for them an irrevocable life span? Yet, the disbelievers insist upon disbelieving.

[17:107] Proclaim, "believe in it, or do not believe in it." Those who possess knowledge from the previous scriptures, when it is recited to them, they fall down to their chins, prostrating.

[18:2] A perfect (scripture) to warn of severe retribution from Him, and to deliver good news to the believers who lead a righteous life, that they have earned a generous recompense.

[18:13] We narrate to you their history, truthfully. They were youths who believed in their Lord, and we increased their guidance.

[18:56] We only send the messengers as simply deliverers of good news, as well as warners. Those who disbelieve argue with falsehood to defeat the truth, and they take My proofs and warnings in vain.

[18:102] Do those who disbelieve think that they can get away with setting up My servants as Gods beside Me? We have prepared for the disbelievers Hell as an eternal abode.

[18:105] Such are the ones who disbelieved in the revelations of their Lord and in meeting Him. Therefore, their works are in vain;

on the Day of Resurrection, they have no weight.

[19:39] Warn them about the day of remorse, when judgment will be issued. They are totally oblivious; they do not believe.

[19:60] Only those who repent, believe, and lead a righteous life will enter Paradise, without the least injustice.

[19:73] When our revelations are recited to them, clearly, those who disbelieve say to those who believe, "Which of us is more prosperous? Which of us is in the majority?"

[19:83] Do you not see how we unleash the devils upon the disbelievers to stir them up?

[20:56] We showed him all our proofs, but he disbelieved and refused.

[20:127] We thus requite those who transgress and refuse to believe in the revelations of their Lord. The retribution in the Hereafter is far worse and everlasting.

And from water we made all living things. Would they believe?

[21:88] We responded to him, and saved him from the crisis; we thus save the believers.

[22:14] GOD admits those who believe and lead a righteous life into gardens with flowing streams. Everything is in accordance with GOD's will.

[22:17] Those who believe, those who are Jewish, the converts, the Christians, the Zoroastrians, and the idol worshipers, GOD is the One who will judge among them on the Day of Resurrection. GOD witnesses all things.

APPENDIX – I

[22:25] Surely, those who disbelieve and repulse others from the path of GOD, and from the Sacred Masjid that we designated for all the people-be they natives or visitors-and seek to pollute it and corrupt it, we will afflict them with painful retribution.

[22:38] GOD defends those who believe. GOD does not love any betrayer, unappreciative.

[22:50] Those who believe and lead a righteous life have deserved forgiveness and a generous recompense.

[22:54] Those who are blessed with knowledge will recognize the truth from your Lord, then believe in it, and their hearts will readily accept it. Most assuredly, GOD guides the believers in the right path.

[22:55] As for those who disbelieve, they will continue to harbor doubts until the Hour comes to them suddenly, or until the retribution of a terrible day comes to them.

[22:56] All sovereignty on that day belongs to GOD, and He will judge among them. As for those who believe and lead a righteous life, they have deserved the gardens of bliss.

[22:57] While those who disbelieved and rejected our revelations have incurred a shameful retribution.

[22:77] O you who believe, you shall bow, prostrate, worship your Lord, and work righteousness, that you may succeed.

[23:74] Those who disbelieve in the Hereafter will surely deviate from the right path.

[24:20] GOD showers you with His grace and mercy. GOD is Most Kind towards the believers, Most Merciful.

[24:47] They say, "We believe in GOD and in the messenger, and we obey," but then some of them slide back afterwards. These are not believers.

[24:55] GOD promises those among you who believe and lead a righteous life, that He will make them sovereigns on earth, as He did for those before them, and will establish for them the religion He has chosen for them, and will substitute peace and security for them in place of fear. All this because they worship Me alone; they never set up any idols beside Me. Those who disbelieve after this are the truly wicked.

[24:57] Do not think that those who disbelieve will ever get away with it. Their final abode is Hell; what a miserable destiny.

[25:37] Similarly, when the people of Noah disbelieved the messengers, we drowned them, and we set them up as a sign for the people. We have prepared for the transgressors a painful retribution.

[25:70] Exempted are those who repent, believe, and lead a righteous life. GOD transforms their sins into credits. GOD is Forgiver, Most Merciful.

[25:77] Say, "You attain value at my Lord only through your worship. But if you disbelieve, you incur the inevitable consequences."

[26:102] "If only we could get another chance, we would then believe."

[26:114] "I will never dismiss the believers.

[27:53] We save those who believe and lead a righteous life.

[27:83] The day will come when we summon from every community some of those who did not believe in our proofs, forcibly.

APPENDIX – I

[28:3] We recite to you herein some history of Moses and Pharaoh, truthfully, for the benefit of people who believe.

[28:67] As for those who repent, believe, and lead a righteous life, they will end up with the winners.

[28:80] As for those who were blessed with knowledge, they said, "Woe to you, GOD's recompense is far better for those who believe and lead a righteous life." None attains this except the steadfast.

[29:7] Those who believe and lead a righteous life, we will certainly remit their sins, and will certainly reward them generously for their righteous works.

[29:9] Those who believe and lead a righteous life, we will certainly admit them with the righteous.

[29:11] GOD will most certainly distinguish those who believe, and He will most certainly expose the hypocrites.

[29:24] The only response from his people was their saying, "Kill him, or burn him." But GOD saved him from the fire. This should provide lessons for people who believe. (Abraham)

[29:44] GOD created the heavens and the earth, truthfully. This provides a sufficient proof for the believers.

[29:46]
And do not argue with the People of the Scripture except in a way that is best, except for those who commit injustice among them, and say, "We believe in that which has been revealed to us and revealed to you. And our God and your God is one; and we are Muslims [in submission] to Him."

[29:58] Those who believe and lead a righteous life, we will surely settle them in Paradise, with mansions and flowing streams. Eternally they abide therein. What a beautiful reward for the workers.

[30:15] As for those who believe and lead a righteous life, they will be in Paradise, rejoicing.

[30:16] As for those who disbelieve, and reject our revelations and the meeting of the Hereafter, they will last in the retribution forever.

[30:37] Do they not realize that GOD increases the provision for whomever He wills, or reduces it? These should be lessons for people who believe.

[30:44] Whoever disbelieves, disbelieves to the detriment of his own soul, while those who lead a righteous life, do so to strengthen and develop their own souls.

[30:45] For He will generously recompense those who believe and lead a righteous life from His bounties. He does not love the disbelievers.

[30:47] We have sent messengers before you to their people, with profound signs. Subsequently, we punished those who transgressed. It is our duty that we grant victory to the believers.

[30:53] Nor can you guide the blind out of their straying. You can only be heard by those who believe in our revelations, and decide to become submitters.

[30:58] Thus, we have cited for the people in this Quran all kinds of examples. Yet, no matter what kind of proof you present to the disbelievers, they say, "You are falsifiers."

APPENDIX – I

[31:8] Surely, those who believe and lead a righteous life have deserved the gardens of bliss.

[31:23] As for those who disbelieve, do not be saddened by their disbelief. To us is their ultimate return, then we will inform them of everything they had done. GOD is fully aware of the innermost thoughts.

[32:18] Is one who is a believer the same as one who is wicked? They are not equal.

[32:19] As for those who believe and lead a righteous life, they have deserved the eternal Paradise. Such is their abode, in return for their works.

[32:20] As for the wicked, their destiny is Hell. Every time they try to leave it, they will be forced back. They will be told, "Taste the agony of Hell which you used to disbelieve in."

[33:11] That is when the believers were truly tested; they were severely shaken up.

[33:22] When the true believers saw the parties (ready to attack), they said, "This is what GOD and His messenger have promised us, and GOD and His messenger are truthful." This (dangerous situation) only strengthened their faith and augmented their submission.

[33:23] Among the believers there are people who fulfill their pledges with GOD. Some of them died, while others stand ready, never wavering.

[33:41] O you who believe, you shall remember GOD frequently.*

[33:43] He is the One who helps you, together with His angels, to lead you out of darkness into the light. He is Most Merciful towards the believers.

[33:47] Deliver good news to the believers, that they have deserved from GOD a great blessing.

[34:4] Most certainly, He will reward those who believe and lead a righteous life. These have deserved forgiveness and a generous provision.

[34:21] He never had any power over them. But we thus distinguish those who believe in the Hereafter from those who are doubtful about it.* Your Lord is in full control of all things.

[34:37] It is not your money or your children that bring you closer to us. Only those who believe and lead a righteous life will receive the reward for their works, multiplied manifold. In the abode of Paradise they will live in perfect peace.

[35:7] Those who disbelieve have incurred a severe retribution, and those who believe and lead a righteous life have deserved forgiveness and a great recompense.

[35:25] If they disbelieve you, those before them have also disbelieved. Their messengers went to them with clear proofs, and the Psalms, and the enlightening scriptures.

[36:47] When they are told, "Give from GOD's provisions to you," those who believe say to those who believe, "Why should we give to those whom GOD could feed, if He so willed? You are really far astray."

[37:148] They did believe, and we let them enjoy this life.

APPENDIX – I

[38:2] Those who disbelieve have plunged into arrogance and defiance.

[38:27] We did not create the heaven and the earth, and everything between them, in vain. Such is the thinking of those who disbelieve. Therefore, woe to those who disbelieve; they will suffer in Hell.

[38:28] Shall we treat those who believe and lead a righteous life as we treat those who commit evil on earth? Shall we treat the righteous as we treat the wicked?

[39:3] Absolutely, the religion shall be devoted to GOD alone. Those who set up idols beside Him say, "We idolize them only to bring us closer to GOD; for they are in a better position!" GOD will judge them regarding their disputes. GOD does not guide such liars, disbelievers.

[39:7] If you disbelieve, GOD does not need anyone. But He dislikes to see His servants make the wrong decision. If you decide to be appreciative, He is pleased for you. No soul bears the sins of any other soul. Ultimately, to your Lord is your return, then He will inform you of everything you had done. He is fully aware of the innermost thoughts.

[39:33] As for those who promote the truth, and believe therein, they are the righteous.

[39:45] When GOD ALONE is mentioned, the hearts of those who do not believe in the Hereafter shrink with aversion. But when others are mentioned beside Him, they become satisfied.*

[39:52] Do they not realize that GOD is the One who increases the provision for whomever He chooses, and withholds? These are lessons for people who believe.

[39:63] To Him belongs all decisions in the heavens and the earth, and those who disbelieved in GOD's revelations are the real losers.

[40:7] Those who serve the throne and all those around it glorify and praise their Lord, and believe in Him. And they ask forgiveness for those who believe: "Our Lord, Your mercy and Your knowledge encompass all things. Forgive those who repent and follow Your path, and spare them the retribution of Hell.

[40:12] This is because when GOD ALONE was advocated, you disbelieved, but when others were mentioned beside Him, you believed. Therefore, GOD's judgment has been issued; He is the Most High, the Great.

[40:14] Therefore, you shall devote your worship absolutely to GOD ALONE, even if the disbelievers dislike it.

[40:22] That is because their messengers went to them with clear proofs, but they disbelieved. Consequently, GOD punished them. He is Mighty, strict in enforcing retribution.

[40:25] And when he showed them the truth from us, they said, "Kill the sons of those who believed with him, and spare their daughters." Thus, the scheming of the disbelievers is always wicked.

[40:27] Moses said, "I seek refuge in my Lord and your Lord, from every arrogant one who does not believe in the Day of Reckoning."

[40:35] They argue against GOD's revelations, without any basis. This is a trait that is most abhorred by GOD and by those who believe. GOD thus seals the hearts of every arrogant tyrant.

[40:37] "I want to reach the heaven, and take a look at the God of Moses. I believe he is a liar." Thus were the evil works of Pharaoh

APPENDIX – I

adorned in his eyes, and thus was he kept from following (the right) path. Pharaoh's scheming was truly evil.

[40:51] Most assuredly, we will give victory to our messengers and to those who believe, both in this world and on the day the witnesses are summoned.

[40:52] On that day, the apologies of the disbelievers will not benefit them. They have incurred condemnation; they have incurred the worst destiny.

[40:58] Not equal are the blind and the seer. Nor are those who believe and work righteousness equal to the sinners. Rarely do you take heed.

[40:59] Most certainly, the Hour (Day of Judgment) is coming, no doubt about it, but most people do not believe.

[40:70] They are the ones who have disbelieved in the scripture, and in the messages we have sent with our messengers. Therefore, they will surely find out.

[40:85] Their belief then could not help them in the least, once they saw our retribution. Such is GOD's system that has been established to deal with His creatures; the disbelievers are always doomed.

[41:7] "Who do not give the obligatory charity (Zakat), and with regard to the Hereafter, they are disbelievers."

[41:8] As for those who believe and lead a righteous life, they receive a well deserved recompense.

[41:18] We always save those who believe and lead a righteous life.

[42:15] This is what you shall preach, and steadfastly maintain what you are commanded to do, and do not follow their wishes. And proclaim: "I believe in all the scriptures sent down by GOD. I was commanded to judge among you equitably. GOD is our Lord and your Lord. We have our deeds and you have your deeds. There is no argument between us and you. GOD will gather us all together; to Him is the ultimate destiny."

[42:18] Challenging it are those who do not believe in it. As for those who believe, they are concerned about it, and they know that it is the truth. Absolutely, those who deny the Hour have gone far astray.

[42:22] You will see the transgressors worried about everything they had committed; everything will come back and haunt them. As for those who believed and led a righteous life, they will be in the gardens of Paradise. They will receive whatever they wish from their Lord. This is the great blessing.

[42:23] This is the good news from GOD to His servants who believe and lead a righteous life. Say, "I do not ask you for any wage. I do ask each of you to take care of your own relatives." Anyone who does a righteous work, we multiply his reward for it. GOD is Forgiver, Appreciative.

[42:45] You will see them facing it, humiliated and debased, and looking, yet trying to avoid looking. Those who believed will proclaim: "The real losers are those who lost their souls and their families on the Day of Resurrection. The transgressors have deserved an everlasting retribution."

[45:3] The heavens and the earth are full of proofs for the believers.

APPENDIX – I

[45:11] This is a beacon, and those who disbelieve in these revelations of their Lord have incurred condemnation and a painful retribution.

[45:21] Do those who work evil expect that we will treat them in the same manner as those who believe and lead a righteous life? Can their life and their death be the same?* Wrong indeed is their judgment.

[45:30] As for those who believe and work righteousness, their Lord will admit them into His mercy. This is the great triumph.

[46:31] "O our people, respond to the call of GOD, and believe in Him. He will then forgive your sins, and spare you a painful retribution."

[47:1] Those who disbelieve and repel from the path of GOD, He nullifies their works.

[47:3] This is because those who disbelieve are following falsehood, while those who believe are following the truth from their Lord. GOD thus cites for the people, their examples.

[47:7] O you who believe, if you support GOD, He will support you, and strengthen your foothold.

[47:8] Those who disbelieve incur misery; He causes their works to be utterly in vain.

[47:33] O you who believe, you shall obey GOD, and obey the messenger. Otherwise, all your works will be in vain.

[47:36] This worldly life is no more than play and vanity. But if you believe and lead a righteous life, He will reward you, without asking you for any money.

[48:4] He is the One who places contentment into the hearts of believers to augment more faith, in addition to their faith. To GOD belongs all forces of the heavens and the earth. GOD is Omniscient, Most Wise.

[48:9] That you people may believe in GOD and His messenger, and reverence Him, and observe Him, and glorify Him, day and night.

[48:20] GOD has promised you many spoils that you will gain. He thus advanced some benefits for you in this life, and He has withheld the people's hands of aggression against you, and has rendered this a sign for the believers. He thus guides you in a straight path.

[48:22] If the disbelievers ever fought you, they would turn around and flee. They have no Lord and Master; they have no helper.

[49:10] The believers are members of one family; you shall keep the peace within your family and reverence GOD, that you may attain mercy.

[49:11] O you who believe, no people shall ridicule other people, for they may be better than they. Nor shall any women ridicule other women, for they may be better than they. Nor shall you mock one another, or make fun of your names. Evil indeed is the reversion to wickedness after attaining faith. Anyone who does not repent after this, these are the transgressors.

[49:14] The Arabs said, "We are Mu'mens (believers)." Say, "You have not believed; what you should say is, 'We are Muslims (submitters),' until belief is established in your hearts." If you obey GOD and His messenger, He will not put any of your works to waste. GOD is Forgiver, Most Merciful.

APPENDIX – I

[49:15] Mu'mens (believers) are those who believe in GOD and His messenger, then attain the status of having no doubt whatsoever, and strive with their money and their lives in the cause of GOD. These are the truthful ones.

[52:21] For those who believed, and their children also followed them in belief, we will have their children join them. We never fail to reward them for any work. Every person is paid for what he did.

[57:7] believe in GOD and His messenger, and give from what He has bestowed upon you. Those among you who believe and give (to charity) have deserved a great recompense.

[57:8] Why should you not believe in GOD when the messenger is inviting you to believe in your Lord? He has taken a pledge from you, if you are believers.

[60:5] "Our Lord, let us not be oppressed by those who disbelieved, and forgive us. You are the Almighty, Most Wise."

[61:2] O you who believe, why do you say what you do not do?

[61:8] They wish to put out GOD's light with their mouths. But GOD insists upon perfecting His light, in spite of the disbelievers.

[61:11] believe in GOD and His messenger and strive in the cause of GOD with your money and your lives. This is the best deal for you, if you only knew.

[61:13] Additionally, you get something you truly love: support from GOD and guaranteed victory. Give good news to the believers.

[61:14] O you who believe, be GOD's supporters, like the disciples of Jesus, son of Mary. When he said to them, "Who are my

supporters towards GOD," they said, "We are GOD's supporters." Thus, a group from the Children of Israel believed, and another group disbelieved. We helped those who believed against their enemy, until they won.

[62:9] O you who believe, when the Congregational Prayer (Salat Al-Jumu'ah) is announced on Friday, you shall hasten to the commemoration of GOD, and drop all business. This is better for you, if you only knew.

[63:3] This is because they believed, then disbelieved. Hence, their minds are blocked; they do not understand.

[63:9] O you who believe, do not be distracted by your money and your children from remembering GOD. Those who do this are the losers.

[64:8] Therefore, you shall believe in GOD and His messenger, and the light that we have revealed herein. GOD is fully Cognizant of everything you do.

[64:9] The day will come when He summons you to the Day of Summoning. That is the Day of Mutual Blaming. Anyone who believes in GOD and leads a righteous life, He will remit his sins, and will admit him into gardens with flowing streams. They abide therein forever. This is the greatest triumph.

[64:11] Nothing happens to you except in accordance with GOD's will. Anyone who believes in GOD, He will guide his heart. GOD is fully aware of all things.

[65:11] a messenger* who recites to you GOD's revelations, clearly, to lead those who believe and work righteousness out of the darkness into the light. Anyone who believes in GOD and leads a righ-

APPENDIX – I

teous life, He will admit him into gardens with flowing streams; they abide therein forever. GOD will generously reward him.

[66:11] And GOD cites as an example of those who believed the wife of Pharaoh. She said, "My Lord, build a home for me at You in Paradise, and save me from Pharaoh and his works; save me from the transgressing people."

[67:29] Say, "He is the Most Gracious; we believe in Him, and we trust in Him. You will surely find out who is really far astray."

[72:13] "'When we heard the guidance, we believed therein. Anyone who believes in his Lord will never fear any injustice, nor any affliction.

[73:20] Your Lord knows that you meditate during two-thirds of the night, or half of it, or one-third of it, and so do some of those who believed with you. GOD has designed the night and the day, and He knows that you cannot always do this. He has pardoned you. Instead, you shall read what you can of the Quran. He knows that some of you may be ill, others may be traveling in pursuit of GOD's provisions, and others may be striving in the cause of GOD. You shall read what you can of it, and observe the contact prayers (Salat), give the obligatory charity (Zakat), and lend GOD a loan of righteousness. Whatever good you send ahead on behalf of your souls, you will find it at GOD far better and generously rewarded. And implore GOD for forgiveness. GOD is Forgiver, Most Merciful.

[75:5] But the human being tends to believe only what he sees in front of him.

[84:25] As for those who believed and led a righteous life, they receive a recompense that is well deserved.

[85:11] Surely, those who believed and led a righteous life, have deserved gardens with flowing streams. This is the greatest triumph.

[95:6] Except those who believe and lead a righteous life; they receive a reward that is well deserved.

[98:7] Those who believed and led a righteous life are the best creatures.

Appendix – II

Daily Prayers

In Islam we pray five times a day. Prayer is like food for the soul. Some people may say we pray too much. Considering the fact that we eat three times a day with many snacks in between, I believe we have just the right amount prayers.

I have written this section mainly for people who are interested in a simple and basic prayer in Islam. There are many websites, YouTube videos, and Internet sites where you can find more elaborate prayers. The Quran does not give a specific instruction in prayer. The main prayer of the Quran that is used in prayer is the first chapter of the Quran, *Hamd* (1).

In the Quran each chapter is called a *Surah* and has a number and a name. The Quran has 114 chapters or *Surahs*. In your prayers, after *Hamd* you can use any of the other *Surahs* of the Quran to continue your prayer. I am going to keep it as basic and simple as I can for the first-time users, so they can get started. It's just like riding a bicycle. Once you learn the basics, you can do all the fancy tricks or prayers on your own.

Below is the summary of prayers and number of times each *rakat* (also rak'ah) has to be read. *A rakat* is a single unit of prayer. It is a combination of words and movements. You need to wash first before you start your prayer. There are also rituals in washing before prayer, the place of prayer, and how to cover up in clothing, which I am not going to detail here, as, again, there are plenty of websites explaining these things in detail. But I am going to put down the basic English prayer for those who are interested. I know many non-Muslims wonder what we say in our prayers, and many second-generation Muslims cannot read Arabic but want to pray and do not know how. Here is the summary of the daily prayers required in Islam:

Morning: 2 rakats

Noon: 4 rakats

Afternoon: 4 rakats

Dusk (sun going down): 3 rakats

Night: 4 rakats

As explained each *rakat* is a single unit of prayer. The prayer itself has a series of acts and prayers in standing, bowing, sitting, and prostration positions.

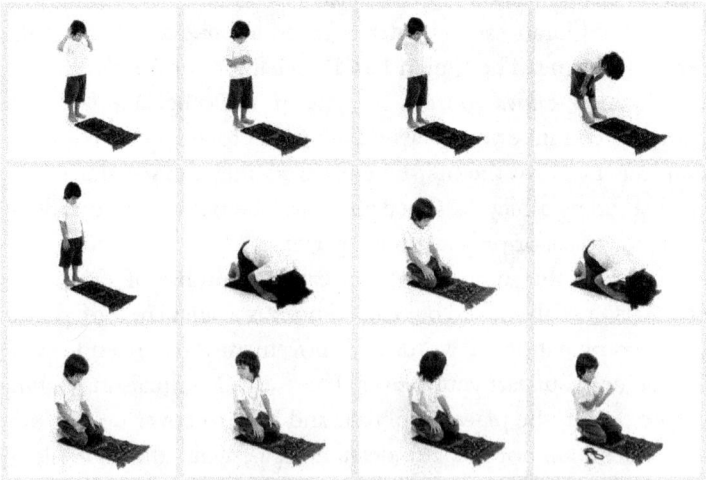

APPENDIX – II

Before the prayer, you have to perform the washing or *wudhu* (Arabic).

In morning prayer, which is only *2 rakats, you finish the prayer after the second sitting (will explain).*

In 3 and 4 rakat prayers, you sit down after the second sitting and say what is called the *Tashahhud* (testimony). After saying the "testimony" you stand up and add another 1 rakat for a 3 rakat prayer or 2 rakats for a 4 rakat prayer. You finish the 3 or 4 rakat prayers after your last sittings.

I will share the basics for all of them for those who are interested. Some people add extra surah from the Quran or many types of compliments or praises of God during the bowing, sitting, or prostration.

So basically, although we pray five times, we only have 2, 3, and 4 rakat prayers. Instead of mentioning the differences between them, I will simply list all of them from start to finish so there is no confusion.

To start with, you need to find or choose clean ground in your space with no clutter. If you do not have a prayer rug, a nice thick clean towel big enough that you can stand, sit, and prostrate on is good enough, until you buy your own prayer rug.

You need to do the pre-wash before the prayer, called *wudhu*. It is basically washing your hands up to your elbow, face, ears, top of your hair, and feet up to your ankles. Please check the Internet for the rituals with all the pictures, if you do not have anyone to show you.

You are to dress properly and be covered respectfully, as you are standing in front of God for your daily meeting. No gym shorts or tank tops for guys or girls. Ladies need a scarf to cover their hair and be covered. You do not have to wear a burqa. Internet sites can give some good general guidance.

For men, despite the Internet sites' depictions of Muslim men, you do not have to grow a beard, wear Arabic clothing, or even wear a cap! Some men wear a cap, as they say Muhammad liked to wear a cap when praying, as it would get cold at night in the desert, so they like to do the same. That is their choice but is not mandatory or necessary for you. Now you are ready. Different Islamic faiths have slightly different ways of standing in front of God. I am going to put down the way Muhammad reportedly did his prayer, before there was ever a Sunni or Shia or any other sect in Islam.

Before saying the prayer, there is the *Azan*. The *Azan* is a call to people that the prayer is about to start. The Azan is not mandatory when you are saying your prayers, but it is good to do. However, it is important to have it in the mosque for the group prayers as a call to prayer. It is perhaps similar to Christians and the sound of the bell in church.

Here is the Azan in English:

God is the greatest, God is the greatest
God is the greatest, God is the greatest
I bear witness that there is none worthy of worship but God
I bear witness that there is none worthy of worship but God
I bear witness that Muhammad is the prophet of God
I bear witness that Muhammad is the prophet of God
Come to prayer,
Come to prayer,
Come to success,
Come to success,
God is the greatest, God is the greatest
There is no deity but God.

After saying your Azan, now you are ready to start your prayer.

You point your prayer rug toward *Qibla*, which is the direction of the Kaaba in Mecca. You stand on your rug facing toward Kaaba, with your hands crossed on your midsection or on your chest. They say that is how Muhammad prayed. And you start by,

APPENDIX – II

1- Stating your intention: I offer ___ number of rakats (2, 4, 4, 3, 4 rakats) of _____ (time of the day: morning, noon, afternoon, dusk, or night) seeking closeness to God.
So for example, for a morning prayer you would say:
I offer "2 rakats" of "morning" prayer for closeness to God.

2- Then you raise your hands by your ears, with the palms of your hands facing forward and your eyes directed to the ground in front of your prayer rug.

3- Then you say, "God is Greatest."

4- Then you recite the first chapter of the Quran, *Hamd*:

(Hamd)
In the name of Most Kind and Most merciful God
Praise the Lord, the king of Universe
Most kind and most forgiving
Master of the day of judgement
We only worship you and we only ask help from you
Guide us to the straight path
The path of those who you gave your blessings
Not those who earned your anger
And not those who went astray

After saying the first chapter of the Quran (Hamd), you can recite any other chapters (surahs) of the Quran. The popular chapters are 112, 113, and 114, as they are shorter and easier to remember.

I will include all of them here, and you can read any of them you like after the first chapter (Hamd).

112
In the name of Most kind and most forgiving God
Say He is the One and only God
The One you go to when in need
He does not give birth to anyone and He was not born from anyone
And there is nothing like Him

113
In the name of most kind most forgiving God
I seek refuge in the Lord of the dawn
From the evil of what He has created
From the evil of overtaking darkness
From the evils of those who practice sorcery
From the evil of a jealous who commits jealousy

APPENDIX – II

114
In the name of most kind and most merciful
I seek refuge in the Lord of mankind, the King of mankind, the God of mankind
From the evil of Satan who whispers temptation in the hearts of people
From among the jinn and the men

After finishing with any of the prayers above, you bend with the palms of your hand on your knees and say:

In bent position called *ruku*,

Glory to my Lord, the Almighty

Then you stand up straight, pause, and say,

God listens to those who praise Him (optional, other sayings can also be used)

Then you go down in the prostrate position (called *sujud*). With your forehead on the ground you say,

Glory to my Lord, the Most High

Then you raise your head and upper torso into sitting position. While doing that, you can say,

O' Lord forgive my sins (optional, other sayings can also be used)

Then you go to prostration again for the second time, and repeat.

APPENDIX – II

Glory to my Lord, the Most High

Then you raise your head and upper torso into sitting position. While doing that, you can say:

Anything is possible through God (optional, other sayings can also be used)

Then you stand up to start the second (rakat) section. As you are standing up you say:

God is in total control of everything with power. (optional, other sayings can also be used)

And then you repeat the surah Hamd again (start of second rakat).

In the name of Most Kind and Most merciful God
Praise the Lord, the king of Universe
Most kind and most forgiving
Master of the day of judgement
We only worship you and we only ask help from you
Guide us to the straight path
The path of those who you gave your blessings
Not those who earned your anger
And not those who went astray

Then you can say any of the following Chapters *(Surah)* again

112

In the name of Most kind and most forgiving God
Say He is the One and only God
The One you go to when in need
He does not give birth to anyone and He was not born from anyone
And there is nothing like Him

113

In the name of most kind most forgiving God
I seek refuge in the Lord of the dawn
From the evil of what He has created
From the evil of overtaking darkness
From the evils of those who practice sorcery
From the evil of a jealous who commits jealousy

114

In the name of most kind and most merciful
I seek refuge in the Lord of mankind, the King of mankind, the God of mankind
From the evil of Satan who whispers temptation in the hearts of people
From among the jinn and the men

After finishing with any of the prayers above, you bend with the palms of your hand on your knees and say:

In bent position,

APPENDIX – II

Glory to my Lord, the Almighty

Then you stand up straight, pause, and say,

God listens to those who praise Him (optional, other sayings can also be used)

Then you go down in the prostrate position, and with your forehead on the ground you say,

Glory to my Lord, the Most High

Then you raise your head and upper torso into sitting position. While doing that, you can say:

O' Lord forgive my sins (optional, other sayings can also be used)

Then you go to prostration again, and repeat.

Glory to my Lord, the Most High

Then you repeat while sitting up, and before getting up:

Anything is possible through God (optional, other sayings can also be used)

This is your second sitting. You give your "testimony" before finishing the prayer.

(*Rak'ah* [Arabic] is the same as rakat.)
In a 2 rakat prayer (morning) you give your "testimony" and finish the prayer.

APPENDIX – II

In a 3 rakat prayer (evening) you give your "testimony", then stand up, give one more rakat of prayer. You say the Hamd (first chapter) only, followed by the bend and prostration twice as before, and then finish the prayer.

In a 4 rakat prayer (noon and night), you give your "testimony" at the second sitting and then stand up and repeat 2 more rakats, similar to the 3 rakat prayer, and then finish the prayer.

In order not to create confusion, I have included each 2, 3 and 4 prayer separately, from start to finish.

This is the ""testimony" "

All greetings, prayers and good deeds are for God
Peace and mercy of God be upon you O Muhammad
Peace be upon us and all the God's righteous servants.
I testify there is no God but One God, and I testify that Muhammad is His servant and Messenger.

This following is said when you are ending your prayer in the sitting position for all prayers:

O Lord send peace on Muhammad and his followers, the same way you sent peace on Abraham and his followers. Indeed you are full of praise and majesty.

O Lord bless Muhammad and his followers, the same way you blessed Abraham and his followers. Indeed you are full of praise and majesty.

At the end you turn your face to the right and left and say:

ALCHEMY OF THE QURAN

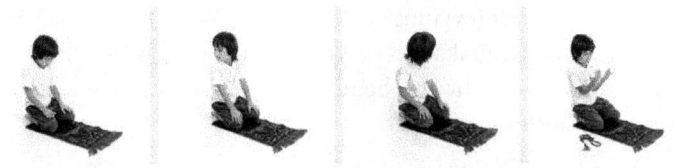

Peace and mercy of God be upon you   (this is the end of prayer)

Now you can make "Dua" (page 91) and ask God for anything you want

APPENDIX – II

The followings are the two, three and four Rakat prayers from start to finish

Two *Rakat* prayer (morning) from start to finish:

I offer "2 rakats" of "morning" prayer for closeness to God.

God is Greatest

ALCHEMY OF THE QURAN

In the name of Most Kind and Most merciful God

Praise the Lord, the king of Universe
Most kind and most forgiving
Master of the day of judgement
We only worship you and we only ask help from you
Guide us to the straight path
The path of those who you gave your blessings
Not those who earned your anger
And not those who went astray

In the name of most kind most forgiving God
I seek refuge in the Lord of the dawn
From the evil of what He has created
From the evil of darkness when it spreads
From the evils of those who practice sorcery
From the evil of a jealous who commits jealousy

In the name of most kind and most merciful
I seek refuge in the Lord of mankind, the King of mankind, the God of mankind
From the evil of Satan who whispers temptation in the hearts of people
From among the jinn and the men

APPENDIX – II

Bend position

Glory to my Lord, the Almighty

God listens to those who praise Him (saying it while straighten up to a straight stand up)

Going down to Prostration with your forehead to ground

Glory to my Lord, the Most High

O' Lord forgive my sins (Rising in sitting position)

Going down to Prostration with your forehead to ground

Glory to my Lord, the Most High

Anything is possible through God (Rising in sitting position)

APPENDIX – II

God is in total control of everything with power (say it as you are standing up to start the 2nd Rakats)

(2nd *Rakats*):

In the name of Most Kind and Most merciful God
Praise the Lord, the king of Universe
Most kind and most forgiving
Master of the day of judgement
We only worship you and we only ask help from you
Guide us to the straight path
The path of those who you gave your blessings
Not those who earned your anger
And not those who went astray

----

(112)
In the name of Most kind and most forgiving God
Say He is the One and only God
The One you go to when in need
He does not give birth to anyone and He was not born from anyone
And there is nothing like Him

Bend position

Glory to my Lord, the Almighty

God listens to those who praise Him (saying it while straighten up to a straight stand up)

APPENDIX – II

Going down to Prostration with your forehead to ground

Glory to my Lord, the Most High

O' Lord forgive my sins (Rising in sitting position)

Going down to Prostration with your forehead to ground

Glory to my Lord, the Most High

Anything is possible through God (Rising in sitting position)

2<u>nd</u> sitting, "testimony".

All greetings, prayers and good deeds are for God
Peace and mercy of God be upon you O Muhammad
Peace be upon us and all the God's righteous servants.
I testify there is no God but One God, and I testify that Muhammad is His servant and Messenger.

Two *Rackats*, end the prayer

APPENDIX – II

O Lord send peace on Muhammad and his followers, the same way you sent peace on Abraham and his followers. Indeed you are full of praise and majesty.

O Lord bless Muhammad and his followers, the same way you blessed Abraham and his followers. Indeed you are full of praise and majesty.

Turn your face to the right and left and say. Peace and mercy of God be upon you.

Now you can make "Dua" (page 91) and ask God for anything you want

Three *Rakats* prayer (evening) start to finish:

I offer "3 rakats" of "Maghrib" prayer for closeness to God.

God is Greatest

In the name of Most Kind and Most merciful God
Praise the Lord, the king of Universe
Most kind and most forgiving
Master of the day of judgement
We only worship you and we only ask help from you
Guide us to the straight path
The path of those who you gave your blessings
Not those who earned your anger
And not those who went astray

APPENDIX – II

In the name of most kind most forgiving God
I seek refuge in the Lord of the dawn
From the evil of what He has created
From the evil of darkness when it spreads
From the evils of those who practice sorcery
From the evil of a jealous who commits jealousy

In the name of most kind and most merciful
I seek refuge in the Lord of mankind, the King of mankind, the God of mankind
From the evil of Satan who whispers temptation in the hearts of people
From among the jinn and the men

Bend position

Glory to my Lord, the Almighty

God listens to those who praise Him (saying it while straighten up to a straight stand up)

Going down to Prostration with your forehead to ground

Glory to my Lord, the Most High

O' Lord forgive my sins (Rising in sitting position)

Going down to Prostration with your forehead to ground

Glory to my Lord, the Most High

APPENDIX – II

Anything is possible through God (Rising in sitting position)

God is in total control of everything with power. (say it as you are standing up to start the 2nd Rakat)

(2nd Rakat):

In the name of Most Kind and Most merciful God
Praise the Lord, the king of Universe
Most kind and most forgiving
Master of the day of judgement
We only worship you and we only ask help from you
Guide us to the straight path
The path of those who you gave your blessings
Not those who earned your anger
And not those who went astray

----

(112)
In the name of Most kind and most forgiving God
Say He is the One and only God
The One you go to when in need
He does not give birth to anyone and He was not born from anyone
And there is nothing like Him

APPENDIX – II

Bend position

Glory to my Lord, the Almighty

God listens to those who praise Him (saying it while straighten up to a straight stand up)

Going down to Prostration with your forehead to ground

Glory to my Lord, the Most High

O' Lord forgive my sins (Rising in sitting position)

Going down to Prostration with your forehead to ground

Glory to my Lord, the Most High

Anything is possible through God (Rising in sitting position)

APPENDIX – II

<u>2nd sitting, "testimony"</u>

All greetings, prayers and good deeds are for God
Peace and mercy of God be upon you O Muhammad
Peace be upon us and all the God's righteous servants.
I testify there is no God but One God, and I testify that Muhammad is His servant and Messenger.

Now you stand up to continue for the 3rd *Rakats*.

God is in total control of everything with power. (say it as you are standing up to start the 3rd Rakat)

(3nd Rakats, Chapter 1, Hamd only):

ALCHEMY OF THE QURAN

In the name of Most Kind and Most merciful God
Praise the Lord, the king of Universe
Most kind and most forgiving
Master of the day of judgement
We only worship you and we only ask help from you
Guide us to the straight path
The path of those who you gave your blessings
Not those who earned your anger
And not those who went astray

Bend position

Glory to my Lord, the Almighty

God listens to those who praise Him (saying it while straighten up to a straight stand up)

APPENDIX – II

Going down to Prostration with your forehead to ground

Glory to my Lord, the Most High

O' Lord forgive my sins (Rising in sitting position)

Going down to Prostration with your forehead to ground

Glory to my Lord, the Most High

Anything is possible through God (Rising in sitting position)

Say the "testimony" again and finish the prayer

All greetings, prayers and good deeds are for God
Peace and mercy of God be upon you O Muhammad
Peace be upon us and all the God's righteous servants.
I testify there is no God but One God, and I testify that Muhammad is His servant and Messenger.

<u>three *Rakats*, end the prayer</u>

O Lord send peace on Muhammad and his followers, the same way you sent peace on Abraham and his followers. Indeed you are full of praise and majesty.

O Lord bless Muhammad and his followers, the same way you blessed Abraham and his followers. Indeed you are full of praise and majesty.

Turn your face to the right and left and say.

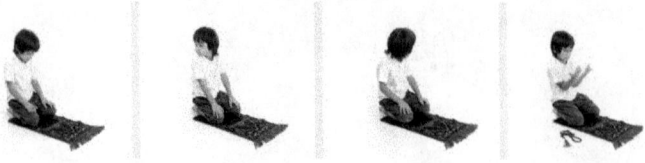

APPENDIX – II

Peace and mercy of God be upon you.

Now you can make "Dua" (page 91) and ask God for anything you want

Four <u>*Rakats* prayer (noon and night) start to finish:</u>

I offer "4 rakats" of "Noon/Afternoon/Night" prayer for closeness to God.

God is Greatest

ALCHEMY OF THE QURAN

In the name of Most Kind and Most merciful God
Praise the Lord, the king of Universe
Most kind and most forgiving
Master of the day of judgement
We only worship you and we only ask help from you
Guide us to the straight path
The path of those who you gave your blessings
Not those who earned your anger
And not those who went astray

In the name of most kind most forgiving God
I seek refuge in the Lord of the dawn
From the evil of what He has created
From the evil of darkness when it spreads
From the evils of those who practice sorcery
From the evil of a jealous who commits jealousy

In the name of most kind and most merciful
I seek refuge in the Lord of mankind, the King of mankind, the God of mankind
From the evil of Satan who whispers temptation in the hearts of people
From among the jinn and the men

APPENDIX – II

Bend position

Glory to my Lord, the Almighty

God listens to those who praise Him (saying it while straighten up to a straight stand up)

Going down to Prostration with your forehead to ground

Glory to my Lord, the Most High

O' Lord forgive my sins (Rising in sitting position)

Going down to Prostration with your forehead to ground

Glory to my Lord, the Most High

Anything is possible through God (Rising in sitting position)

APPENDIX – II

God is in total control of everything with power. (say it as you are standing up to start the second Rakat)

(Second Rakat):

In the name of Most Kind and Most merciful God
Praise the Lord, the king of Universe
Most kind and most forgiving
Master of the day of judgement
We only worship you and we only ask help from you
Guide us to the straight path
The path of those who you gave your blessings
Not those who earned your anger
And not those who went astray

----

(112)
In the name of Most kind and most forgiving God
Say He is the One and only God
The One you go to when in need
He does not give birth to anyone and He was not born from anyone
And there is nothing like Him

Bend position

Glory to my Lord, the Almighty

God listens to those who praise Him (saying it while straighten up to a straight stand up)

APPENDIX – II

Going down to Prostration with your forehead to ground

Glory to my Lord, the Most High

O' Lord forgive my sins (Rising in sitting position)

Going down to Prostration with your forehead to ground

Glory to my Lord, the Most High

Anything is possible through God (Rising in sitting position)

2<u>nd sitting, "testimony".</u>

*All greetings, prayers and good deeds are for God
Peace and mercy of God be upon you O Muhammad
Peace be upon us and all the God's righteous servants.
I testify there is no God but One God, and I testify that Muhammad
is His servant and Messenger.*
<u>Now you stand up to continue for the third Rakat.</u>

God is in total control of everything with power. (say it as you are standing up to start the 3ⁿᵈ Rakat)

APPENDIX – II

(Third *Rakat, Chapter 1, Hamd* only):

In the name of Most Kind and Most merciful God
Praise the Lord, the king of Universe
Most kind and most forgiving
Master of the day of judgement
We only worship you and we only ask help from you
Guide us to the straight path
The path of those who you gave your blessings
Not those who earned your anger
And not those who went astray

Bend position

ALCHEMY OF THE QURAN

Glory to my Lord, the Almighty

God listens to those who praise Him (saying it while straighten up to a straight stand up)

Going down to Prostration with your forehead to ground

Glory to my Lord, the Most High

O' Lord forgive my sins (Rising in sitting position)

APPENDIX – II

Going down to Prostration with your forehead to ground

Glory to my Lord, the Most High

Anything is possible through God (Rising in sitting position)

<u>Now you stand up to continue for the fourth *Rakat*.</u>

ALCHEMY OF THE QURAN

God is in total control of everything with power. (say it as you are standing up to start the fourth Rakat)

(fourth Rakat, Chapter 1, Hamd only):

In the name of Most Kind and Most merciful God
Praise the Lord, the king of Universe
Most kind and most forgiving
Master of the day of judgement
We only worship you and we only ask help from you
Guide us to the straight path
The path of those who you gave your blessings
Not those who earned your anger
And not those who went astray

Bend position

APPENDIX – II

Glory to my Lord, the Almighty

God listens to those who praise Him (saying it while straighten up to a straight stand up)

Going down to Prostration with your forehead to ground

Glory to my Lord, the Most High

O' Lord forgive my sins (Rising in sitting position)

Going down to Prostration with your forehead to ground

Glory to my Lord, the Most High

Anything is possible through God (Rising in sitting position)

Testify again and finish the prayer
All greetings, prayers and good deeds are for God
Peace and mercy of God be upon you O Muhammad
Peace be upon us and all the God's righteous servants.
I testify there is no God but One God, and I testify that Muhammad is His servant and Messenger.

fourth *Rackat*, end the prayer

APPENDIX – II

O Lord send peace on Muhammad and his followers, the same way you sent peace on Abraham and his followers. Indeed you are full of praise and majesty.

O Lord bless Muhammad and his followers, the same way you blessed Abraham and his followers. Indeed you are full of praise and majesty.

Turn your face to the right and left and say.

Peace and mercy of God be upon you.

Now you can make "Dua" (page 91) and ask God for anything you want

References

1. Quran: Sahih International, English, Arabic
2. Quran: Muhammad Sarwar, English, Arabic
3. Quran: Yusuf Ali, English, Arabic
4. Quran: Baha'edin Khoramshahi, Farsi, Arabic
5. Quran: http://www.allahsquran.com/learn/
6. Quran: http://corpus.quran.com/translation.jsp
7. Quran: http://www.clearquran.com/
8. Masnavi Molavi, Molana, jalaledeen Balkhi, (Rumi), Farsi
9. Koleyat, Hafez, Farsi
10. Golestan, Saadi, Farsi
11. Makhzan Ol Asrar, Nezami Ganjavi, Farsi
12. Who wrote the Bible, Richard Elliott Freidman, English
13. The Bible with Sources Revealed, Richard Elliott Friedman, English
14. The Bible, The Quran and Science, Dr. Maurice Bucaille
15. The science of the Quran, Ahmad Hassan

16. Bible, King James, English

17. Shahnameh, Ferdowsi. Farsi

Biography

❖

Faramarz Franco Davati is an engineer and a theologian. He holds a Bachelor of Science in Engineering from Purdue and a Master of Science in Aerospace Engineering from San Diego State University. He is the managing president and founder of Failure & Damage Analysis Inc., a company that investigates industrial and commercial accidents. He also has several websites providing continuing education to professional engineers, architects, land surveyors, and geologists. Although he lectures in forensic sciences around the country, his lifetime passion and interest has always been studying religion and theology.